BBC

DOCTOR WHO

THE THIRTEENTH DOCTOR

"As The Doctor would say, brilliant!"
BIG COMIC PAGE

"Rachael Stott does an excellent job and makes a strong impression from the very first panel. "
SciFi PULSE

"This is one book newcomers and old fans alike are sure to enjoy. 9/10!"
EXPLORE THE MULTIVERSE

"This comic captures the energy and dramatic elements of the recent Doctor Who series. All of the creative team work together to produce a solid adventure which is sure to win the hearts of the fans."
MONKEYS FIGHTING ROBOTS

"Perfectly captures the look and voices of the characters!"
ADVENTURES IN POOR TASTE

"If you're a fan overflowing with love for the new Doctor, this is a great place to get an extra dose of Doctor Who."
COMICBOOK.COM

"Highly recommended... Bold, sassy, intelligent, and accessible to new fans. 5 out of 5!"
GEEK SYNDICATE

"A perfect continuation of what they've come to love about Series 11. 5 out of 5!"
KABOOOOOM

"Rachael Stott's artwork is excellent, bringing Jodie Whittaker's mannerisms to life in startling detail. Remarkable. 9 out of 10!"
SciFi BULLETIN

"The kind of comic we need right now."
ROGUES PORTAL

Editors
Jonathan Stevenson
Jessica Burton

Senior Designer
Andrew Leung

Titan Comics

Editor Emeritus
Andrew James

Senior Editor
Martin Eden

Production Assistant
Rhiannon Roy

Production Controller
Peter James

Senior Production Controller
Jackie Flook

Art Director
Oz Browne

Sales & Circulation Manager
Steve Tothill

Senior Publicist
Will O'Mullane

Publicist
Imogen Harris

Senior Brand Manager
Chris Thompson

Marketing Assistant
Charlie Raspin

Ads & Marketing Assistant
Bella Hoy

Commercial Manager
Michelle Fairlamb

Head Of Rights
Jenny Boyce

Publishing Manager
Darryl Tothill

Publishing Director
Chris Teather

Operations Director
Leigh Baulch

Executive Director
Vivian Cheung

Publisher
Nick Landau

For rights information contact Jenny Boyce
jenny.boyce@titanemail.com

Special thanks to Chris Chibnall, Matt Strevens, Sam Hoyle, Mandy Thwaites,
Gabby De Matteis, Ross McGlinchey, David Wilson-Nunn, Kirsty Mullan and Kate Bush
for their invaluable assistance.

BBC Worldwide

Director Of Editorial Governance
Nicolas Brett

Director Of Consumer Products And Publishing
Andrew Moultrie

Head Of UK Publishing
Chris Kerwin

Publisher
Mandy Thwaites

Publishing Co-Ordinator
Eva Abramik

DOCTOR WHO: THE THIRTEENTH DOCTOR VOL. 1: A NEW BEGINNING
STANDARD EDITION ISBN: 9781785866760
FP EDITION ISBN: 9781787732339

Published by Titan Comics, a division of Titan Publishing Group, Ltd. 144 Southwark Street, London, SE1 0UP.
Titan Comics is a registered trademark. All rights reserved.

A CIP catalogue record for this title is available from the British Library.
First edition: May 2019.

10 9 8 7 6 5 4 3 2 1

Printed in Spain

Titan Comics does not read or accept unsolicited DOCTOR WHO submissions of ideas, stories or artwork.

BBC
DOCTOR WHO

THE THIRTEENTH DOCTOR

WRITER
JODY HOUSER

ARTIST
RACHAEL STOTT

WITH
GIORGIA SPOSITO

AND
VALERIA FAVOCCIA

COLORIST
ENRICA EREN ANGIOLINI

COLOR ASSISTANT
VIVIANA SPINELLI

FLATTERS
SARA MICHIELI & ANDREA MORETTO

WITH THANKS TO
ADELE MATERA

LETTERER
COMICRAFT'S SARAH JACOBS
AND JOHN ROSHELL

TITAN®
COMICS

BBC

BBC

DOCTOR WHO

THE THIRTEENTH DOCTOR

PREVIOUSLY...

When the Doctor fell out of the Sheffield sky and into the lives of Graham, Yasmin, and Ryan, they had little idea how much their worlds would change! Now the Doctor and her friends travel through space and time, righting wrongs, facing terrible danger, and witnessing magnificent wonders!

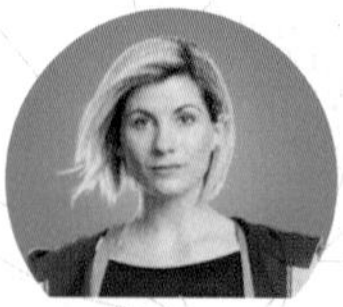

The **Doctor**

The Thirteenth Doctor is a live wire, full of energy and fizzing with excitement and wit! The Doctor is a charismatic and confident explorer, dedicated to seeing all the wonders of the universe, championing fairness and kindness wherever she can. Brave and selfless, this Doctor loves to be surrounded by friends!

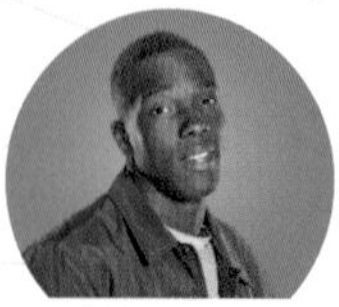

Ryan Sinclair

Ryan is 19 years old, born and bred in Sheffield. He works in a warehouse while studying to become a mechanic. He likes video games and is great with technology! Ryan is dyspraxic, which means he sometimes finds physical co-ordination tricky – but his curiosity and energy always win out over fear.

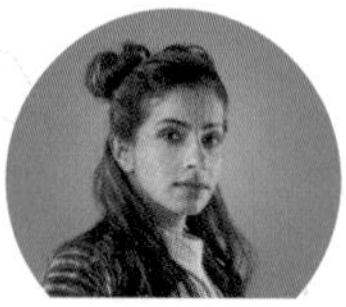

Yasmin **'Yaz'** Khan

Yaz is a 19-year-old Sheffielder, friendly and self-assured, a quick logical thinker and a natural leader – the perfect person to have around in a crisis! Yaz loves her job as a probationary police officer, but wants more – not because she's bored, but because she loves adventure and the thrill of the new!

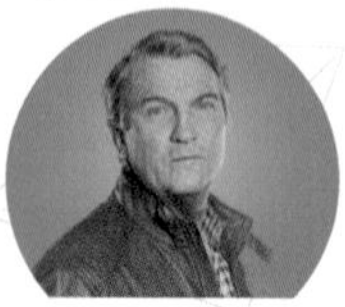

Graham O'Brien

Graham is a funny, charming and cheeky chap from Essex – he's a family man and an ex-bus driver, with a sharp sense of humor and a caring, warm nature. He might be of a different generation (and might sometimes move at a slower pace than Yaz and Ryan), but he's brave, selfless, and wise too – just like the Doctor.

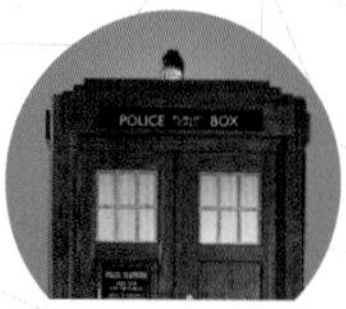

The **TARDIS**

'Time and Relative Dimension in Space'. Bigger on the inside, this unassuming blue police box is your ticket to amazing adventures across time and space! The Doctor likes to think she's in control of her temporal jaunts, but more often than not, the temperamental TARDIS takes her and her friends to where and when they need to be...

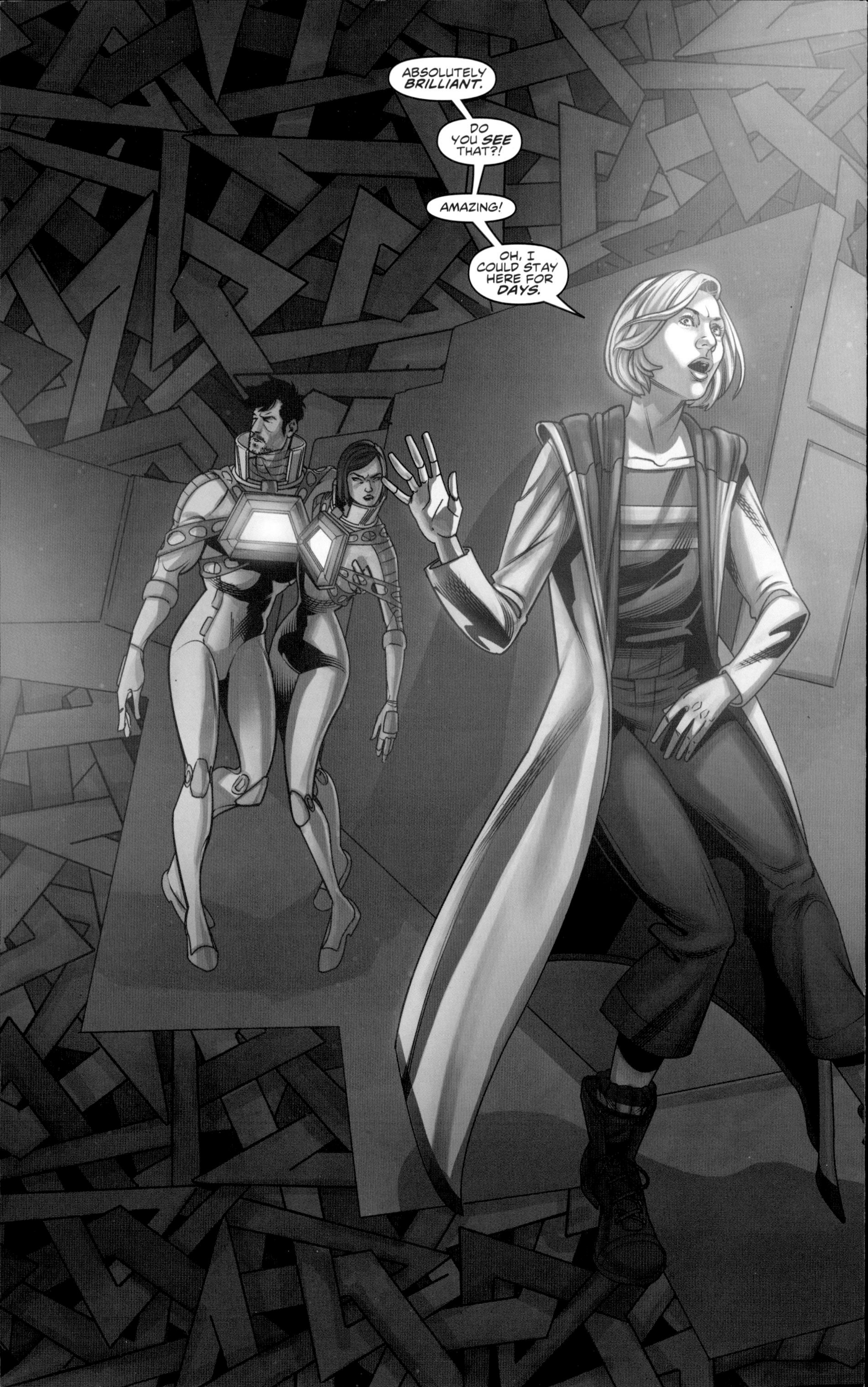
ABSOLUTELY BRILLIANT.
DO YOU SEE THAT?!
AMAZING!
OH, I COULD STAY HERE FOR DAYS.

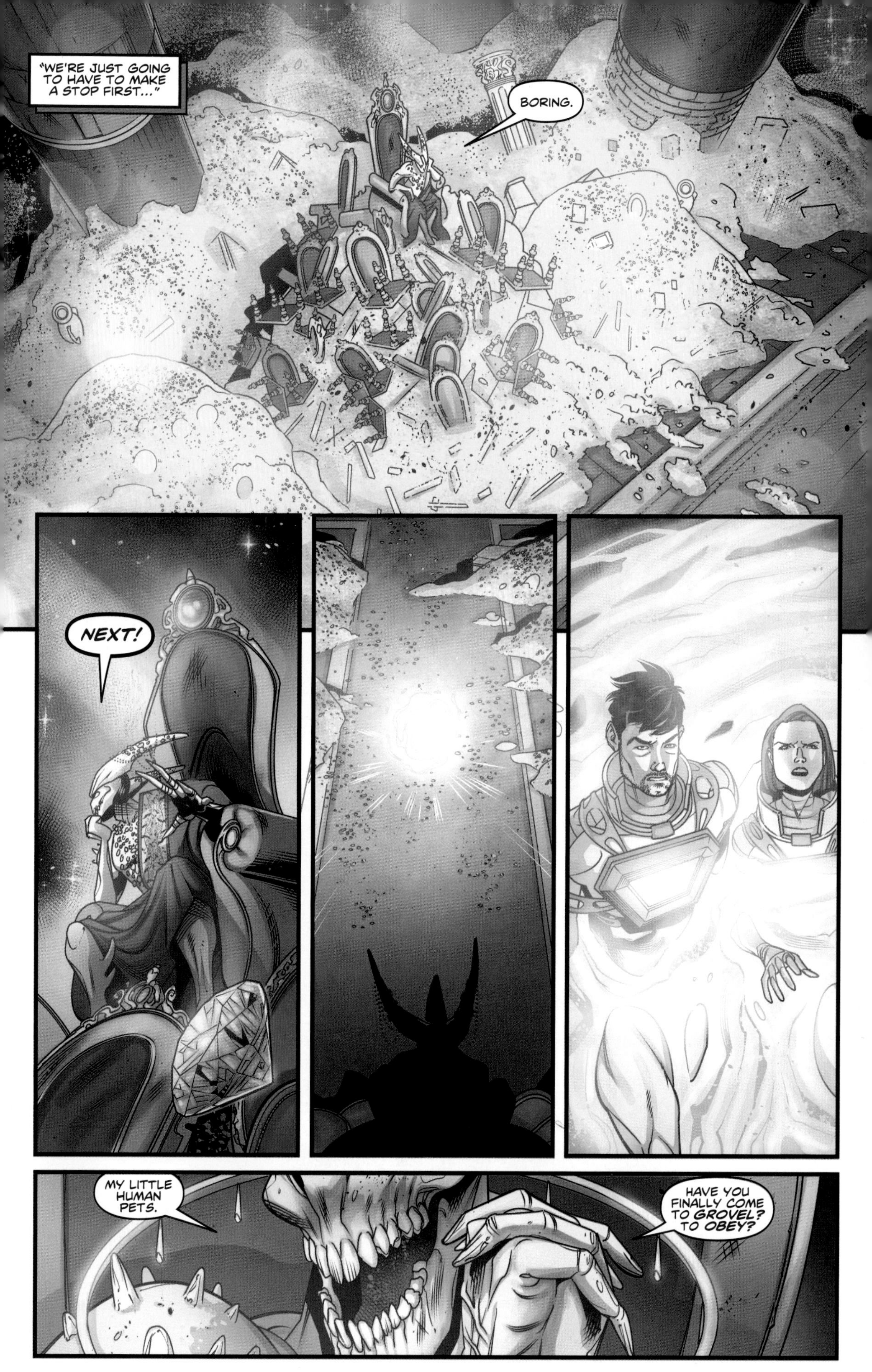
"WE'RE JUST GOING TO HAVE TO MAKE A STOP FIRST..."
BORING.
NEXT!
MY LITTLE HUMAN PETS.
HAVE YOU FINALLY COME TO GROVEL? TO OBEY?

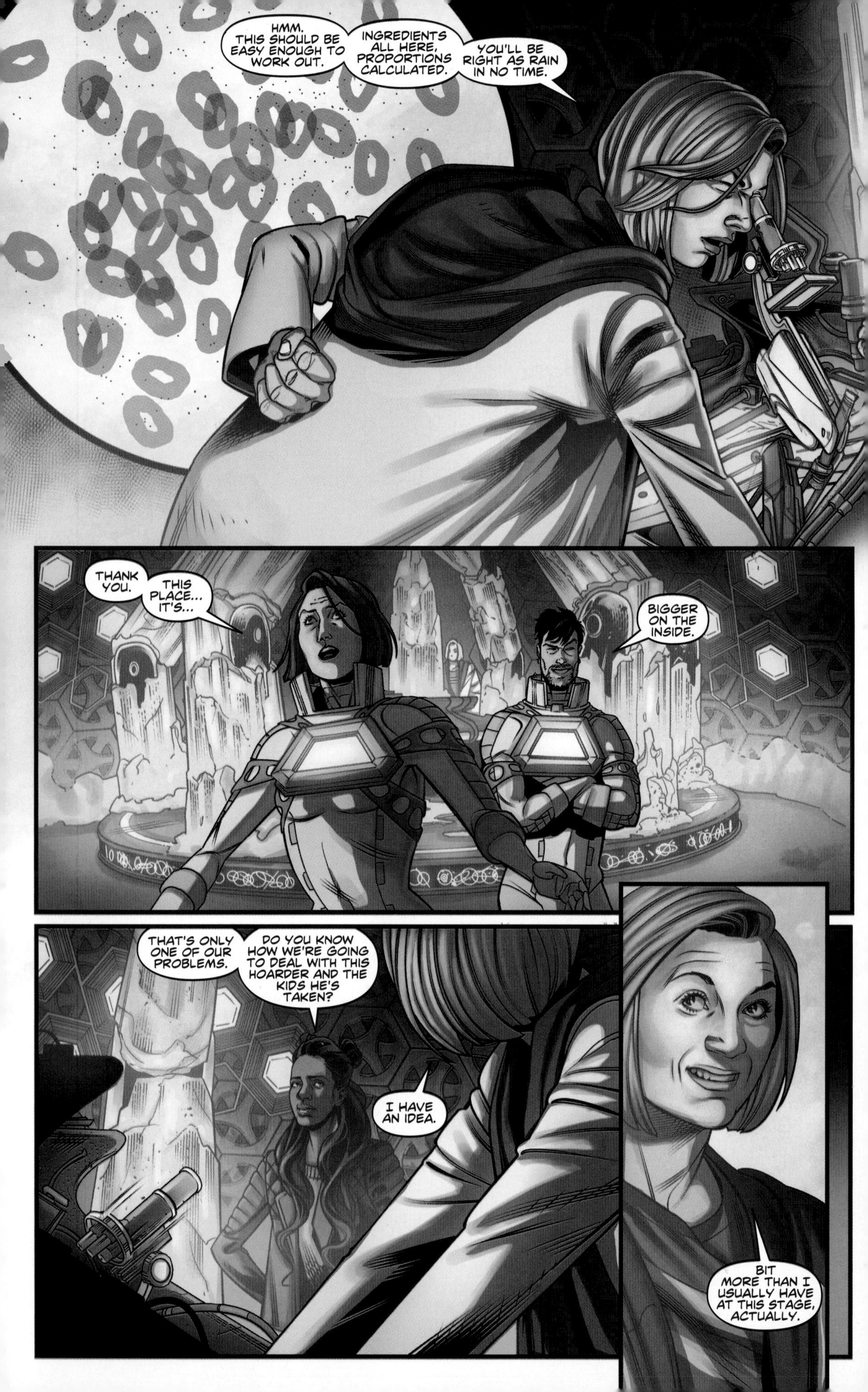
HMM. THIS SHOULD BE EASY ENOUGH TO WORK OUT.
INGREDIENTS ALL HERE, PROPORTIONS CALCULATED.
YOU'LL BE RIGHT AS RAIN IN NO TIME.
THANK YOU.
THIS PLACE... IT'S...
BIGGER ON THE INSIDE.
THAT'S ONLY ONE OF OUR PROBLEMS.
DO YOU KNOW HOW WE'RE GOING TO DEAL WITH THIS HOARDER AND THE KIDS HE'S TAKEN?
I HAVE AN IDEA.
BIT MORE THAN I USUALLY HAVE AT THIS STAGE, ACTUALLY.

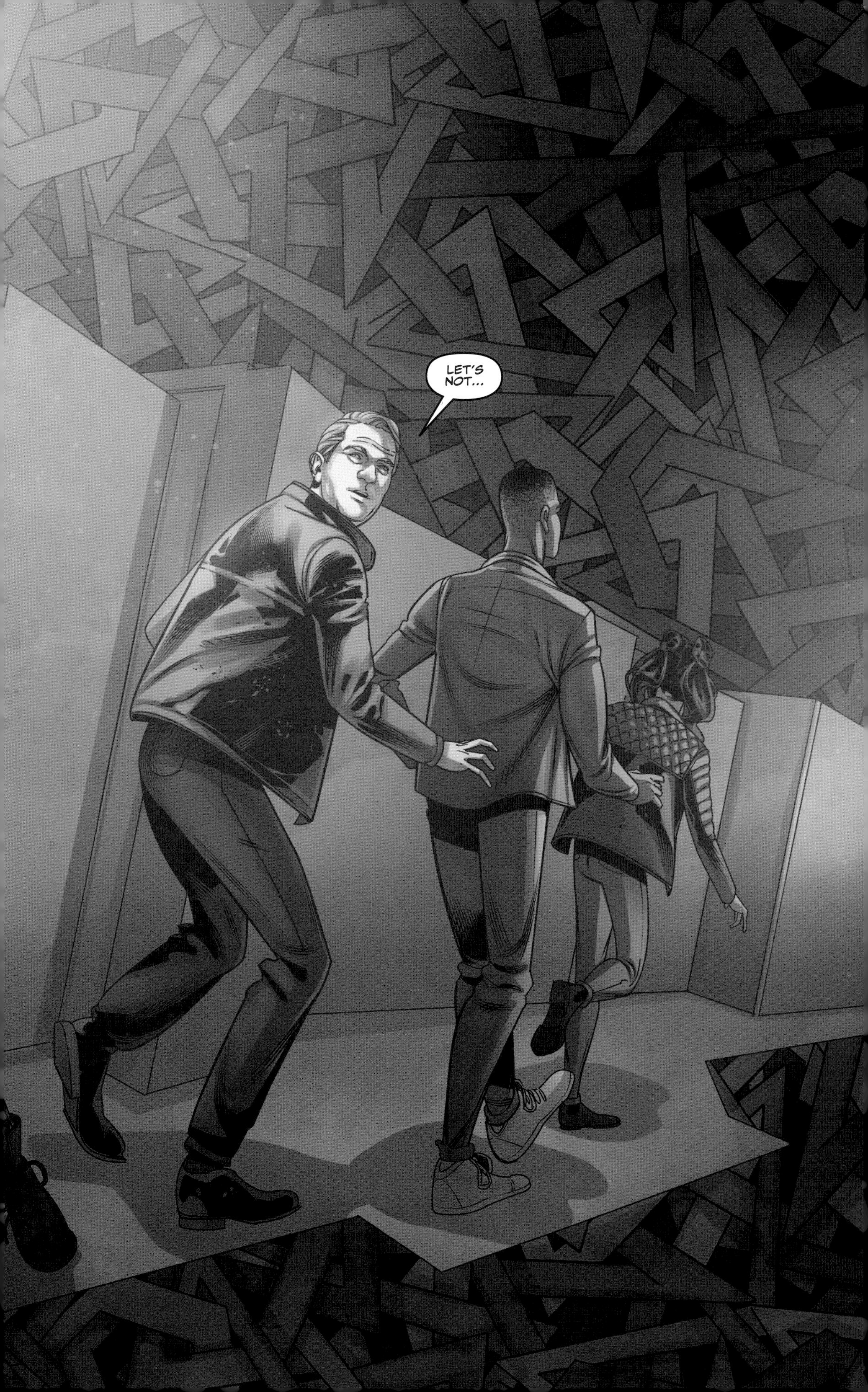
LET'S NOT...

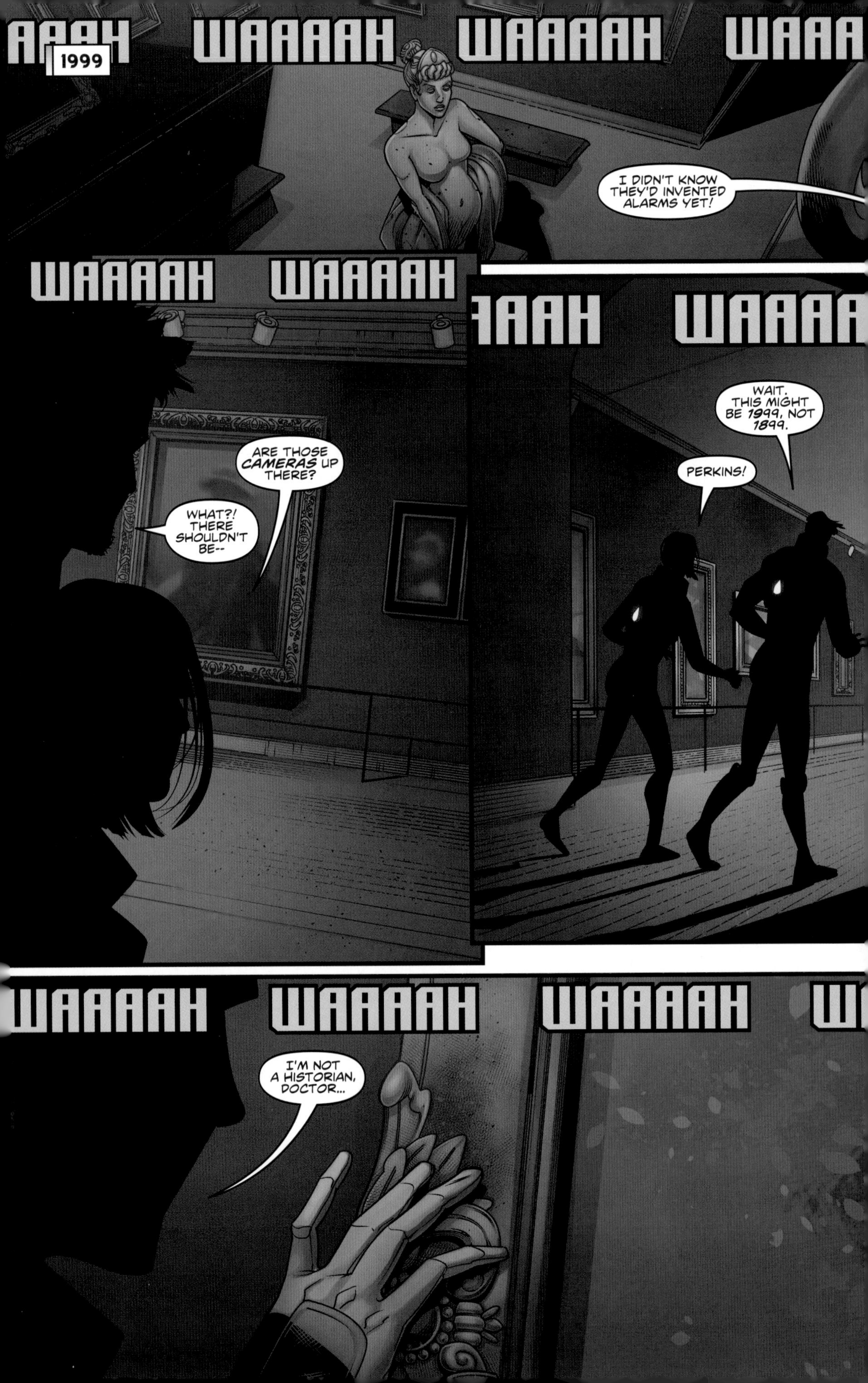

1999
WAAAAH WAAAAH WAAAAH
I DIDN'T KNOW THEY'D INVENTED ALARMS YET!
WAAAAH WAAAAH
WHAT?! THERE SHOULDN'T BE--
ARE THOSE CAMERAS UP THERE?
WAAAAH
PERKINS!
WAIT. THIS MIGHT BE 1999, NOT 1899.
WAAAAH WAAAAH WAAAAH
I'M NOT A HISTORIAN, DOCTOR...

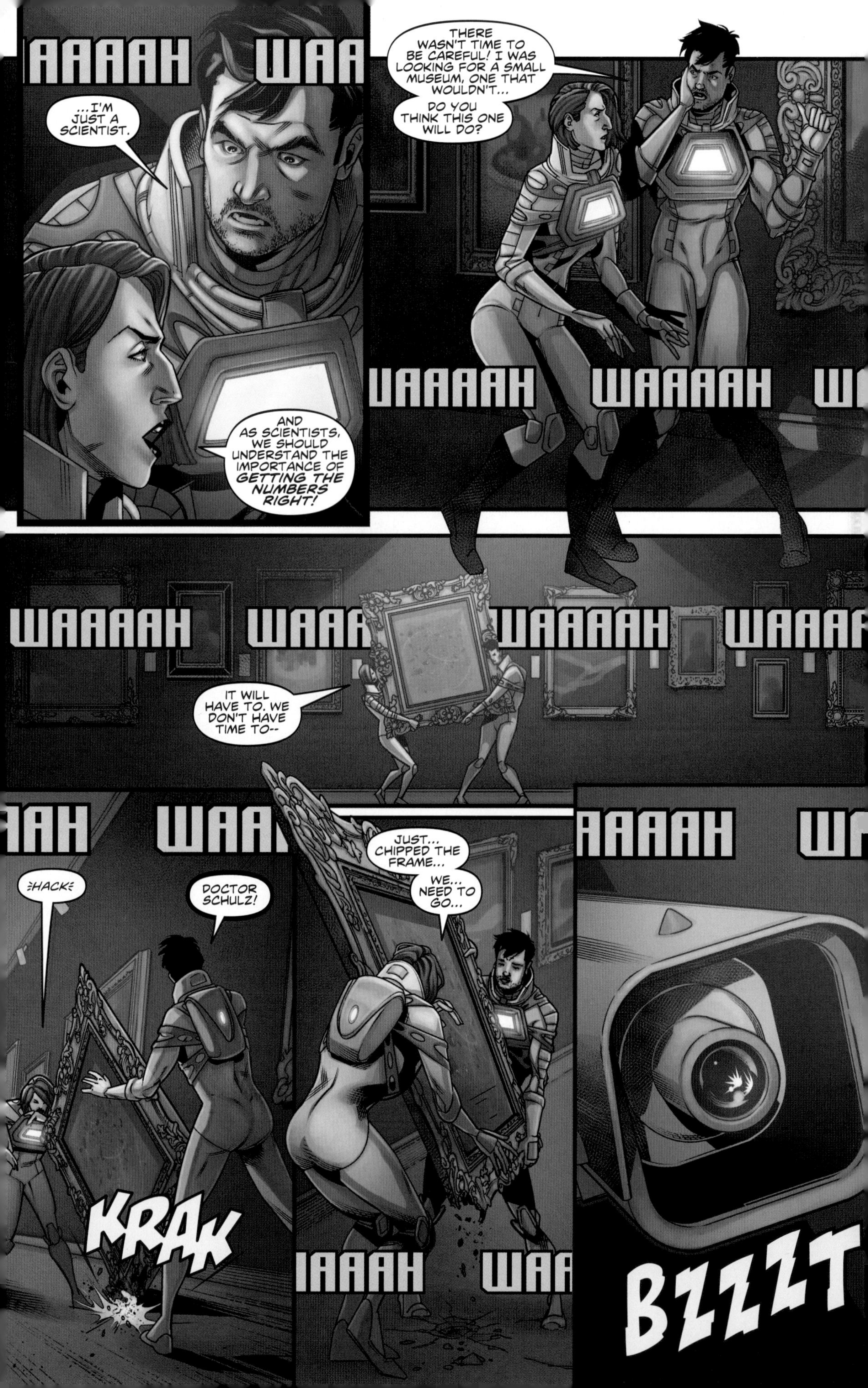

AAAAH WAA
...I'M JUST A SCIENTIST.
AND AS SCIENTISTS, WE SHOULD UNDERSTAND THE IMPORTANCE OF GETTING THE NUMBERS RIGHT!
THERE WASN'T TIME TO BE CAREFUL! I WAS LOOKING FOR A SMALL MUSEUM, ONE THAT WOULDN'T...
DO YOU THINK THIS ONE WILL DO?
WAAAAH WAAAAH W
WAAAAH WAAA WAAAAH WAAA
IT WILL HAVE TO. WE DON'T HAVE TIME TO--
AH WAA
HACK
DOCTOR SCHULZ!
KRAK
JUST... CHIPPED THE FRAME...
WE... NEED TO GO...
AAAH WAA
AAAAH W
BZZZT

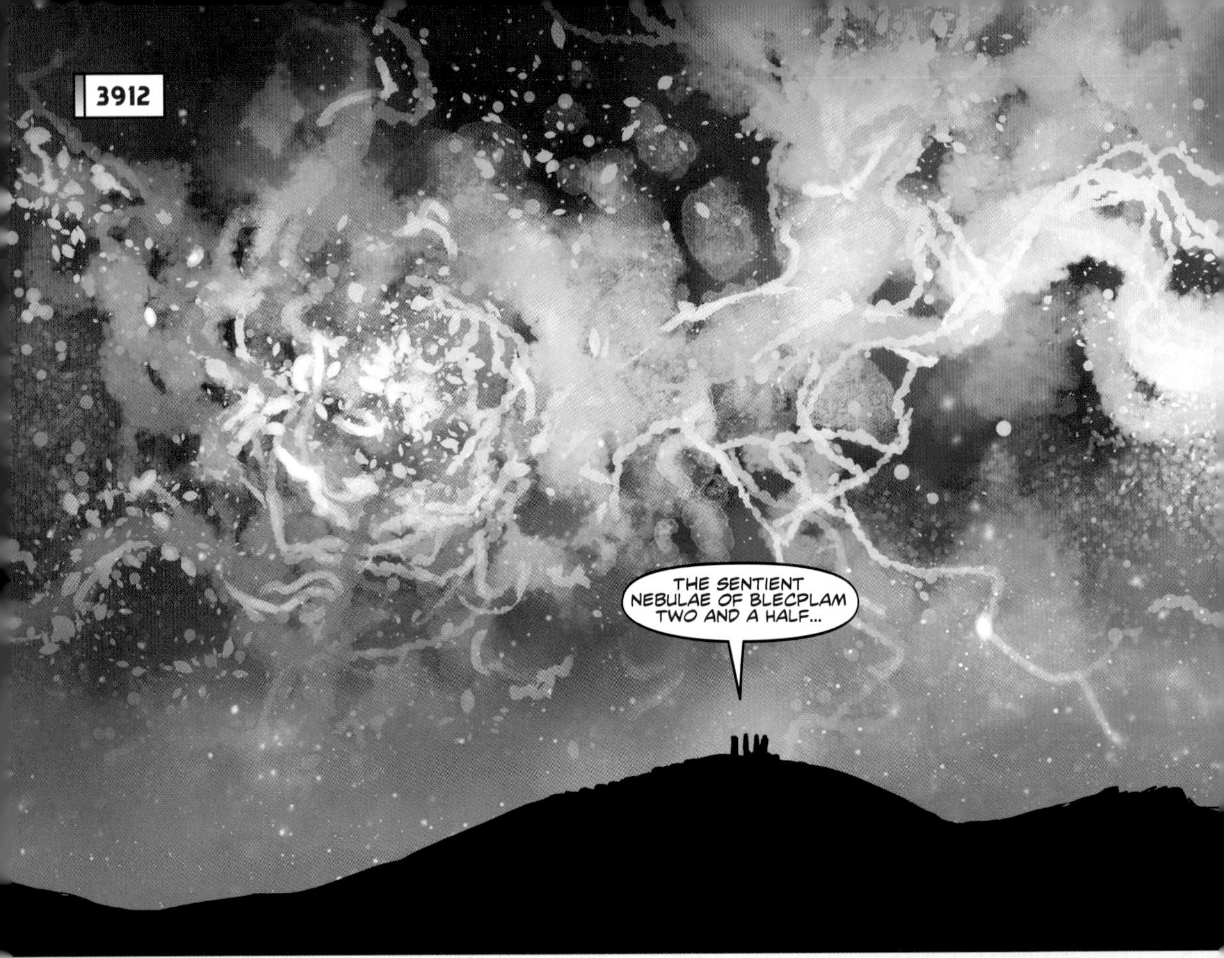
3912
THE SENTIENT NEBULAE OF BLECPLAM TWO AND A HALF...

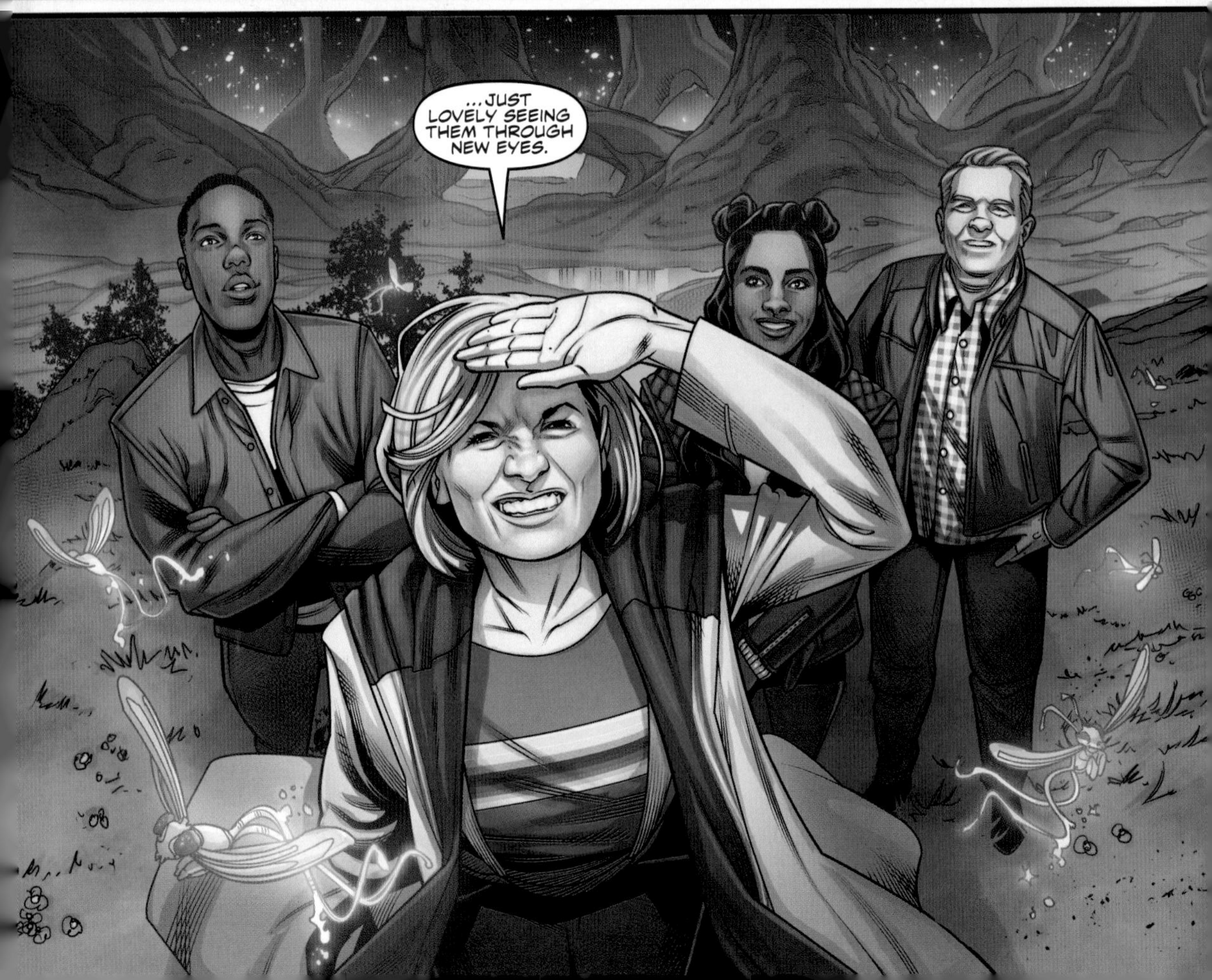
...JUST LOVELY SEEING THEM THROUGH NEW EYES.

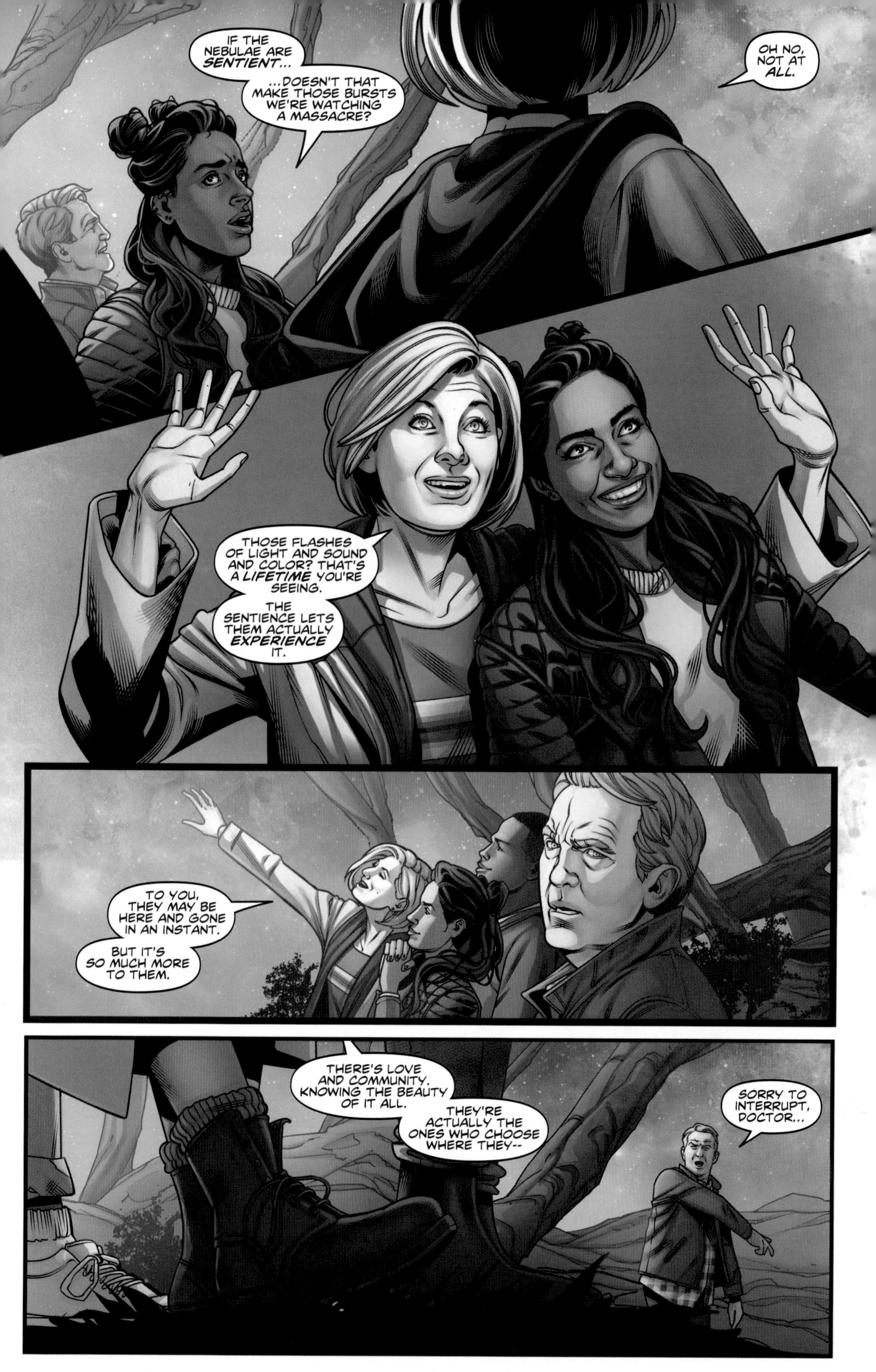
IF THE NEBULAE ARE SENTIENT...
...DOESN'T THAT MAKE THOSE BURSTS WE'RE WATCHING A MASSACRE?
OH NO, NOT AT ALL.
THOSE FLASHES OF LIGHT AND SOUND AND COLOR? THAT'S A LIFETIME YOU'RE SEEING.
THE SENTIENCE LETS THEM ACTUALLY EXPERIENCE IT.
TO YOU, THEY MAY BE HERE AND GONE IN AN INSTANT.
BUT IT'S SO MUCH MORE TO THEM.
THERE'S LOVE AND COMMUNITY. KNOWING THE BEAUTY OF IT ALL.
THEY'RE ACTUALLY THE ONES WHO CHOOSE WHERE THEY--
SORRY TO INTERRUPT, DOCTOR...

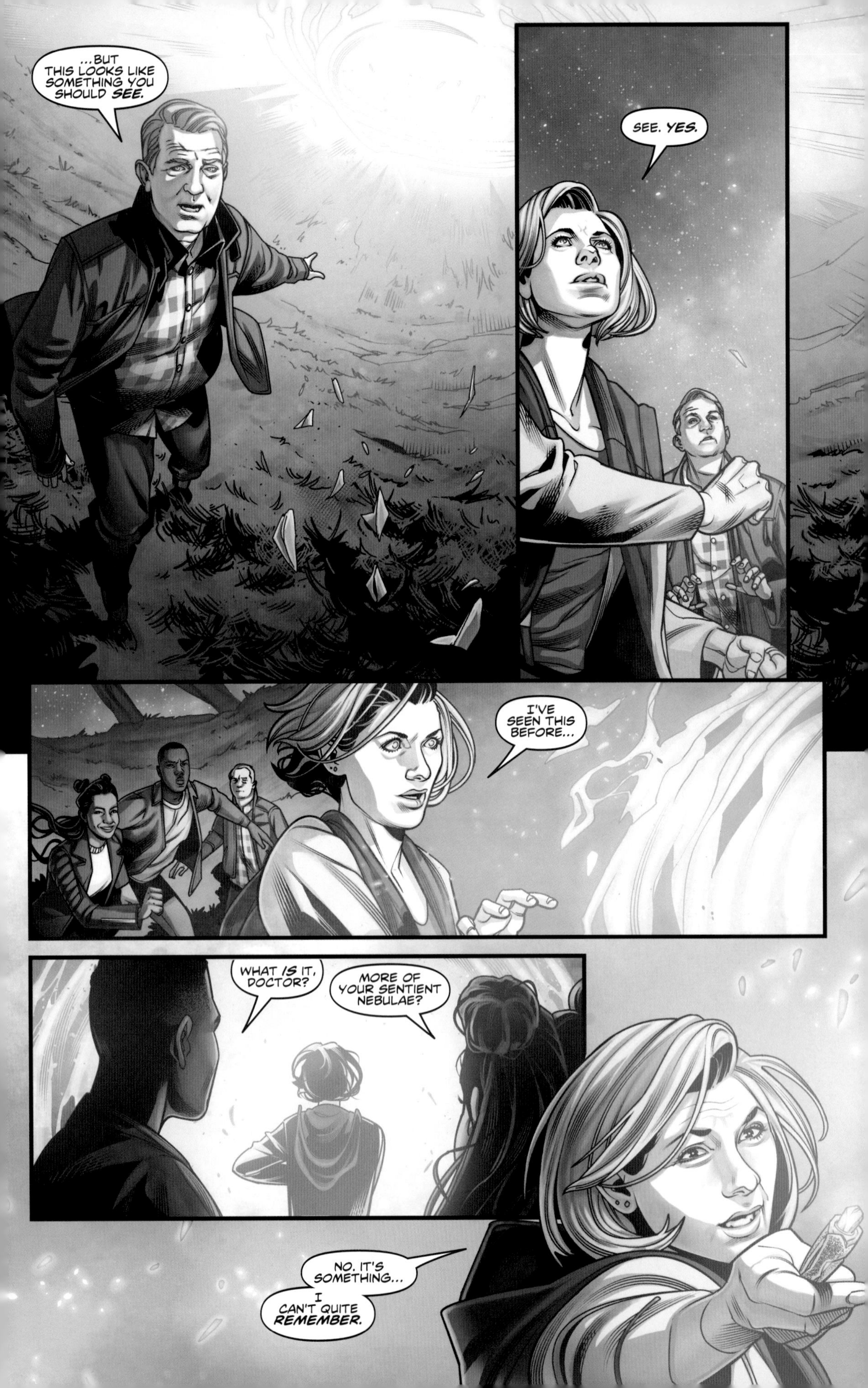
...BUT THIS LOOKS LIKE SOMETHING YOU SHOULD SEE.
SEE. YES.
I'VE SEEN THIS BEFORE...
WHAT IS IT, DOCTOR?
MORE OF YOUR SENTIENT NEBULAE?
NO. IT'S SOMETHING...
I CAN'T QUITE REMEMBER.

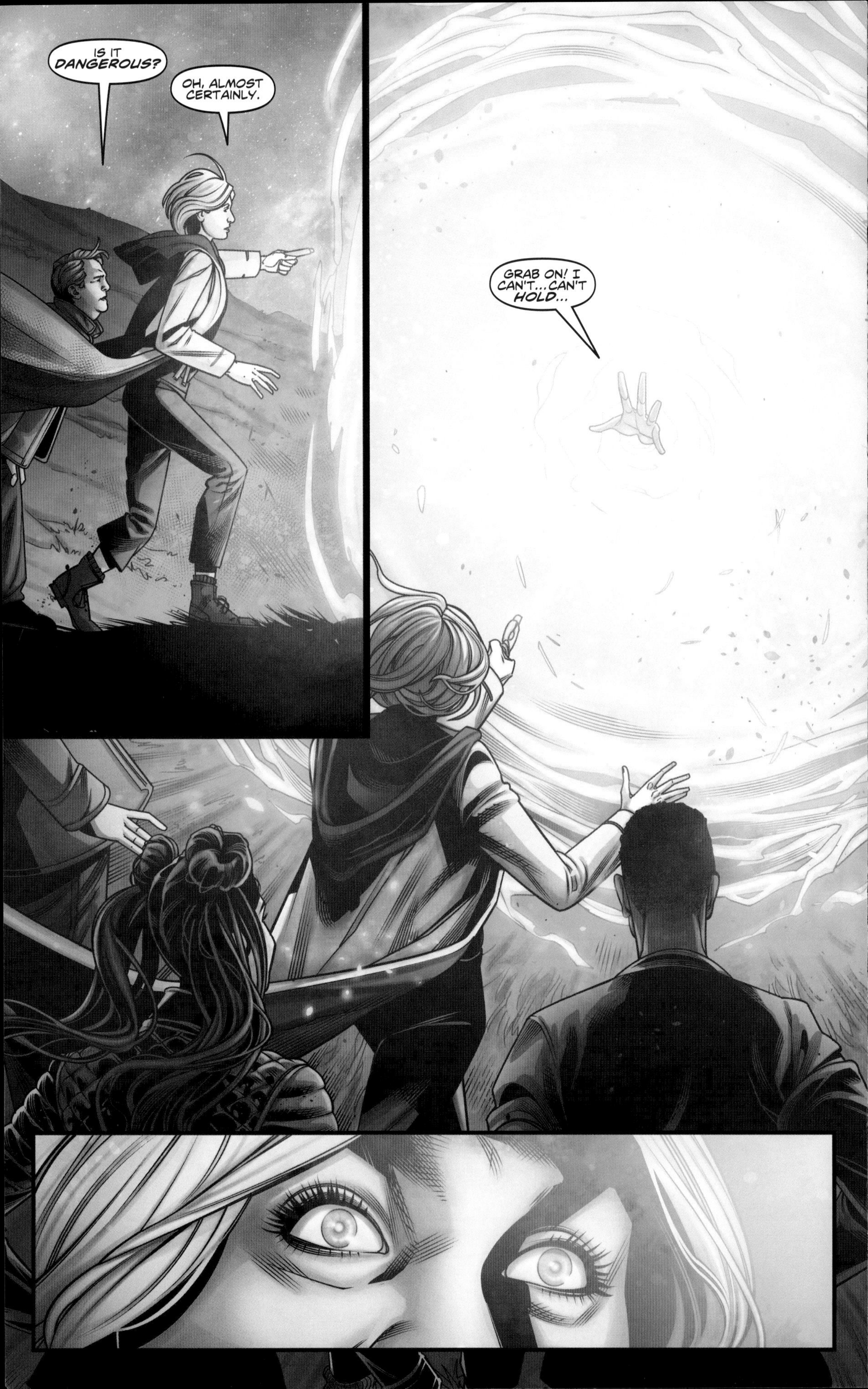
IS IT DANGEROUS?
OH, ALMOST CERTAINLY.
GRAB ON! I CAN'T...CAN'T HOLD...

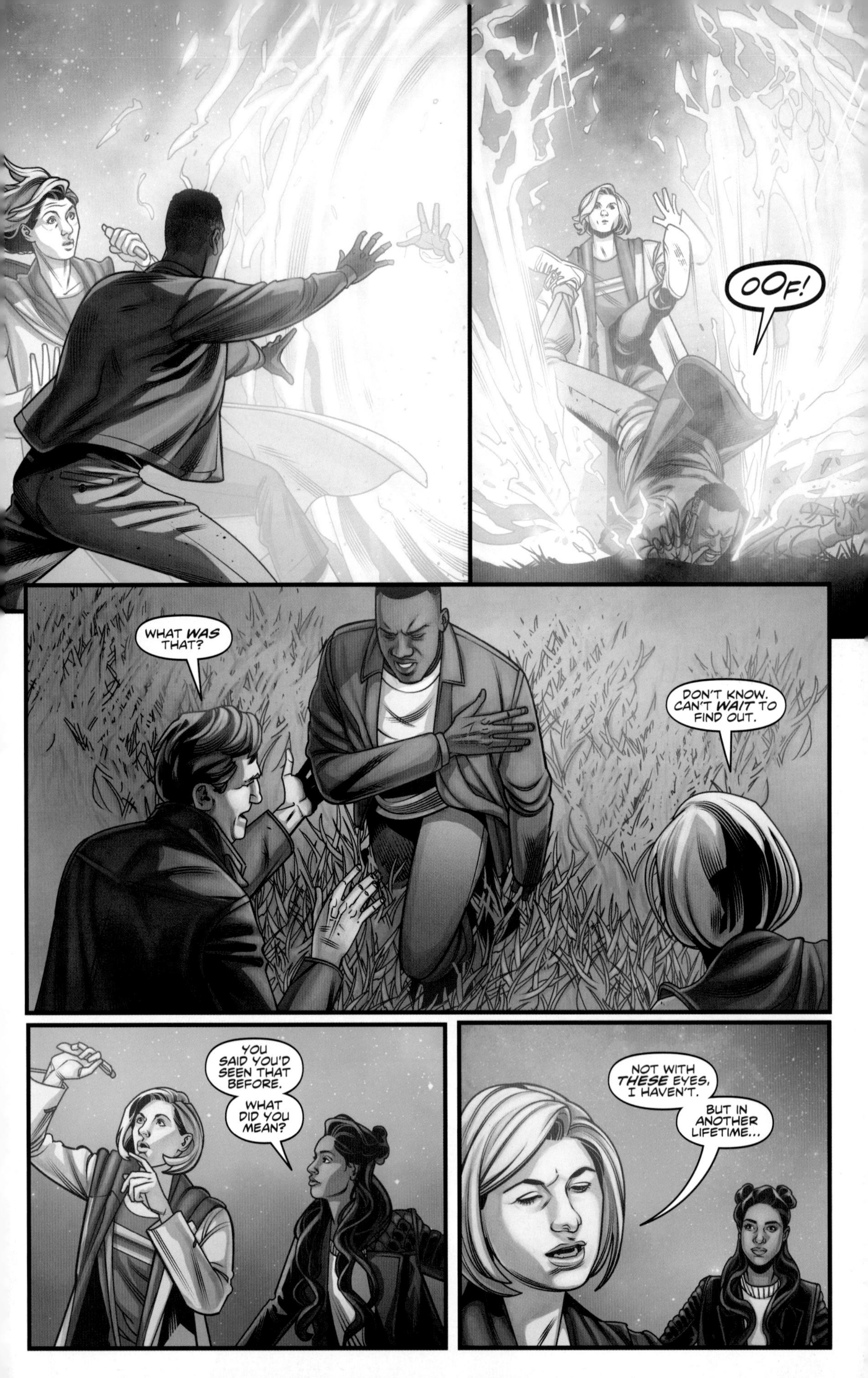

OOF!
WHAT *WAS* THAT?
DON'T KNOW. CAN'T *WAIT* TO FIND OUT.
YOU SAID YOU'D SEEN THAT BEFORE.
WHAT DID YOU MEAN?
NOT WITH *THESE* EYES, I HAVEN'T.
BUT IN ANOTHER LIFETIME...

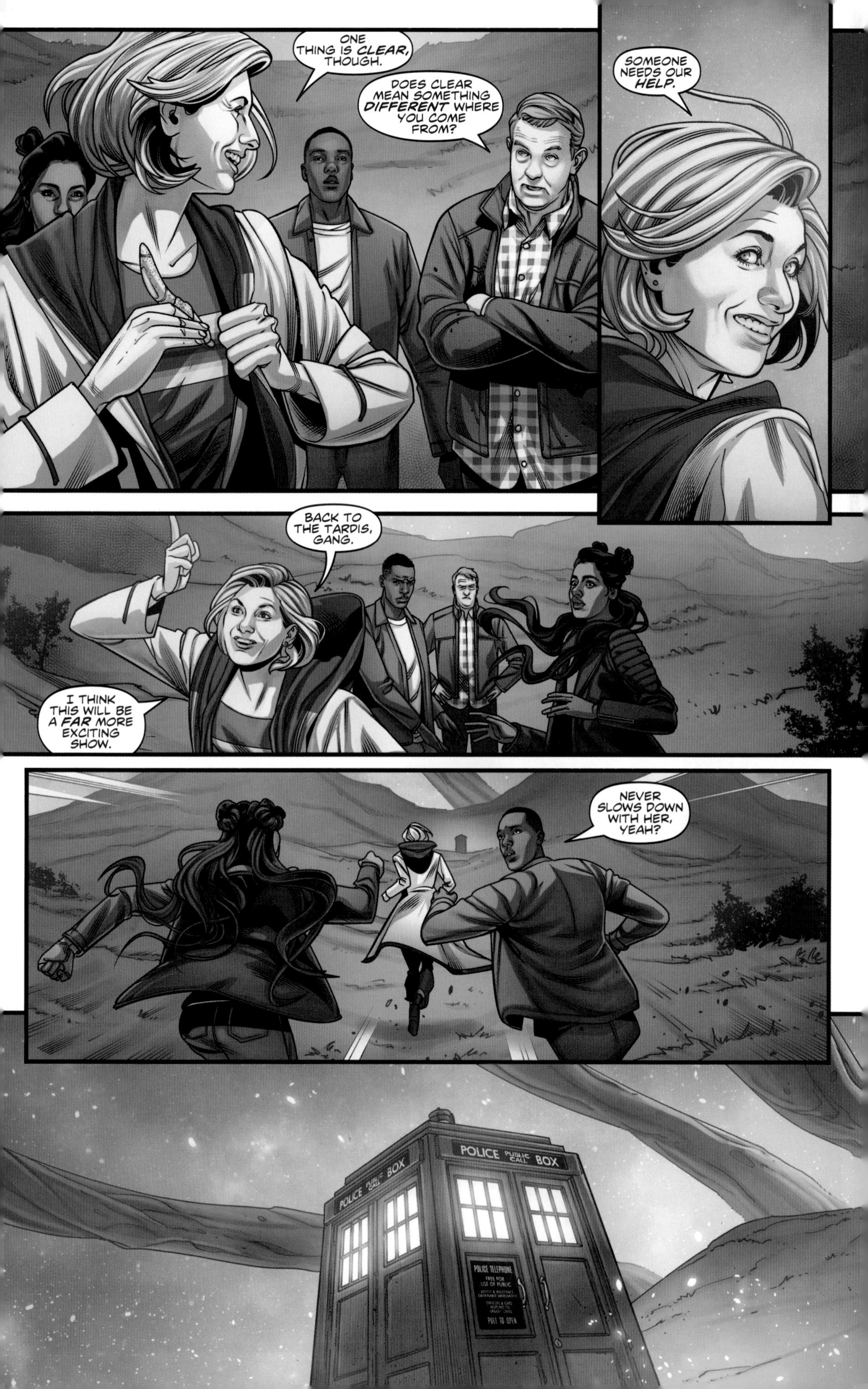
ONE THING IS CLEAR, THOUGH.
DOES CLEAR MEAN SOMETHING DIFFERENT WHERE YOU COME FROM?
SOMEONE NEEDS OUR HELP.
BACK TO THE TARDIS, GANG.
I THINK THIS WILL BE A FAR MORE EXCITING SHOW.
NEVER SLOWS DOWN WITH HER, YEAH?
POLICE PUBLIC CALL BOX
POLICE PUBLIC CALL BOX
POLICE TELEPHONE
FREE FOR USE OF PUBLIC
PULL TO OPEN

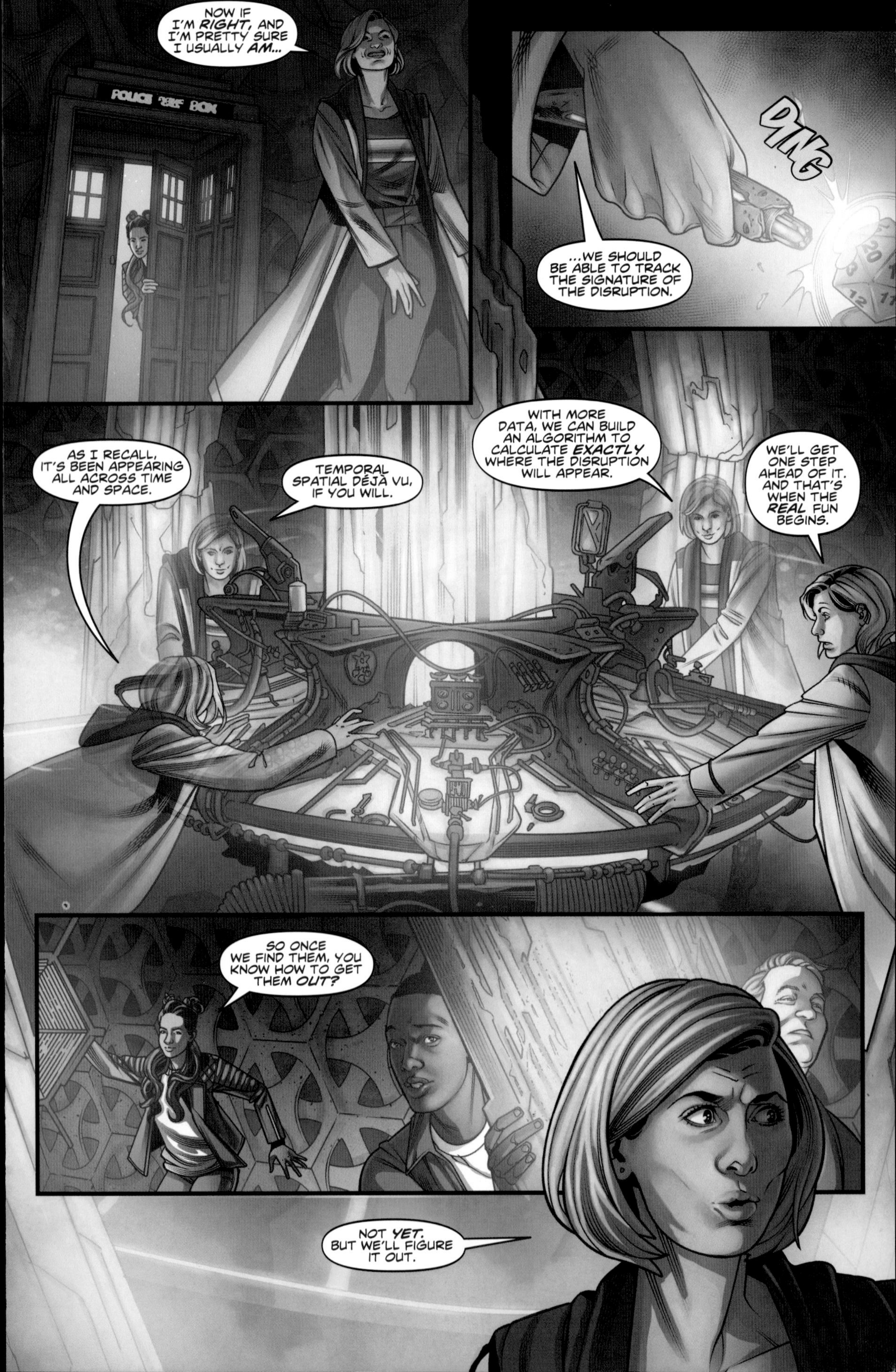
NOW IF I'M *RIGHT,* AND I'M PRETTY SURE I USUALLY *AM...*
POLICE BOX
DING
...WE SHOULD BE ABLE TO TRACK THE SIGNATURE OF THE DISRUPTION.
AS I RECALL, IT'S BEEN APPEARING ALL ACROSS TIME AND SPACE.
TEMPORAL SPATIAL DÉJÀ VU, IF YOU WILL.
WITH MORE DATA, WE CAN BUILD AN ALGORITHM TO CALCULATE *EXACTLY* WHERE THE DISRUPTION WILL APPEAR.
WE'LL GET ONE STEP AHEAD OF IT. AND THAT'S WHEN THE *REAL* FUN BEGINS.
SO ONCE WE FIND THEM, YOU KNOW HOW TO GET THEM *OUT?*
NOT *YET.* BUT WE'LL FIGURE IT OUT.

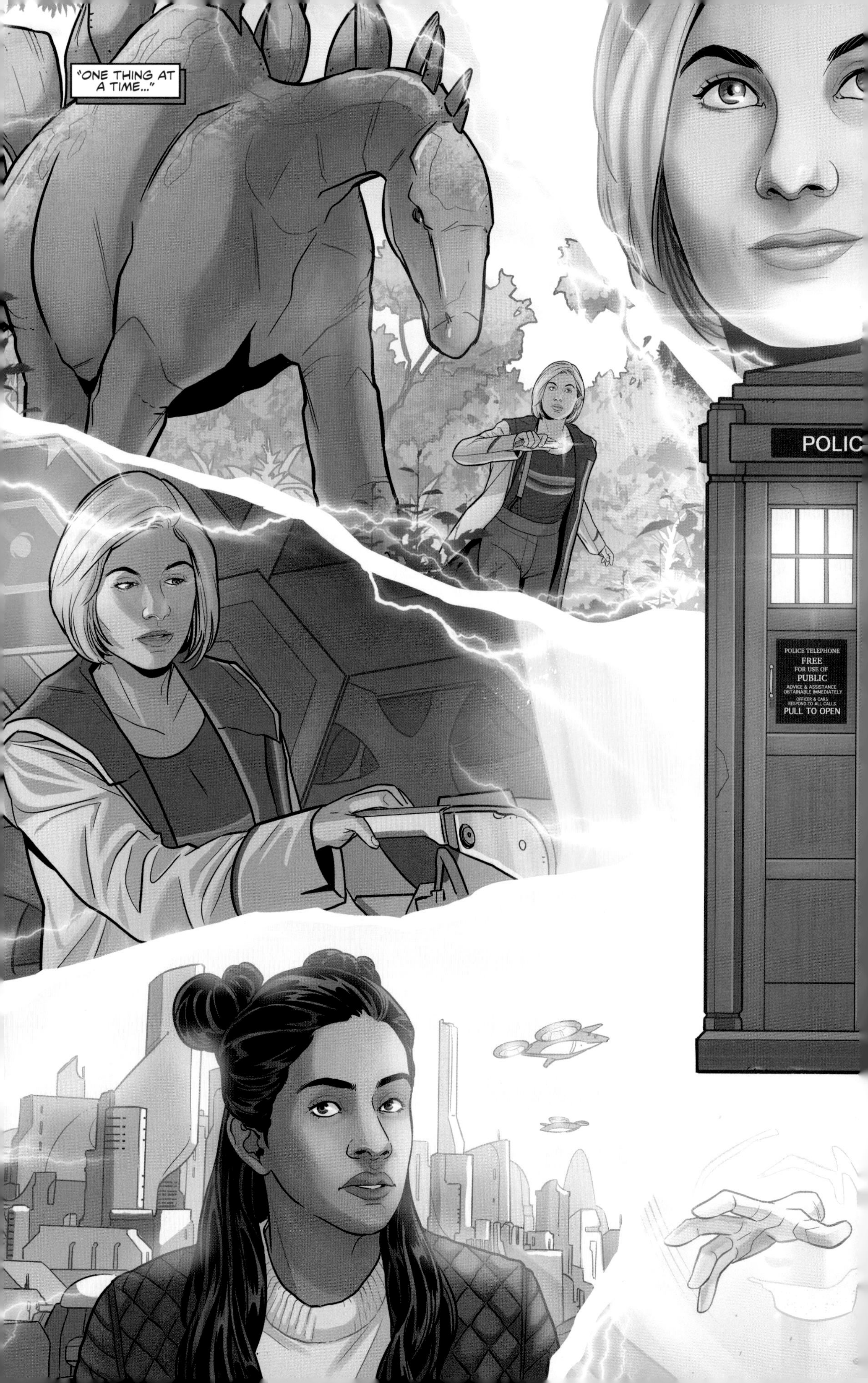
"ONE THING AT A TIME..."
POLIC
POLICE TELEPHONE
FREE
FOR USE OF
PUBLIC
ADVICE & ASSISTANCE OBTAINABLE IMMEDIATELY
OFFICER & CARS RESPOND TO ALL CALLS
PULL TO OPEN

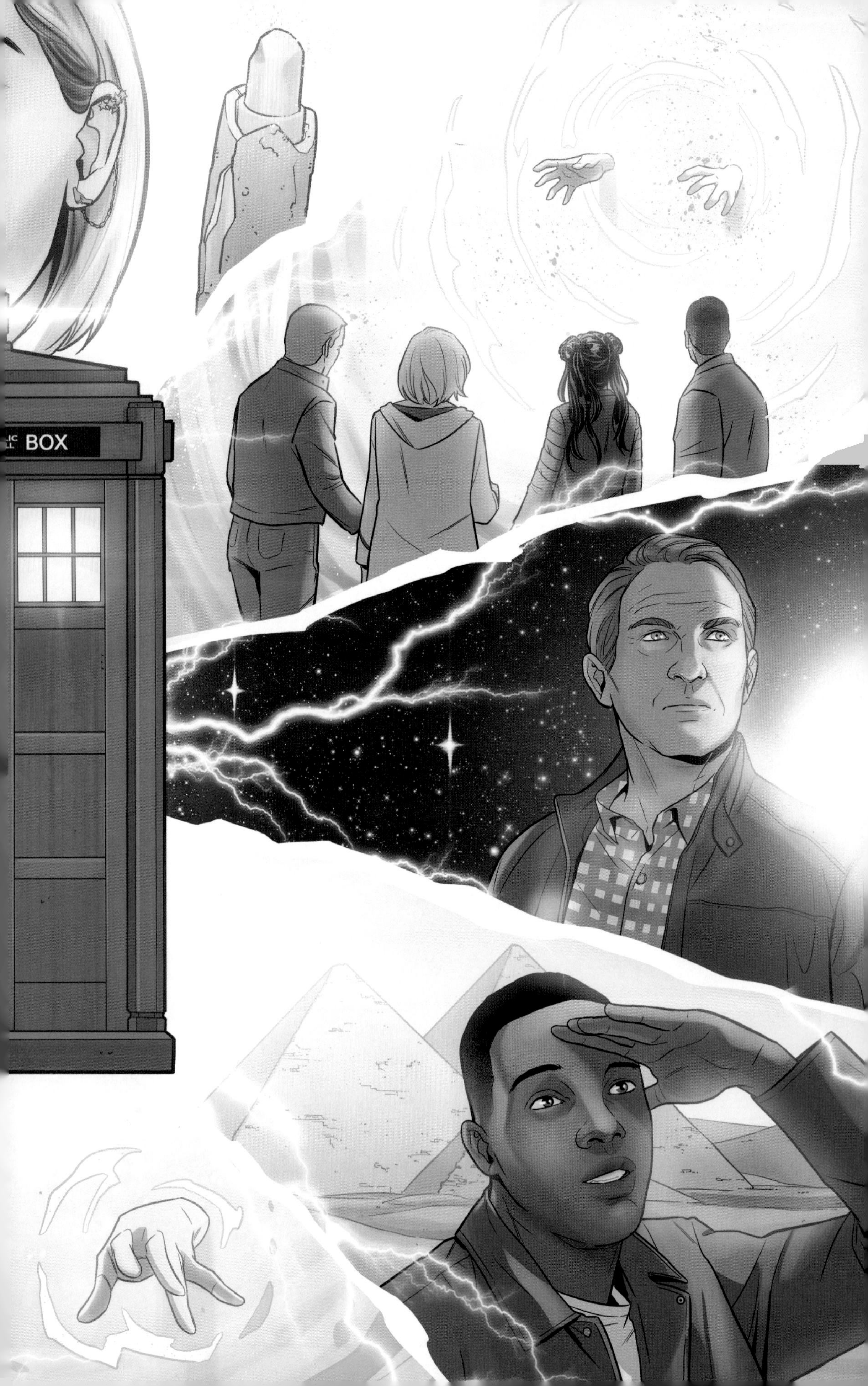
BOX

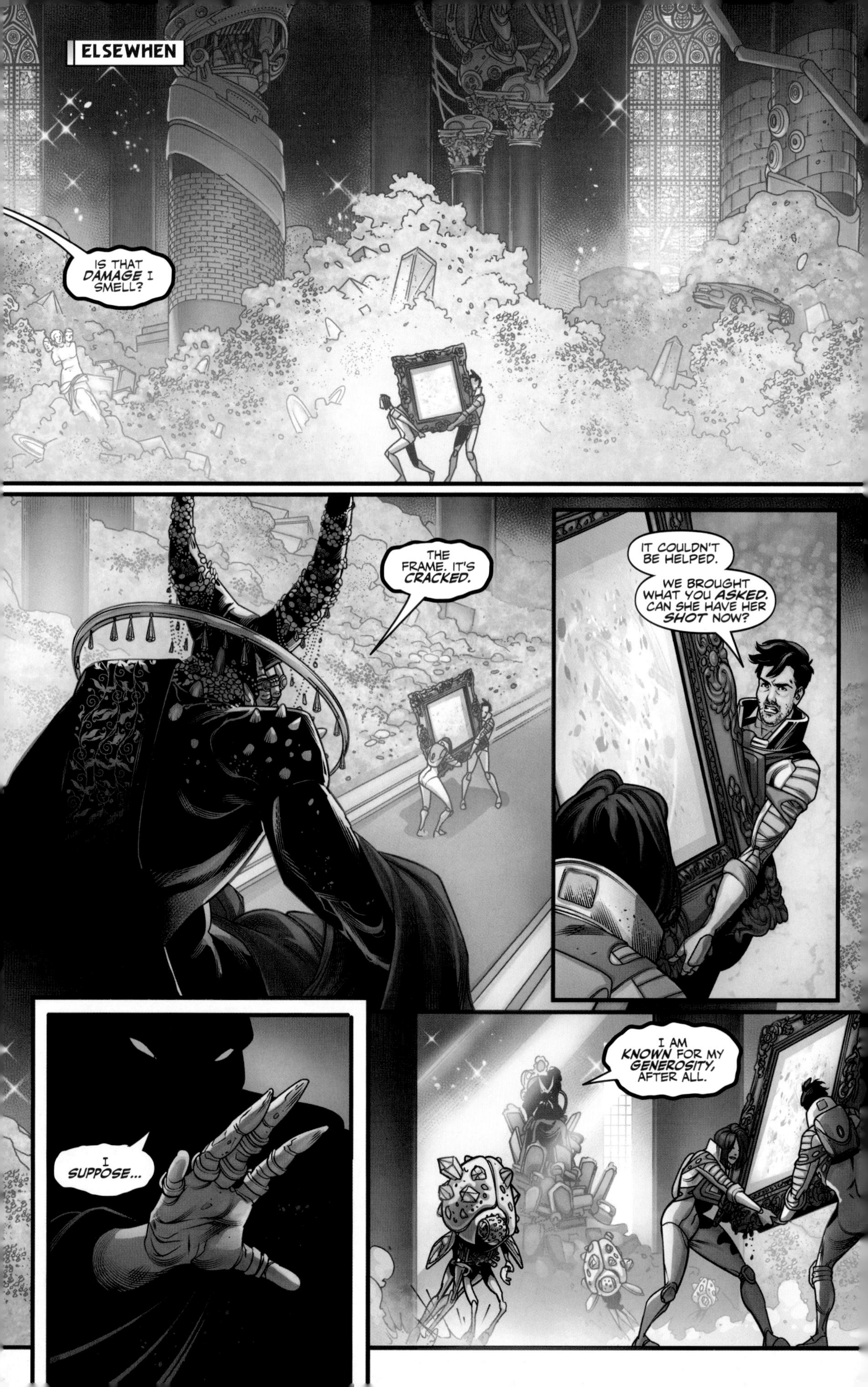
ELSEWHEN
IS THAT DAMAGE I SMELL?
THE FRAME. IT'S CRACKED.
IT COULDN'T BE HELPED.
WE BROUGHT WHAT YOU ASKED. CAN SHE HAVE HER SHOT NOW?
I SUPPOSE...
I AM KNOWN FOR MY GENEROSITY, AFTER ALL.

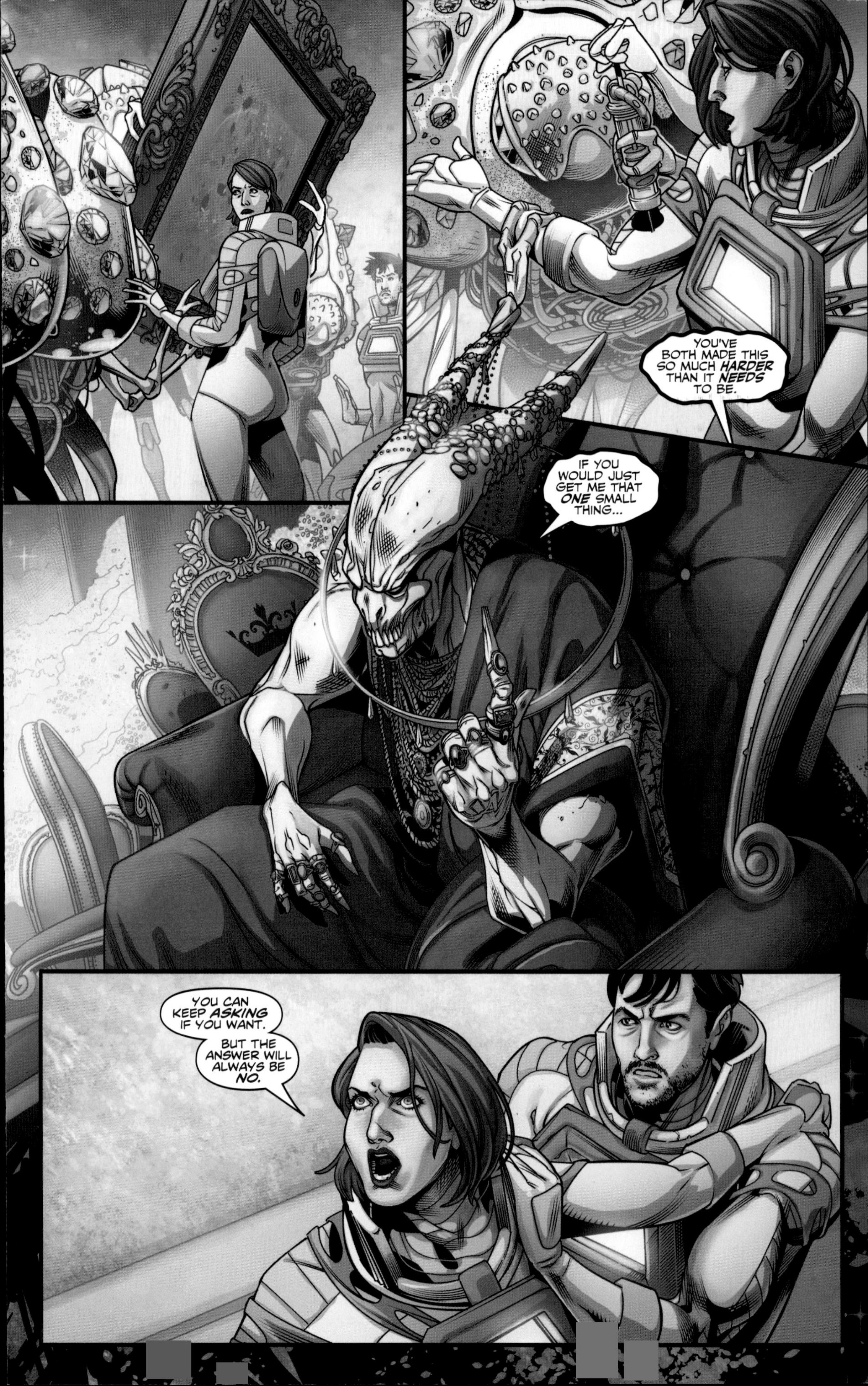
YOU'VE BOTH MADE THIS SO MUCH HARDER THAN IT NEEDS TO BE.
IF YOU WOULD JUST GET ME THAT ONE SMALL THING...
YOU CAN KEEP ASKING IF YOU WANT.
BUT THE ANSWER WILL ALWAYS BE NO.

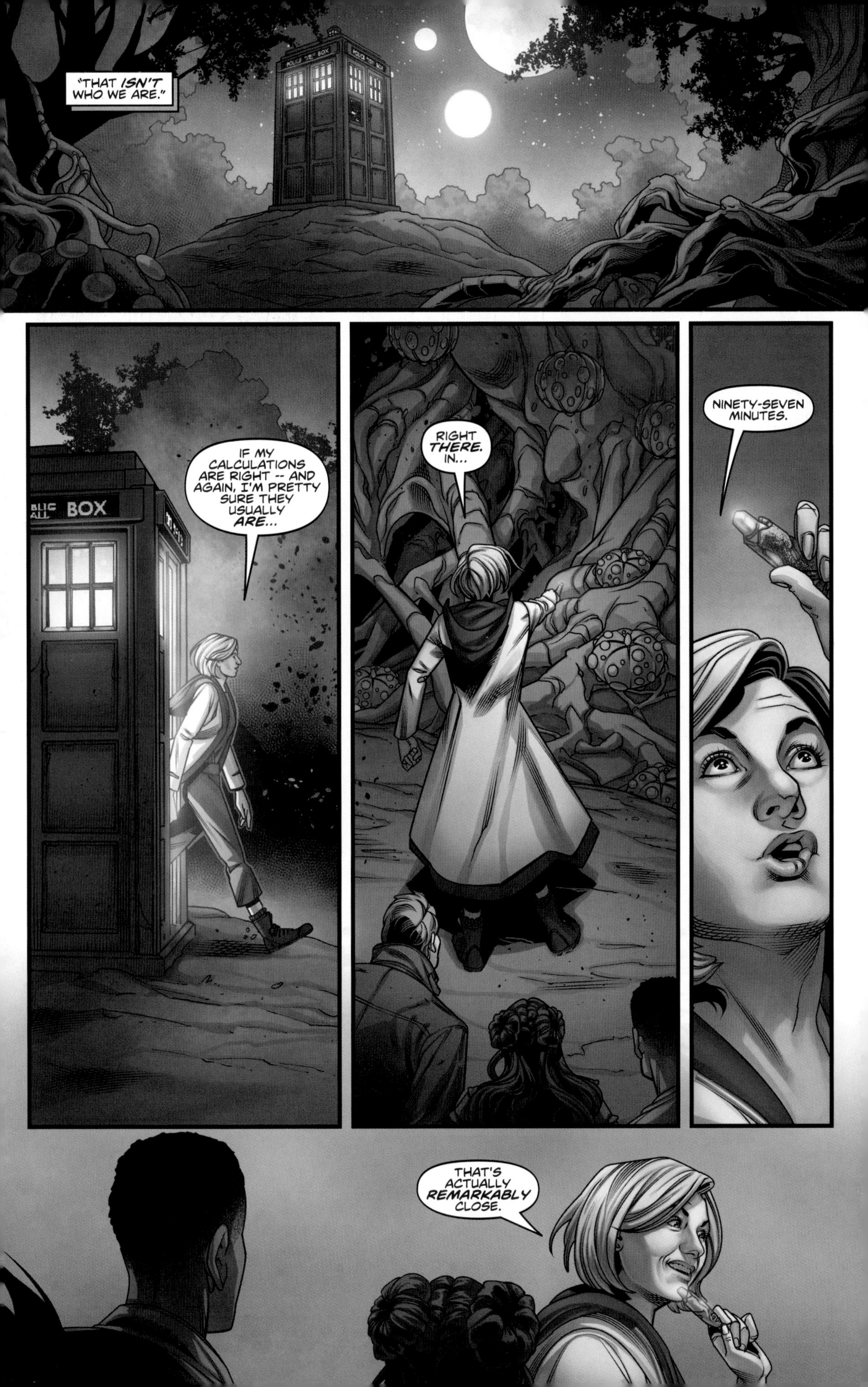
"THAT ISN'T WHO WE ARE."
BOX
IF MY CALCULATIONS ARE RIGHT -- AND AGAIN, I'M PRETTY SURE THEY USUALLY ARE...
RIGHT THERE. IN...
NINETY-SEVEN MINUTES.
THAT'S ACTUALLY REMARKABLY CLOSE.

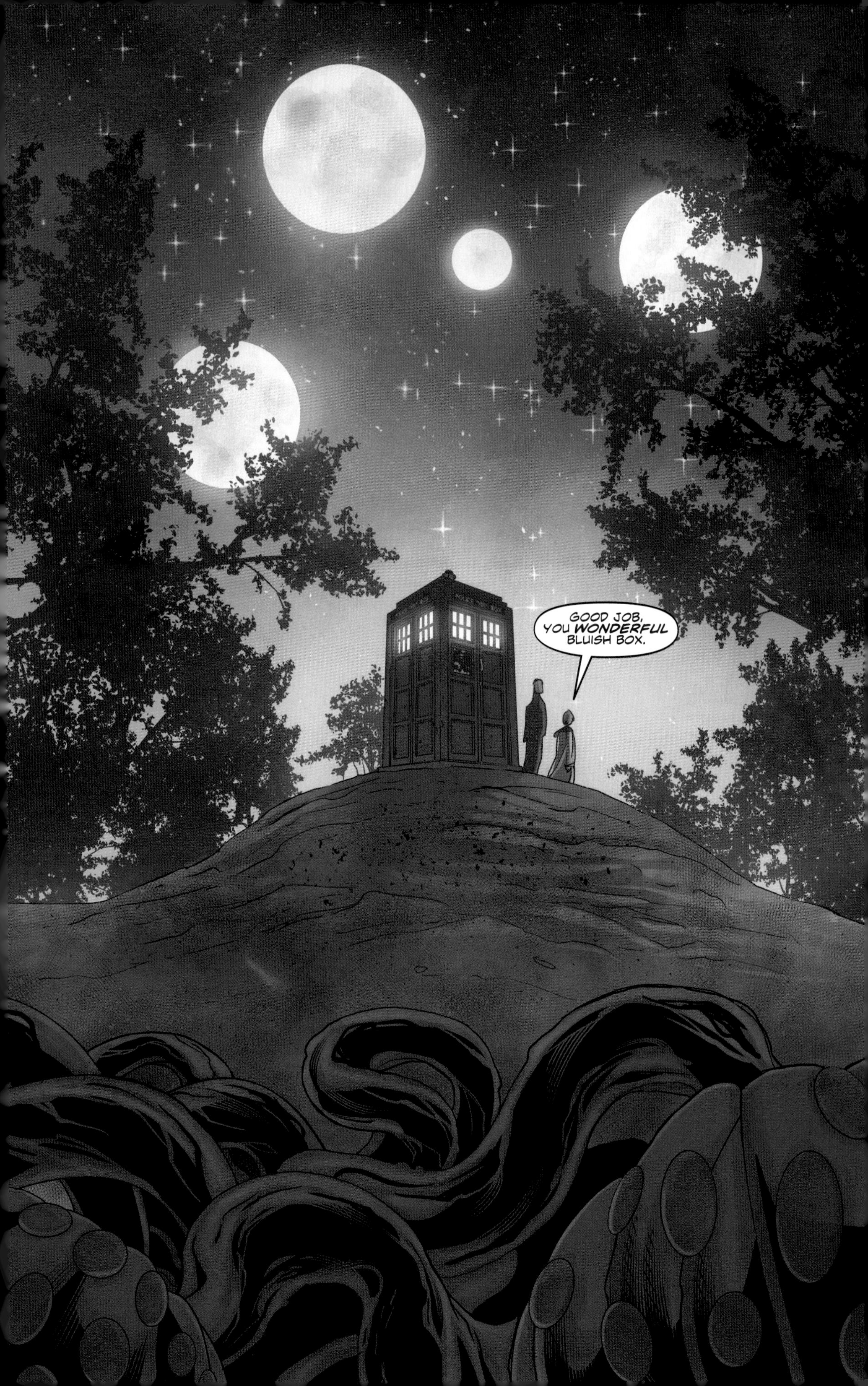
GOOD JOB, YOU WONDERFUL BLUISH BOX.

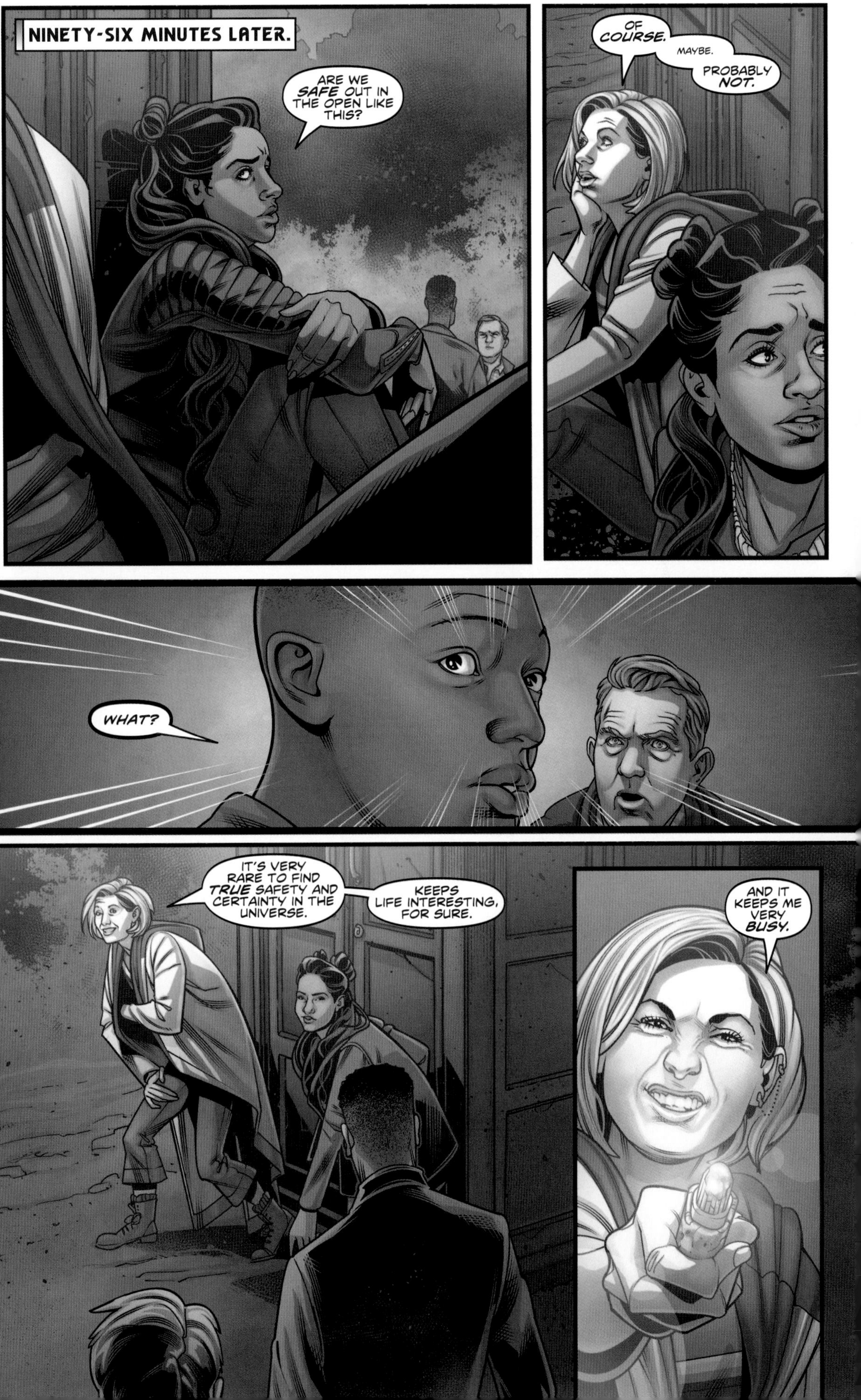
NINETY-SIX MINUTES LATER.
ARE WE SAFE OUT IN THE OPEN LIKE THIS?
OF COURSE.
MAYBE.
PROBABLY NOT.
WHAT?
IT'S VERY RARE TO FIND TRUE SAFETY AND CERTAINTY IN THE UNIVERSE.
KEEPS LIFE INTERESTING, FOR SURE.
AND IT KEEPS ME VERY BUSY.

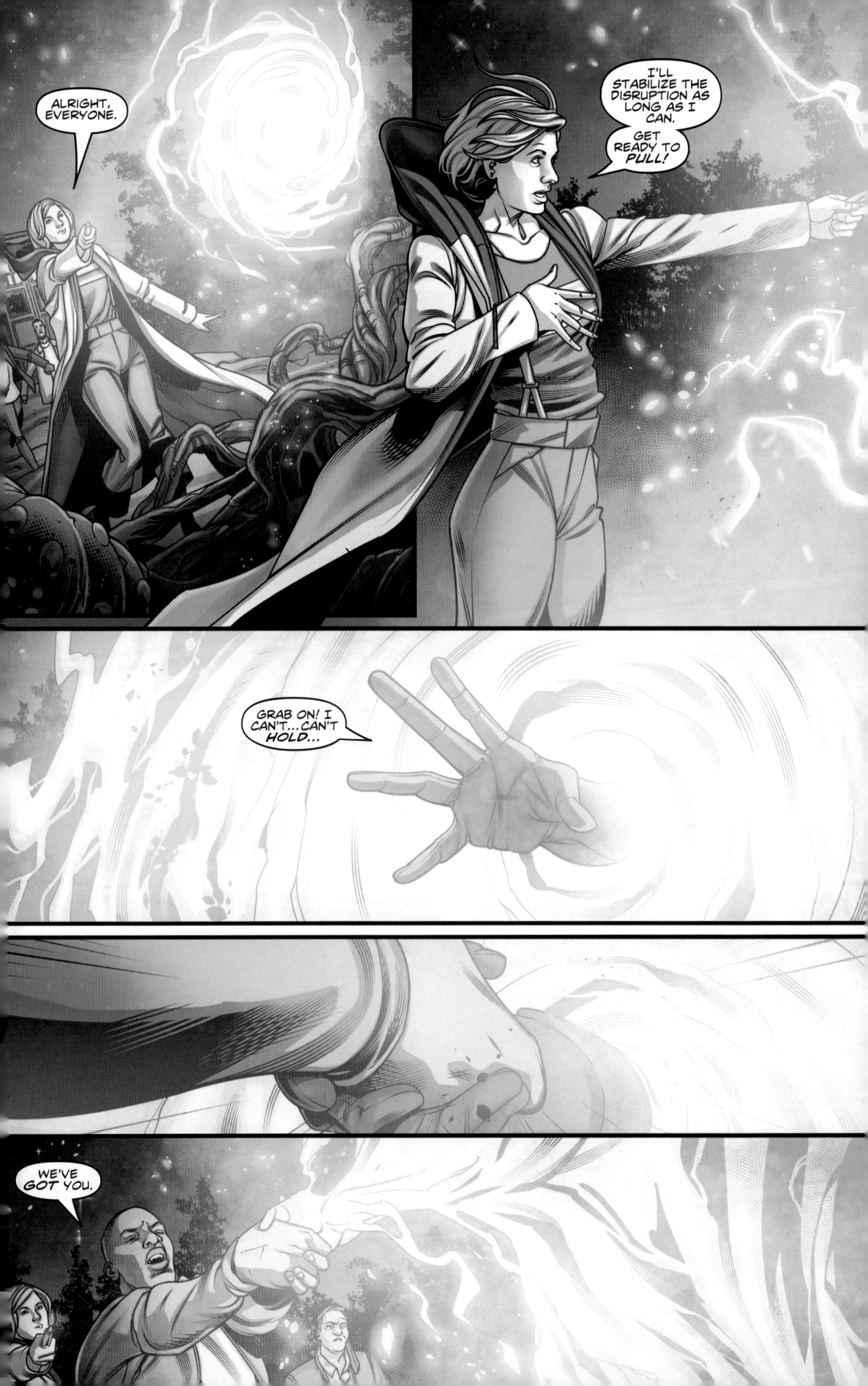
ALRIGHT, EVERYONE.
I'LL STABILIZE THE DISRUPTION AS LONG AS I CAN.
GET READY TO PULL!
GRAB ON! I CAN'T...CAN'T HOLD...
WE'VE GOT YOU.

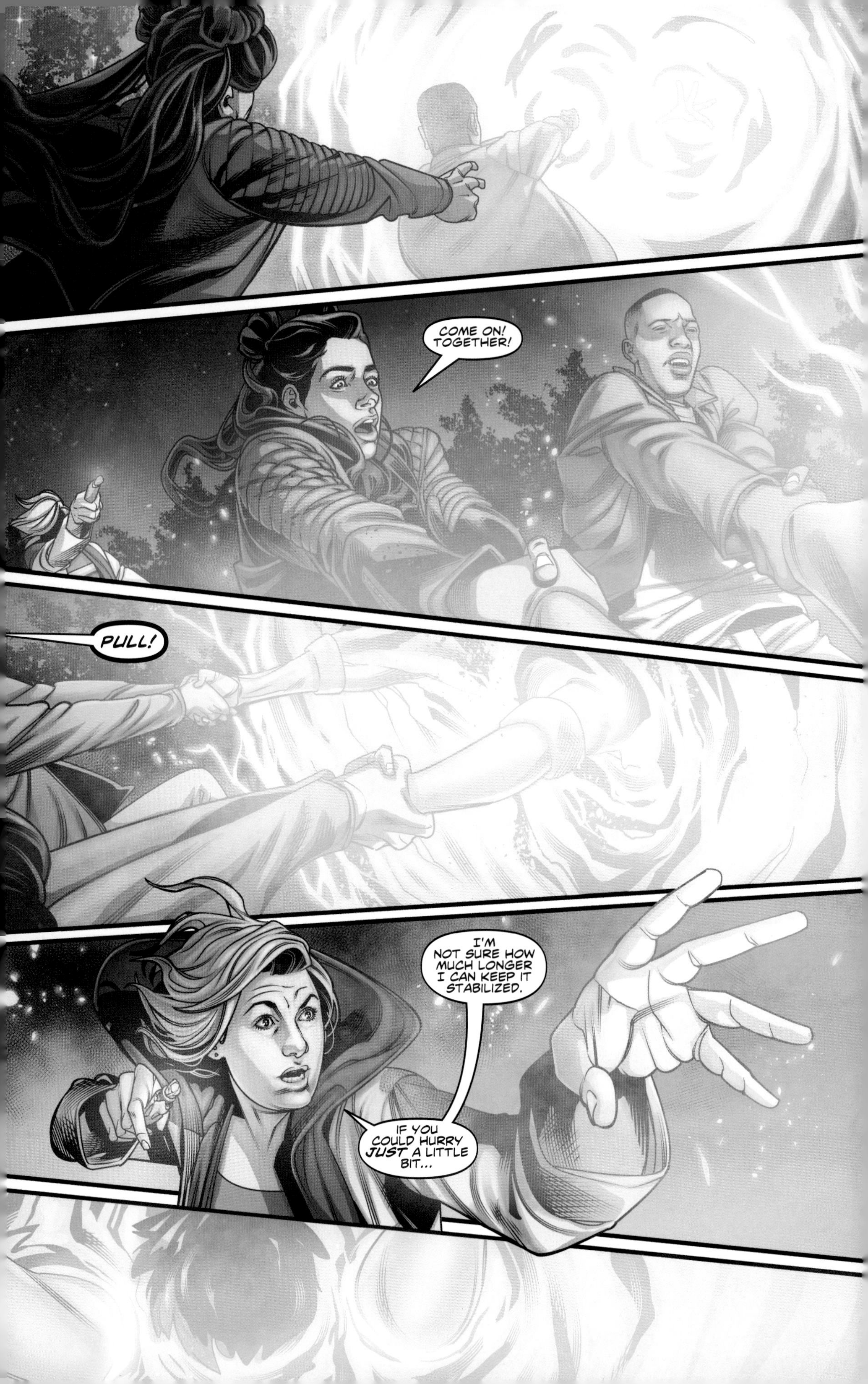

COME ON! TOGETHER!
PULL!
I'M NOT SURE HOW MUCH LONGER I CAN KEEP IT STABILIZED.
IF YOU COULD HURRY JUST A LITTLE BIT...

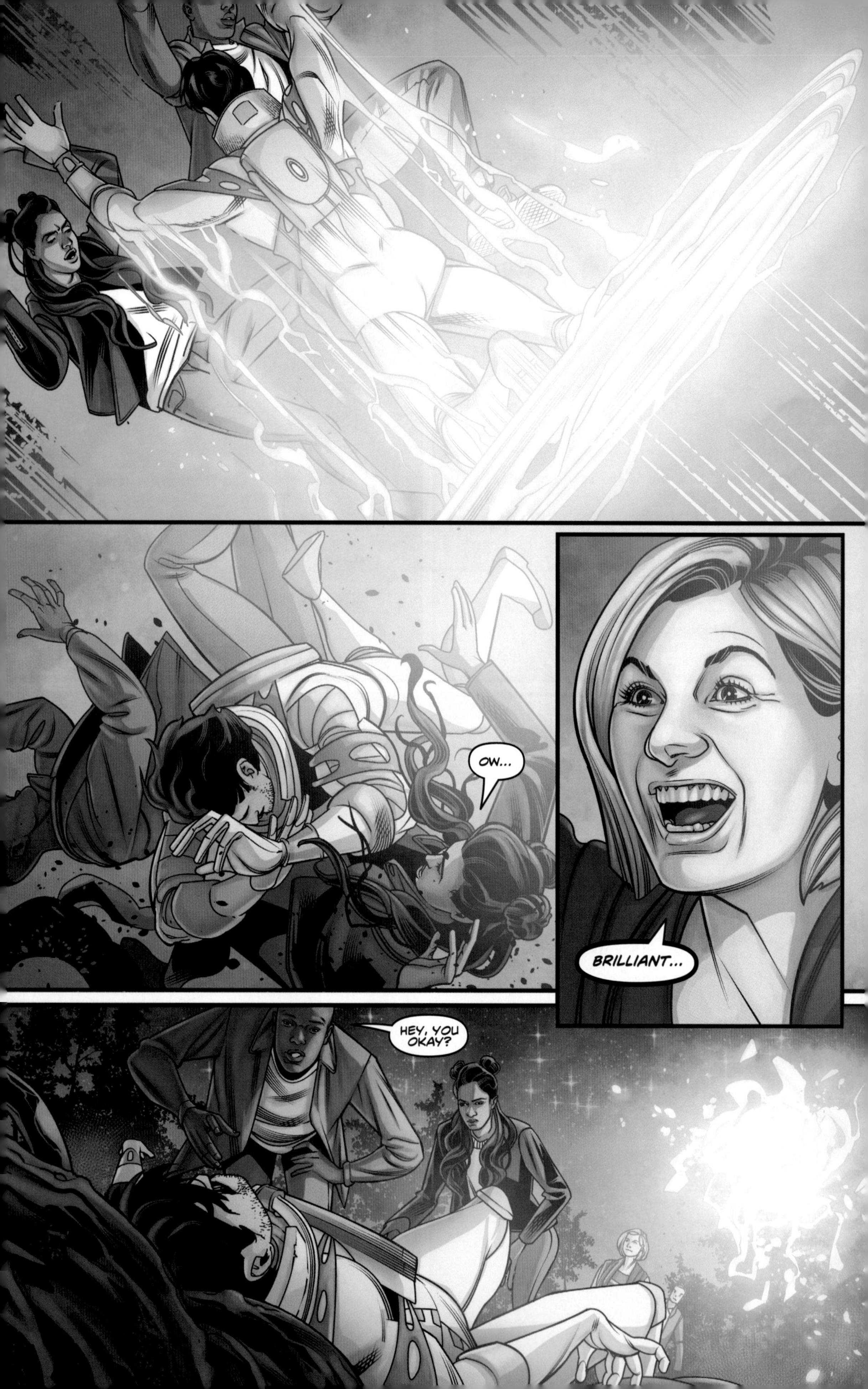
OW...
BRILLIANT...
HEY, YOU OKAY?

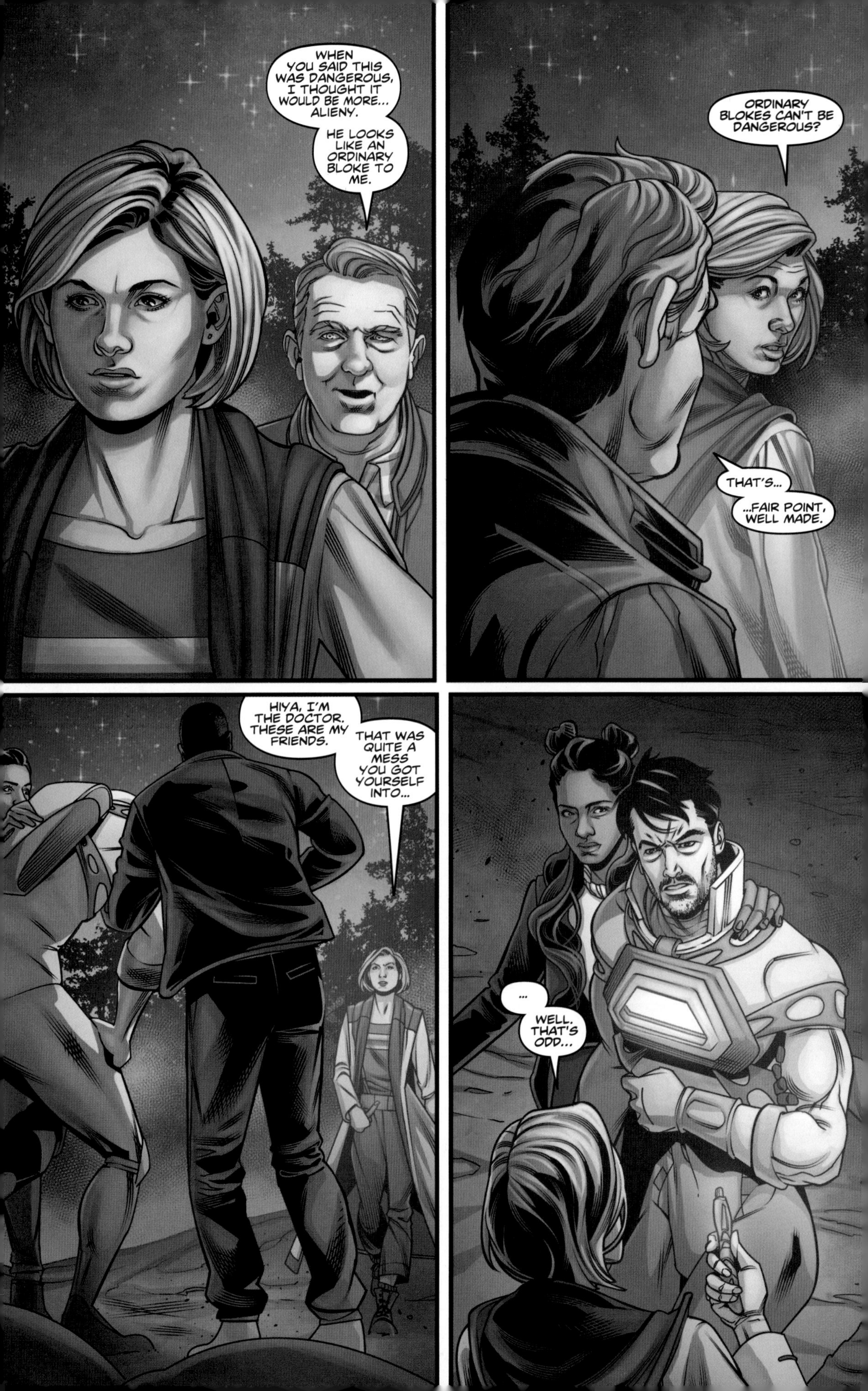

WHEN YOU SAID THIS WAS DANGEROUS, I THOUGHT IT WOULD BE MORE... ALIENY.
HE LOOKS LIKE AN ORDINARY BLOKE TO ME.
ORDINARY BLOKES CAN'T BE DANGEROUS?
THAT'S...
...FAIR POINT, WELL MADE.
HIYA, I'M THE DOCTOR. THESE ARE MY FRIENDS.
THAT WAS QUITE A MESS YOU GOT YOURSELF INTO...
...
WELL, THAT'S ODD...

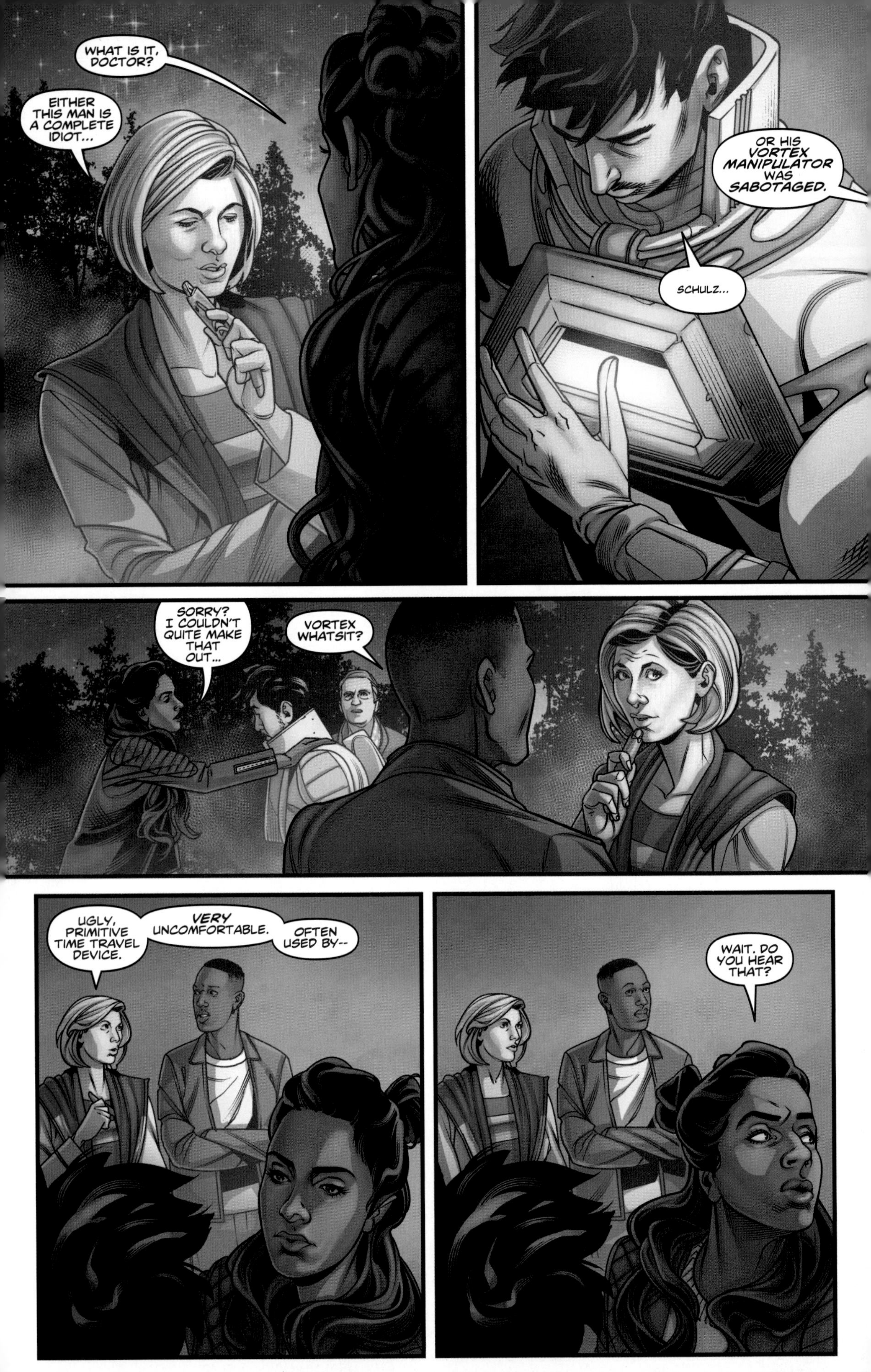
WHAT IS IT, DOCTOR?
EITHER THIS MAN IS A COMPLETE IDIOT...
OR HIS VORTEX MANIPULATOR WAS SABOTAGED.
SCHULZ...
SORRY? I COULDN'T QUITE MAKE THAT OUT...
VORTEX WHATSIT?
UGLY, PRIMITIVE TIME TRAVEL DEVICE.
VERY UNCOMFORTABLE.
OFTEN USED BY--
WAIT. DO YOU HEAR THAT?

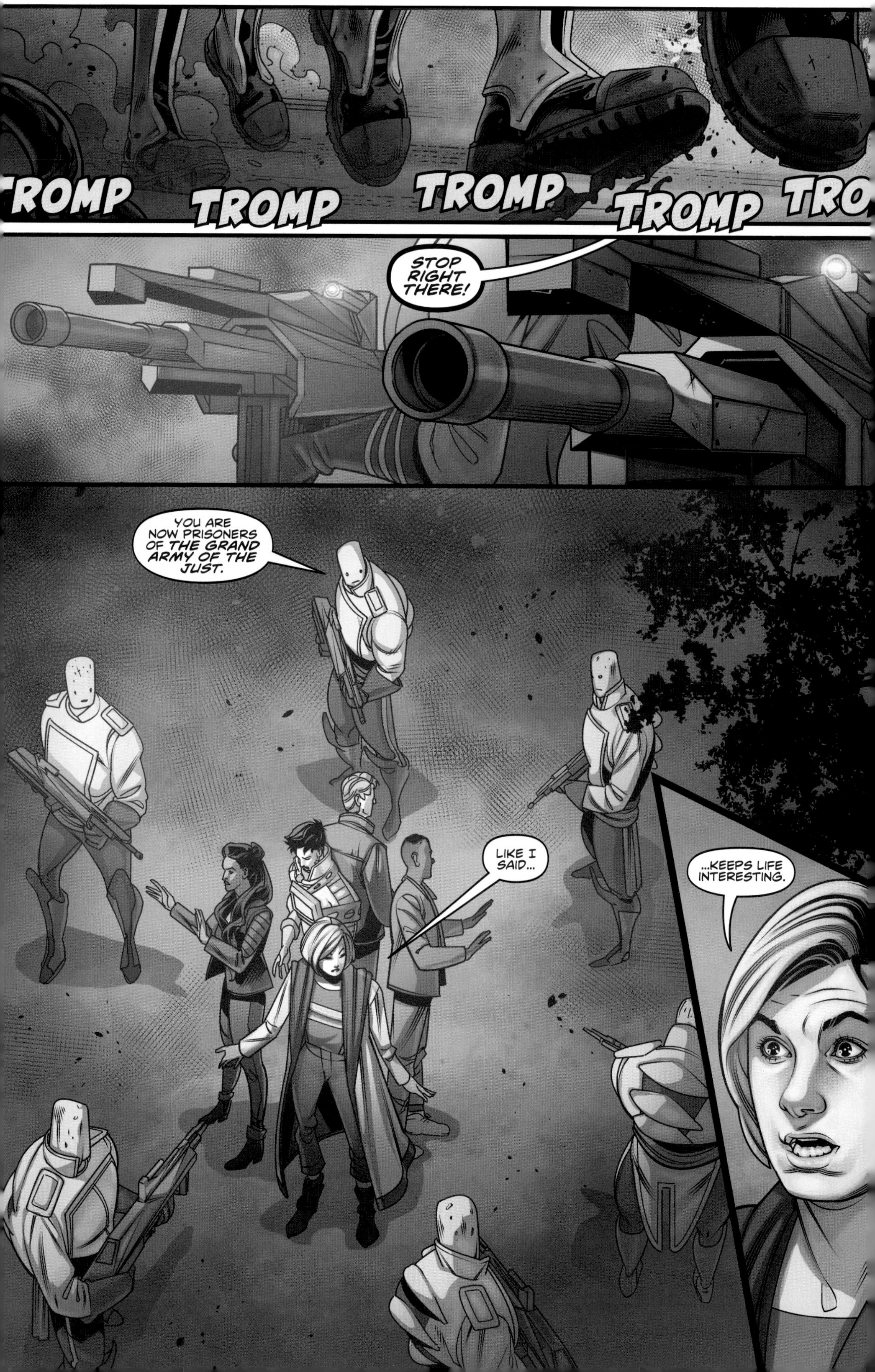
TROMP
TROMP
TROMP
TROMP
TRO
STOP RIGHT THERE!
YOU ARE NOW PRISONERS OF THE GRAND ARMY OF THE JUST.
LIKE I SAID...
...KEEPS LIFE INTERESTING.

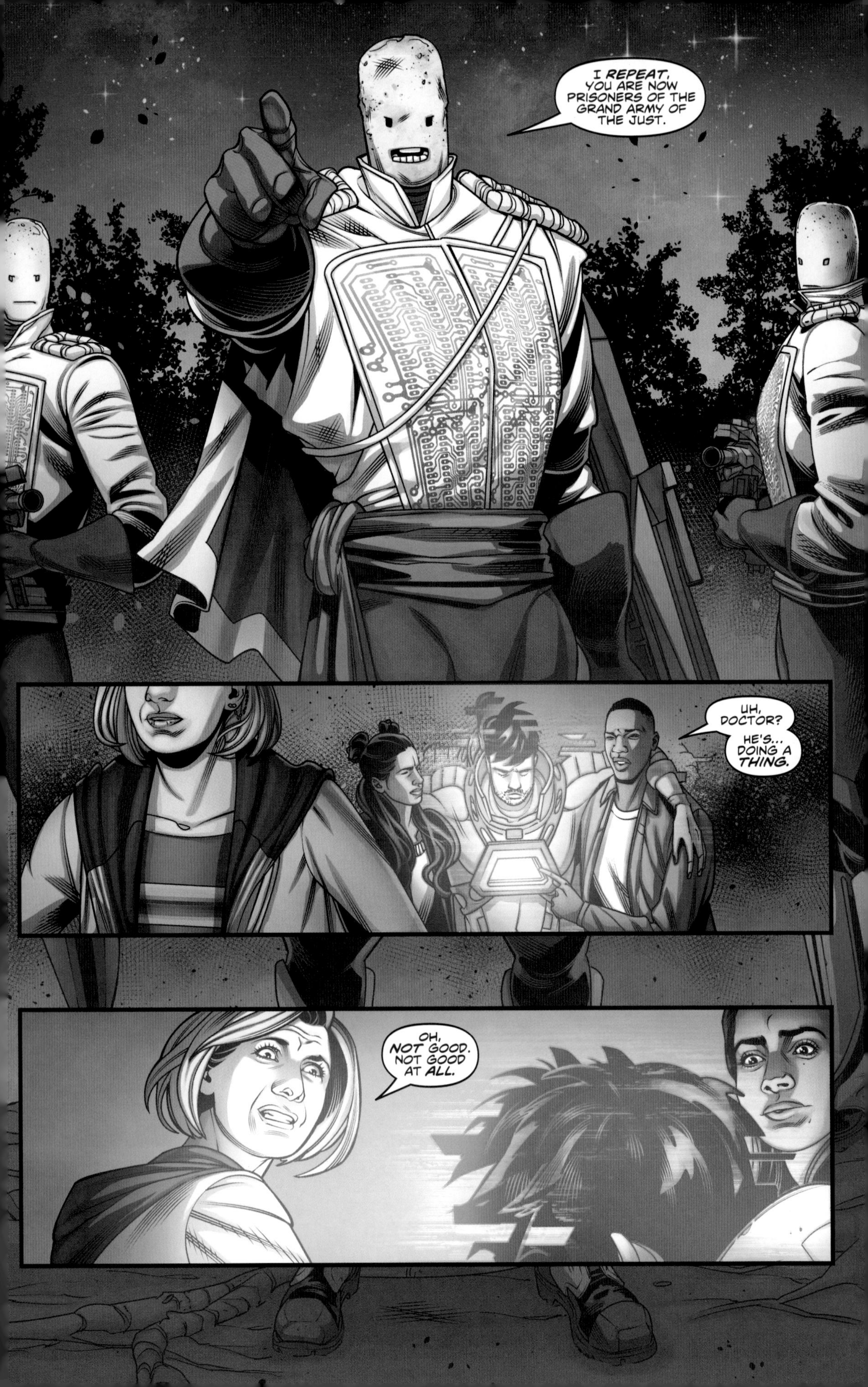
I REPEAT, YOU ARE NOW PRISONERS OF THE GRAND ARMY OF THE JUST.
UH, DOCTOR? HE'S... DOING A THING.
OH, NOT GOOD. NOT GOOD AT ALL.

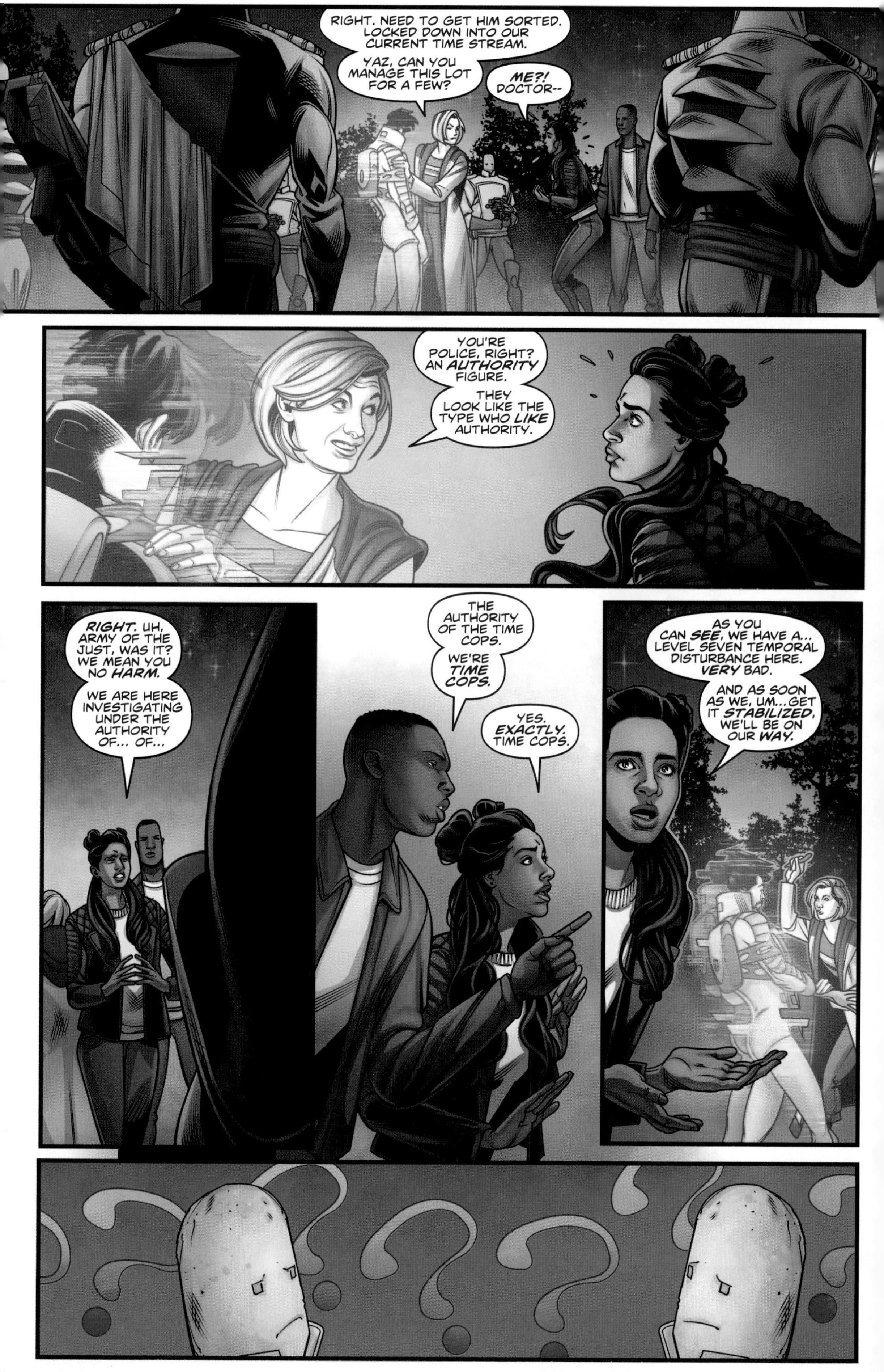
RIGHT. NEED TO GET HIM SORTED. LOCKED DOWN INTO OUR CURRENT TIME STREAM.
YAZ, CAN YOU MANAGE THIS LOT FOR A FEW?
ME?! DOCTOR--
YOU'RE POLICE, RIGHT? AN AUTHORITY FIGURE.
THEY LOOK LIKE THE TYPE WHO LIKE AUTHORITY.
RIGHT. UH, ARMY OF THE JUST, WAS IT? WE MEAN YOU NO HARM.
WE ARE HERE INVESTIGATING UNDER THE AUTHORITY OF... OF...
THE AUTHORITY OF THE TIME COPS.
WE'RE TIME COPS.
YES. EXACTLY. TIME COPS.
AS YOU CAN SEE, WE HAVE A... LEVEL SEVEN TEMPORAL DISTURBANCE HERE. VERY BAD.
AND AS SOON AS WE, UM...GET IT STABILIZED, WE'LL BE ON OUR WAY.

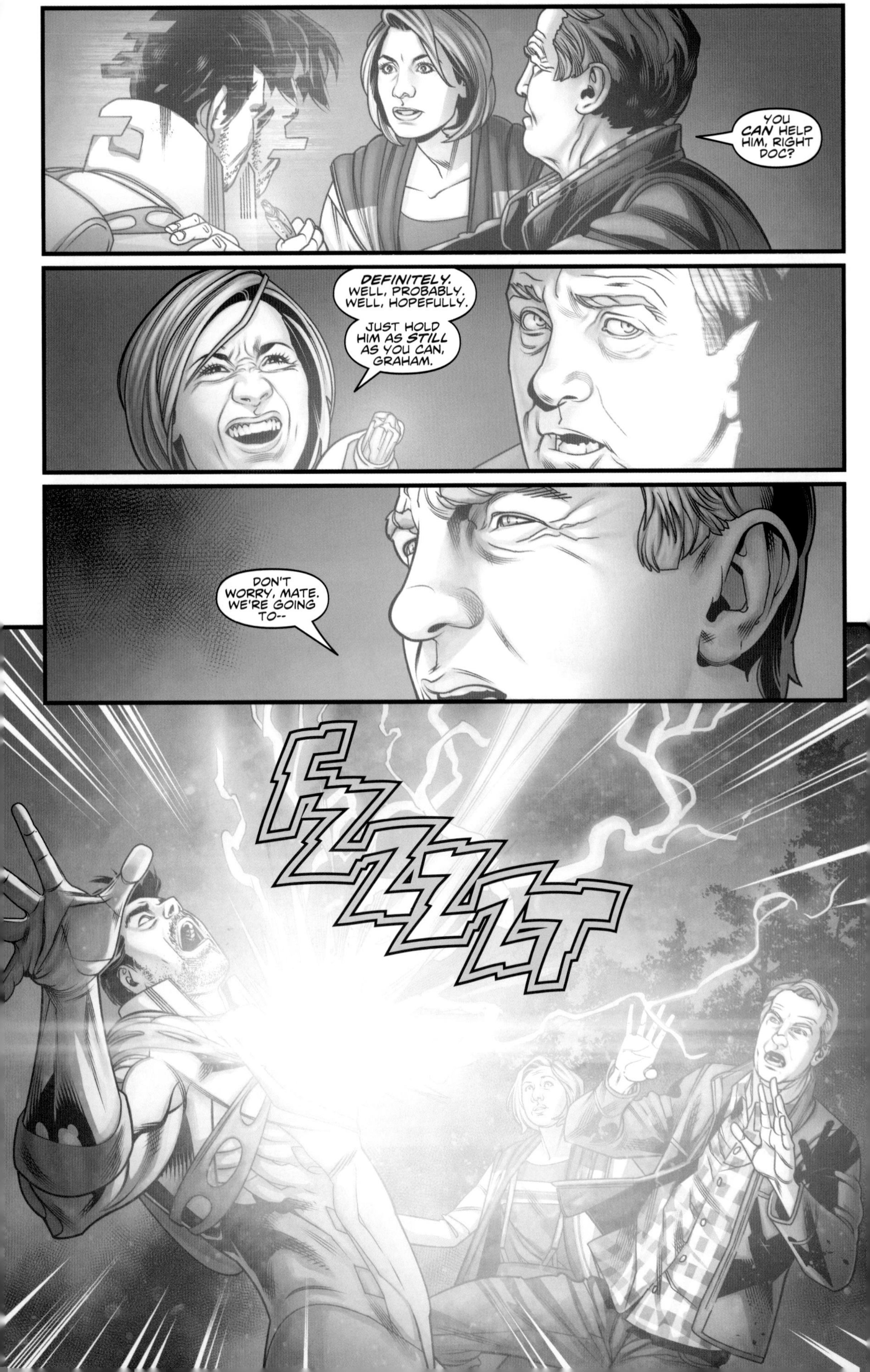
YOU CAN HELP HIM, RIGHT DOC?
DEFINITELY. WELL, PROBABLY. WELL, HOPEFULLY.
JUST HOLD HIM AS STILL AS YOU CAN, GRAHAM.
DON'T WORRY, MATE. WE'RE GOING TO--
FZZZZT

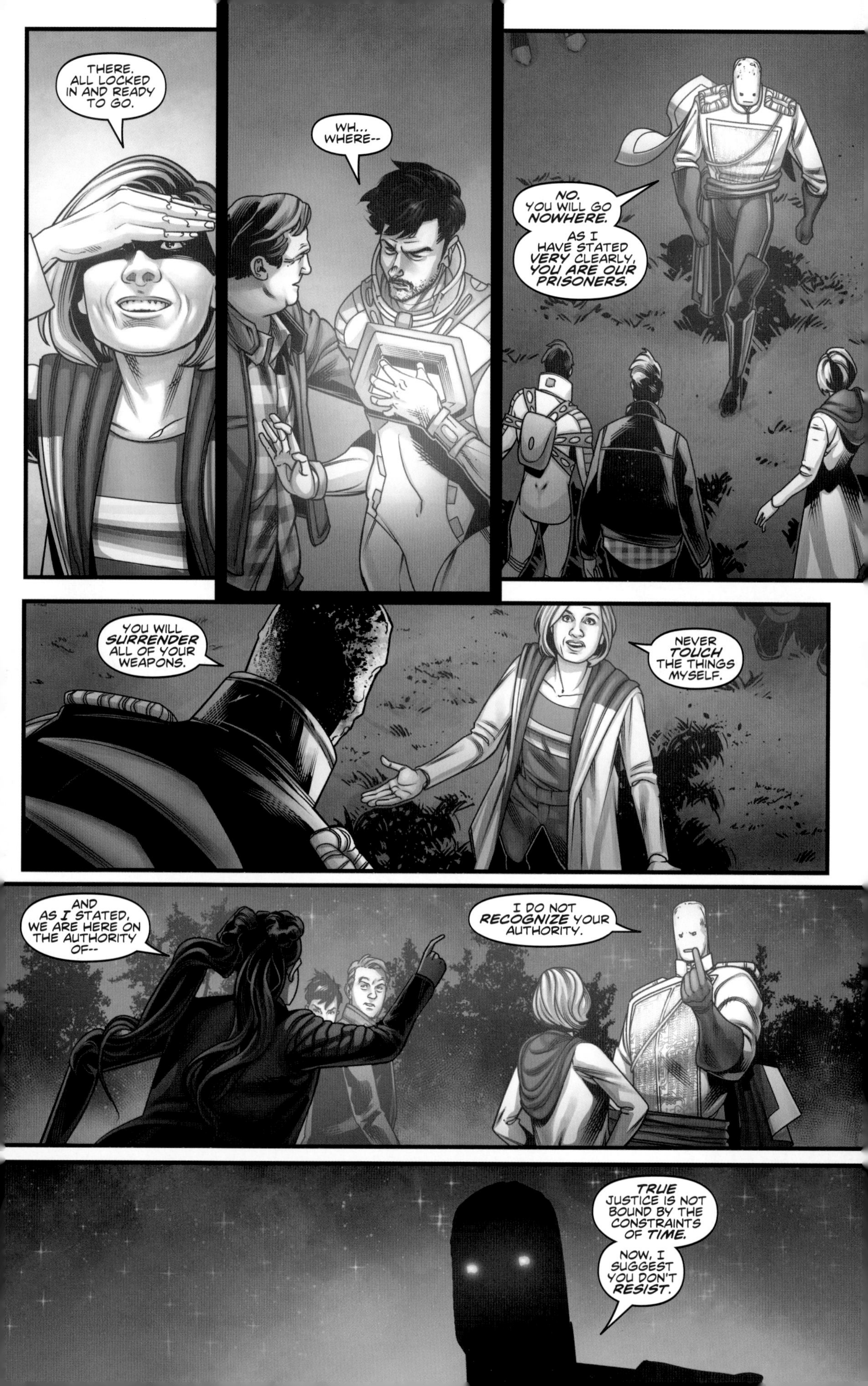
THERE. ALL LOCKED IN AND READY TO GO.
WH... WHERE--
NO. YOU WILL GO NOWHERE.
AS I HAVE STATED VERY CLEARLY, YOU ARE OUR PRISONERS.
YOU WILL SURRENDER ALL OF YOUR WEAPONS.
NEVER TOUCH THE THINGS MYSELF.
AND AS I STATED, WE ARE HERE ON THE AUTHORITY OF--
I DO NOT RECOGNIZE YOUR AUTHORITY.
TRUE JUSTICE IS NOT BOUND BY THE CONSTRAINTS OF TIME.
NOW, I SUGGEST YOU DON'T RESIST.

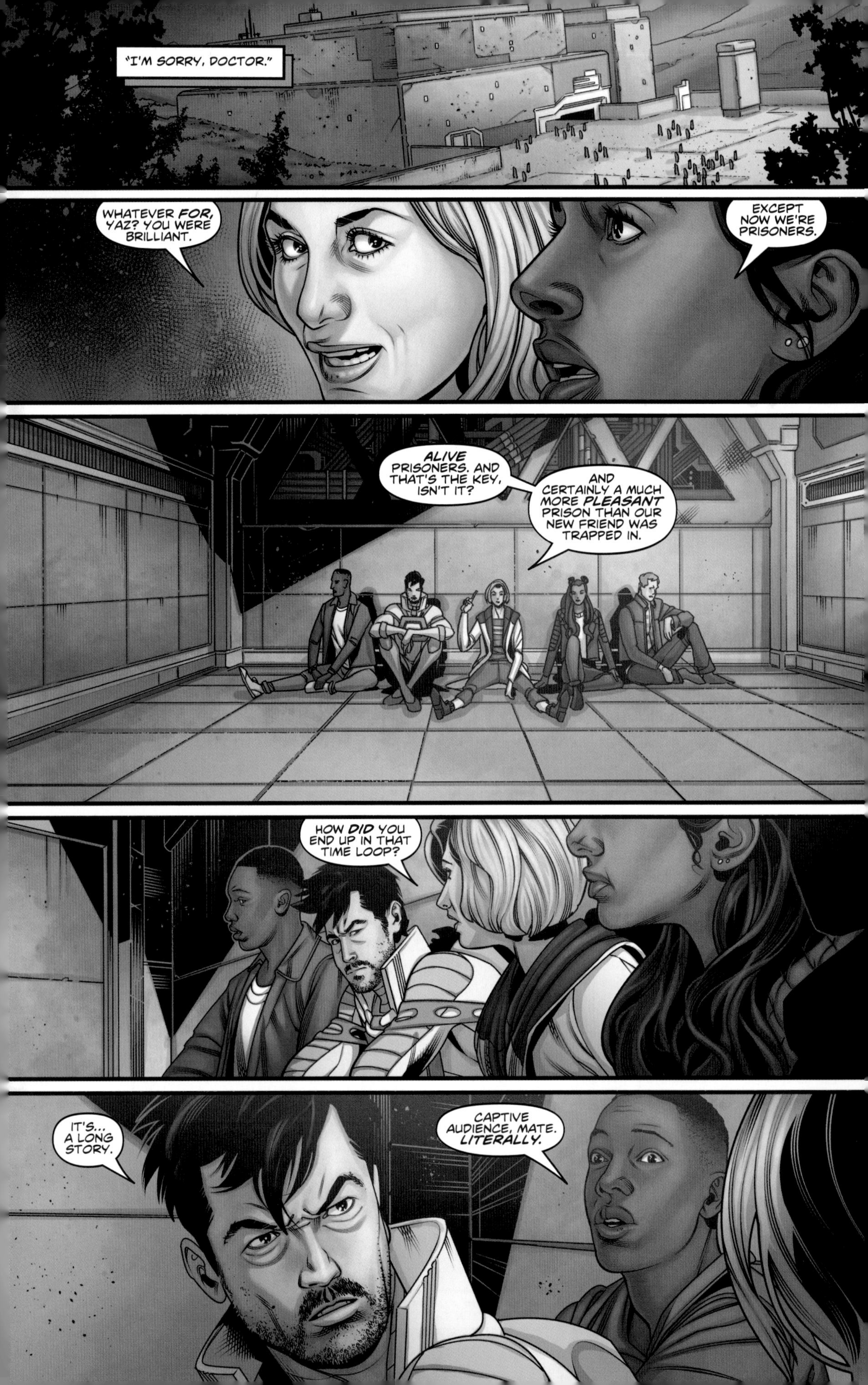
"I'M SORRY, DOCTOR."
WHATEVER FOR, YAZ? YOU WERE BRILLIANT.
EXCEPT NOW WE'RE PRISONERS.
ALIVE PRISONERS. AND THAT'S THE KEY, ISN'T IT?
AND CERTAINLY A MUCH MORE PLEASANT PRISON THAN OUR NEW FRIEND WAS TRAPPED IN.
HOW DID YOU END UP IN THAT TIME LOOP?
IT'S... A LONG STORY.
CAPTIVE AUDIENCE, MATE. LITERALLY.

"MY NAME IS DR. LEON PERKINS.

"I WORK UNDER THE FOREMOST EXPERT ON TEMPORAL PHYSICS, DR. IRENE SCHULZ.

FOREMOST *HUMAN* EXPERT, I TAKE IT.

ERR. YES.

"WE WERE WORKING ON THE LATEST ADVANCEMENT IN, WELL, WHAT YOU MIGHT CALL *TIME TRAVEL*.

"*WEARABLE* TECH.

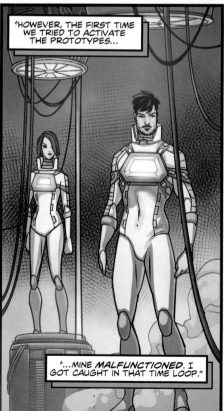

"HOWEVER, THE FIRST TIME WE TRIED TO ACTIVATE THE PROTOTYPES...

"...MINE *MALFUNCTIONED*. I GOT CAUGHT IN THAT TIME LOOP."

THAT'S IT?

ISN'T THAT *ENOUGH?*

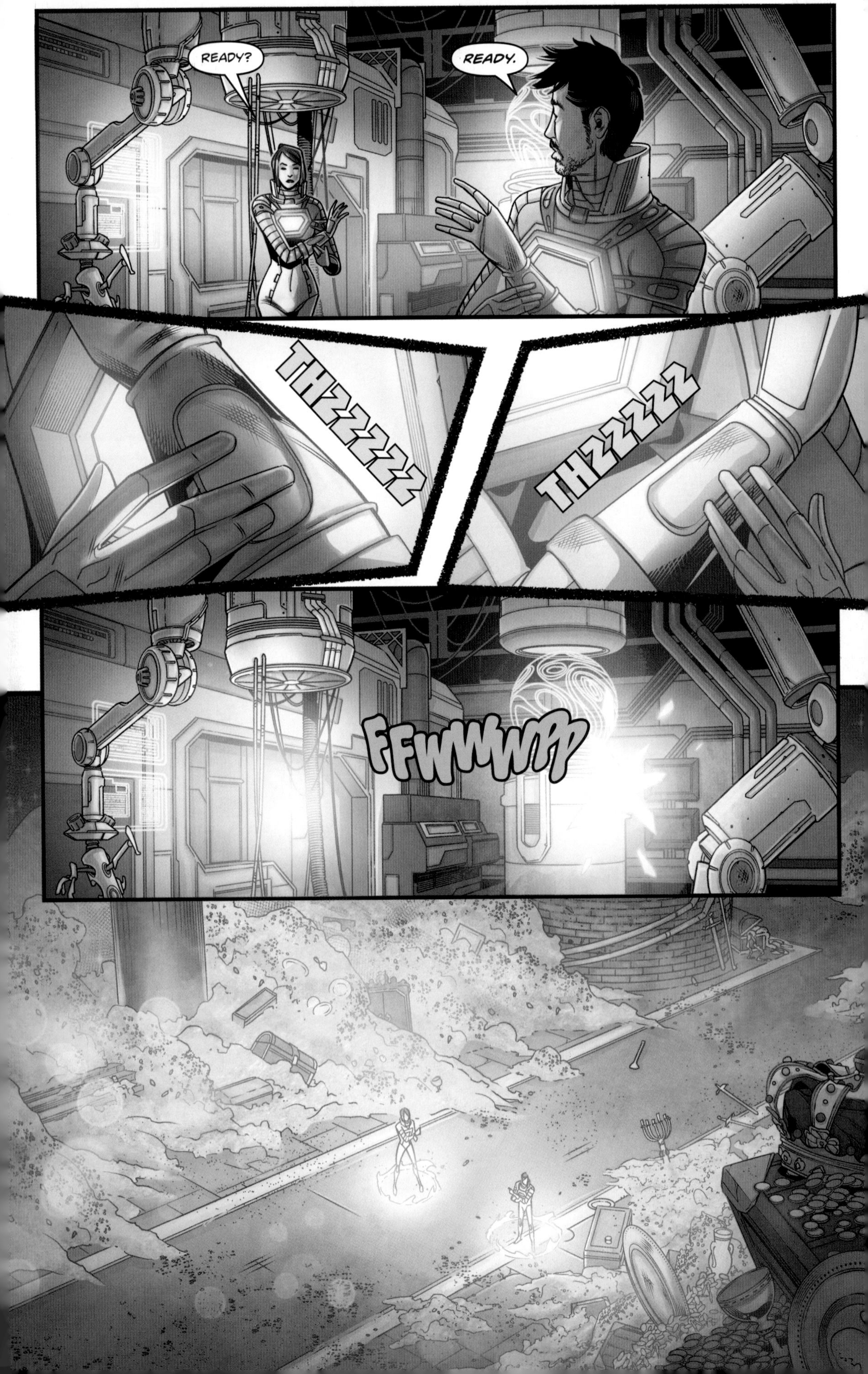
READY?
READY.
THZZZZZZ
THZZZZZZ
FFWWWPP

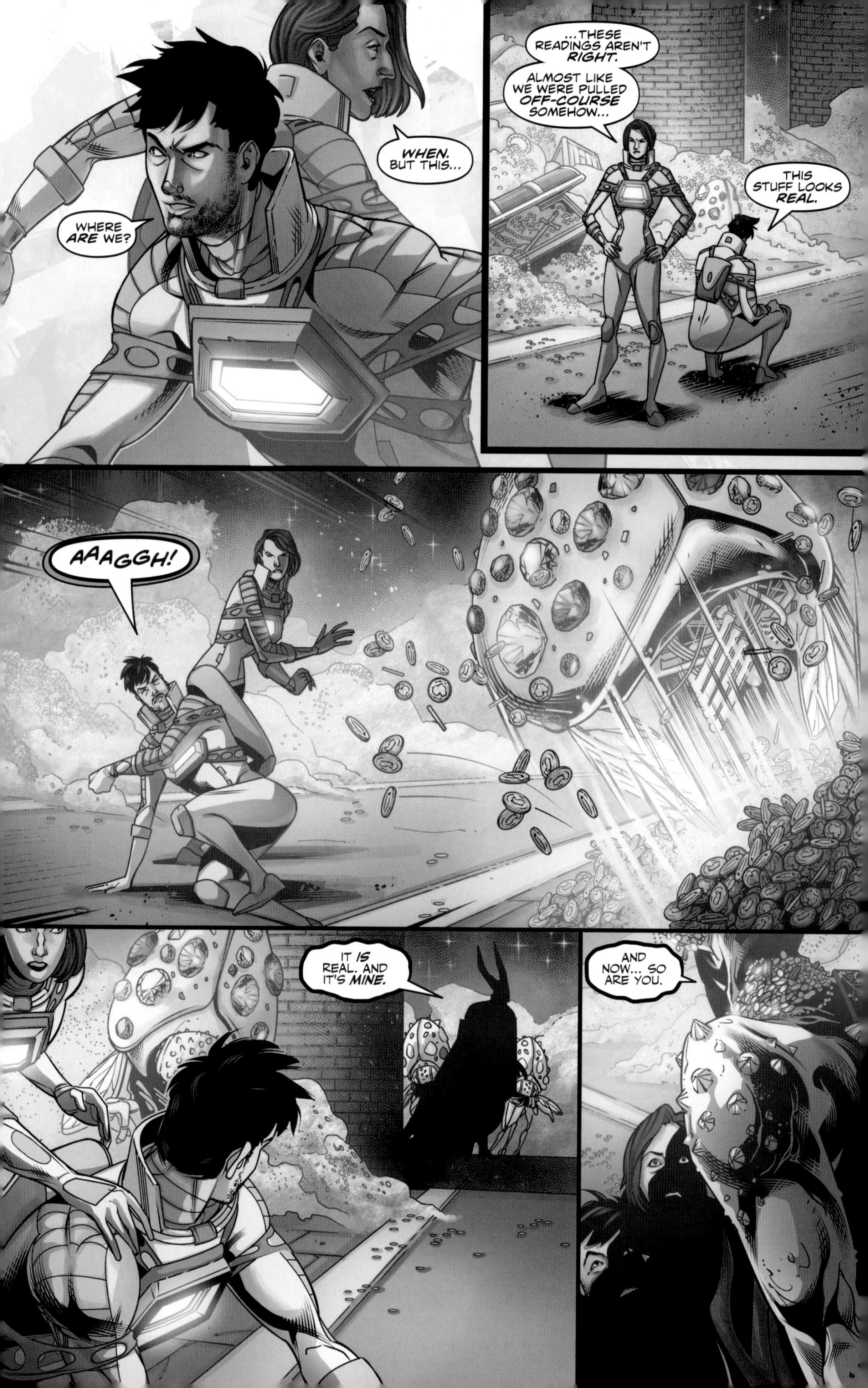
WHERE ARE WE?
WHEN. BUT THIS...
...THESE READINGS AREN'T RIGHT.
ALMOST LIKE WE WERE PULLED OFF-COURSE SOMEHOW...
THIS STUFF LOOKS REAL.
AAAGGH!
IT IS REAL. AND IT'S MINE.
AND NOW... SO ARE YOU.

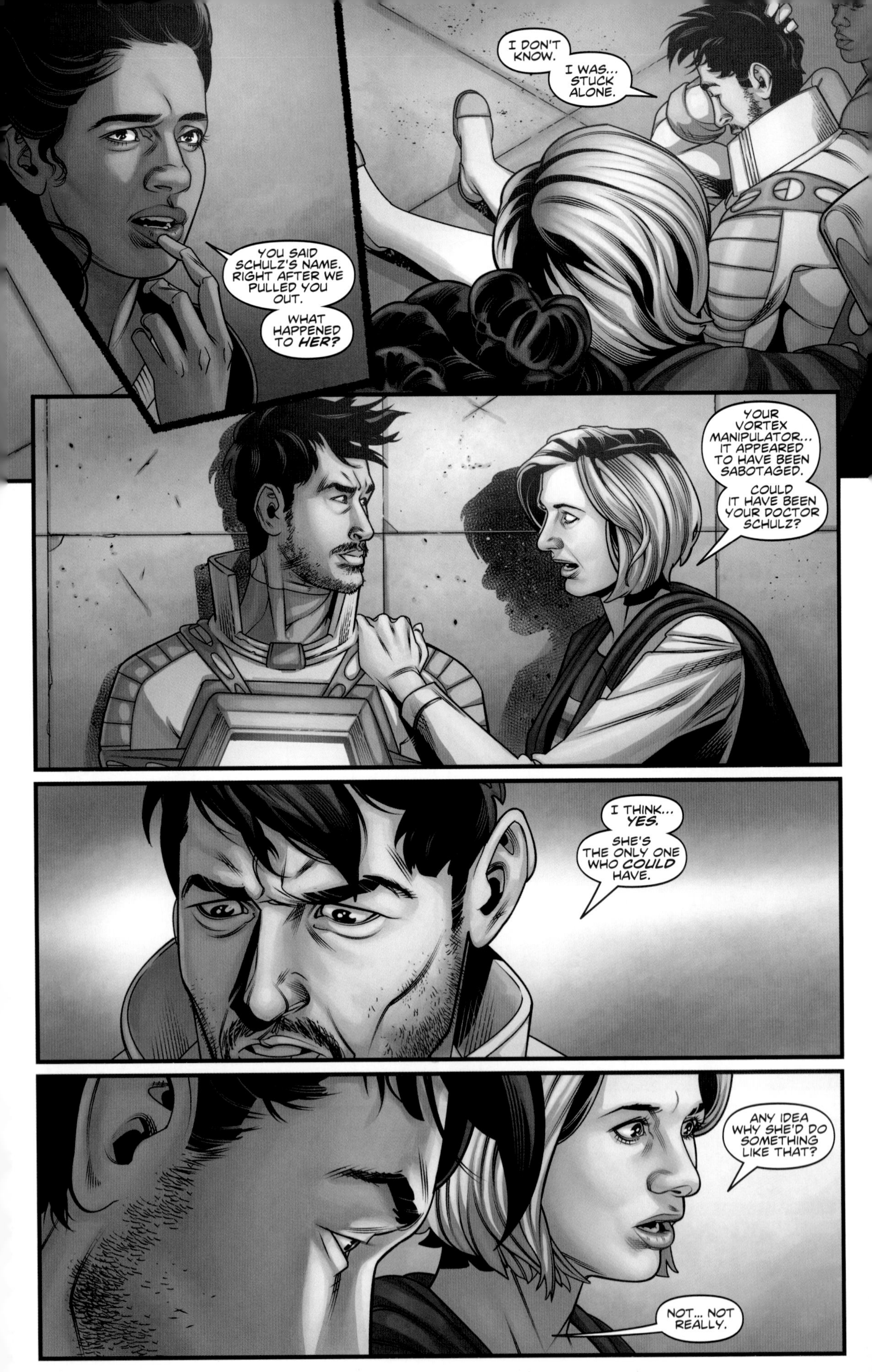
YOU SAID SCHULZ'S NAME. RIGHT AFTER WE PULLED YOU OUT.
WHAT HAPPENED TO HER?
I DON'T KNOW.
I WAS... STUCK ALONE.
YOUR VORTEX MANIPULATOR... IT APPEARED TO HAVE BEEN SABOTAGED.
COULD IT HAVE BEEN YOUR DOCTOR SCHULZ?
I THINK... YES.
SHE'S THE ONLY ONE WHO COULD HAVE.
ANY IDEA WHY SHE'D DO SOMETHING LIKE THAT?
NOT... NOT REALLY.

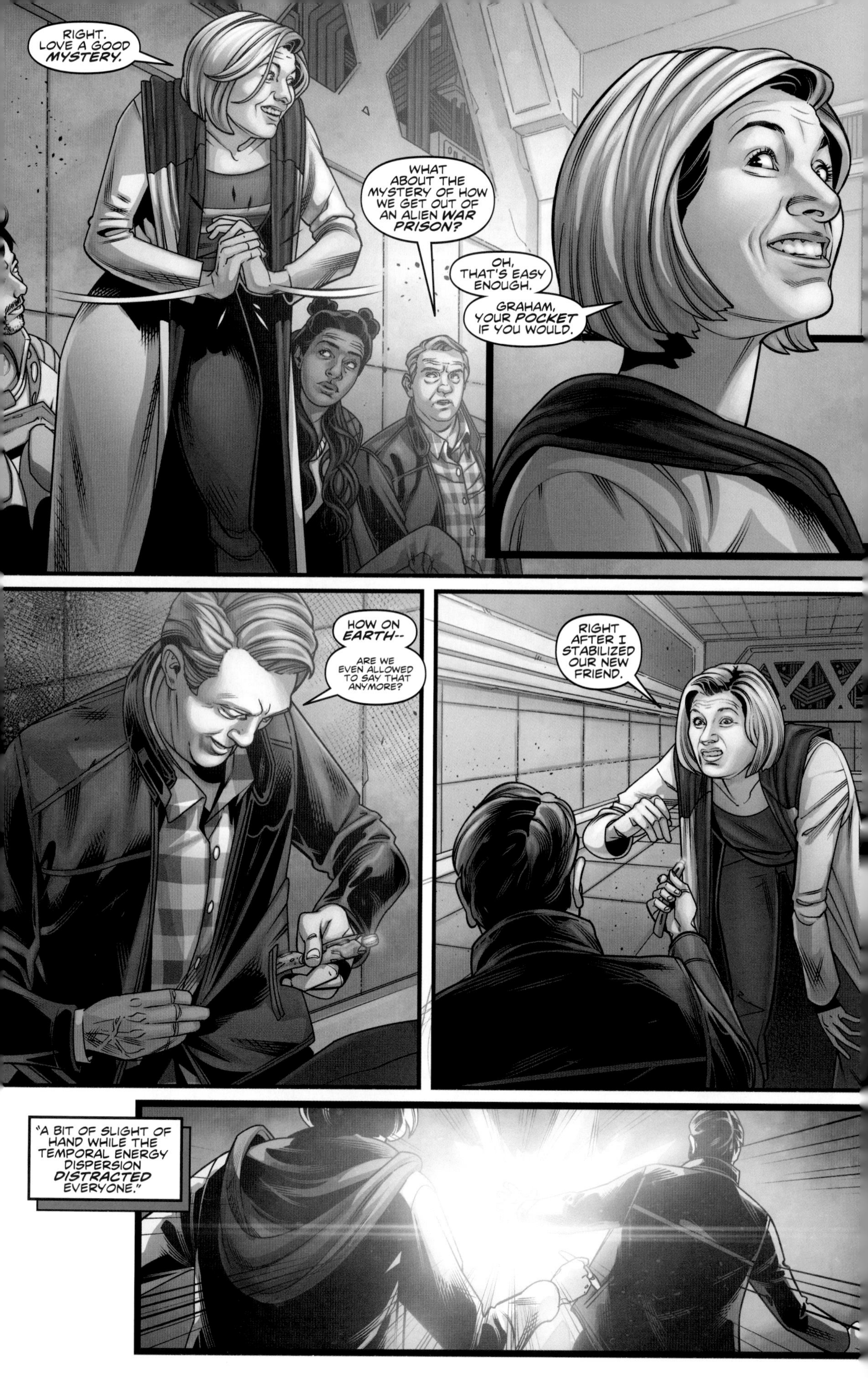
RIGHT. LOVE A GOOD MYSTERY.
WHAT ABOUT THE MYSTERY OF HOW WE GET OUT OF AN ALIEN WAR PRISON?
OH, THAT'S EASY ENOUGH.
GRAHAM, YOUR POCKET IF YOU WOULD.
HOW ON EARTH--
ARE WE EVEN ALLOWED TO SAY THAT ANYMORE?
RIGHT AFTER I STABILIZED OUR NEW FRIEND.
"A BIT OF SLIGHT OF HAND WHILE THE TEMPORAL ENERGY DISPERSION DISTRACTED EVERYONE."

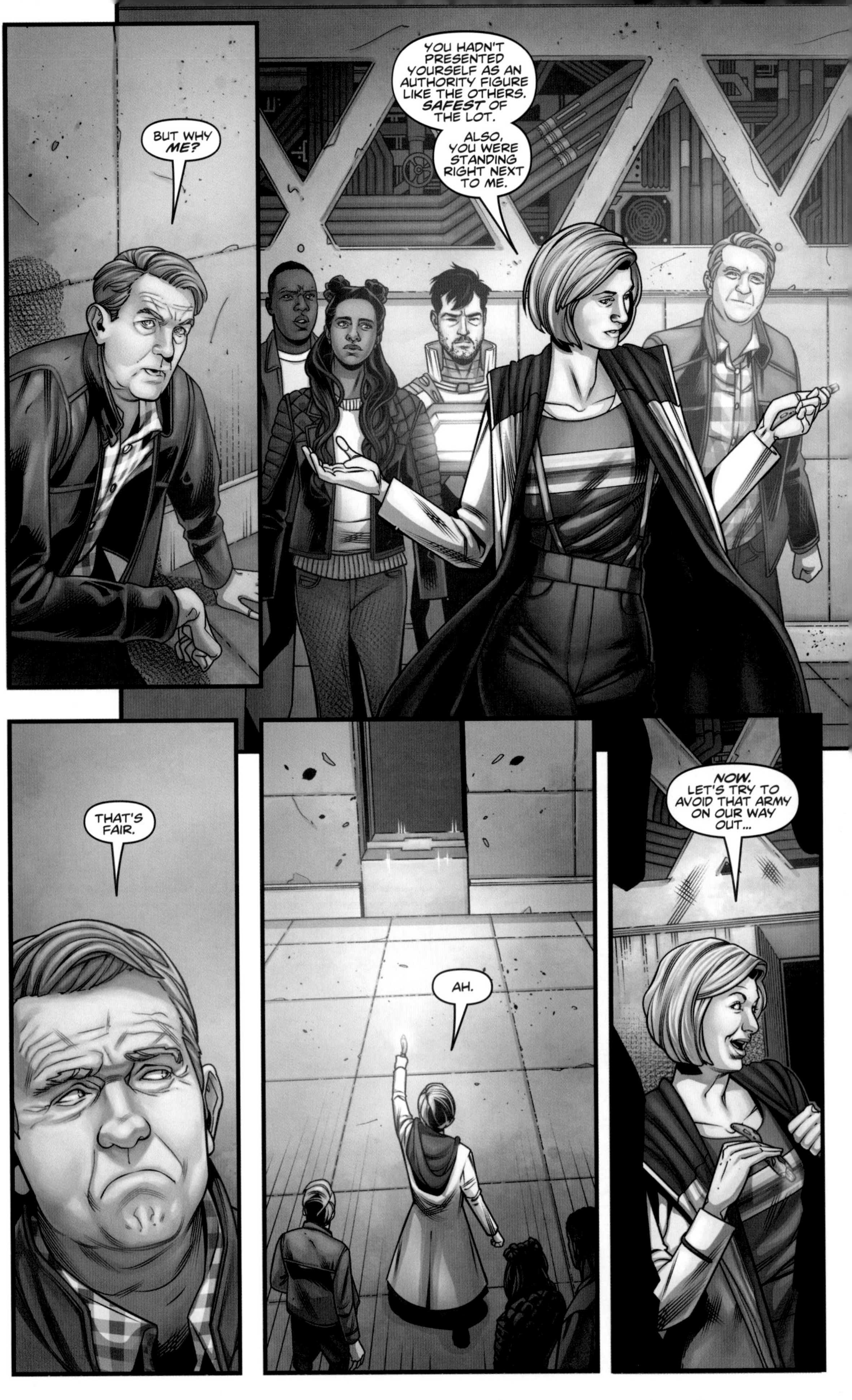
BUT WHY *ME?*
YOU HADN'T PRESENTED YOURSELF AS AN AUTHORITY FIGURE LIKE THE OTHERS. *SAFEST* OF THE LOT.
ALSO, YOU WERE STANDING RIGHT NEXT TO ME.
THAT'S FAIR.
AH.
NOW. LET'S TRY TO AVOID THAT ARMY ON OUR WAY OUT...

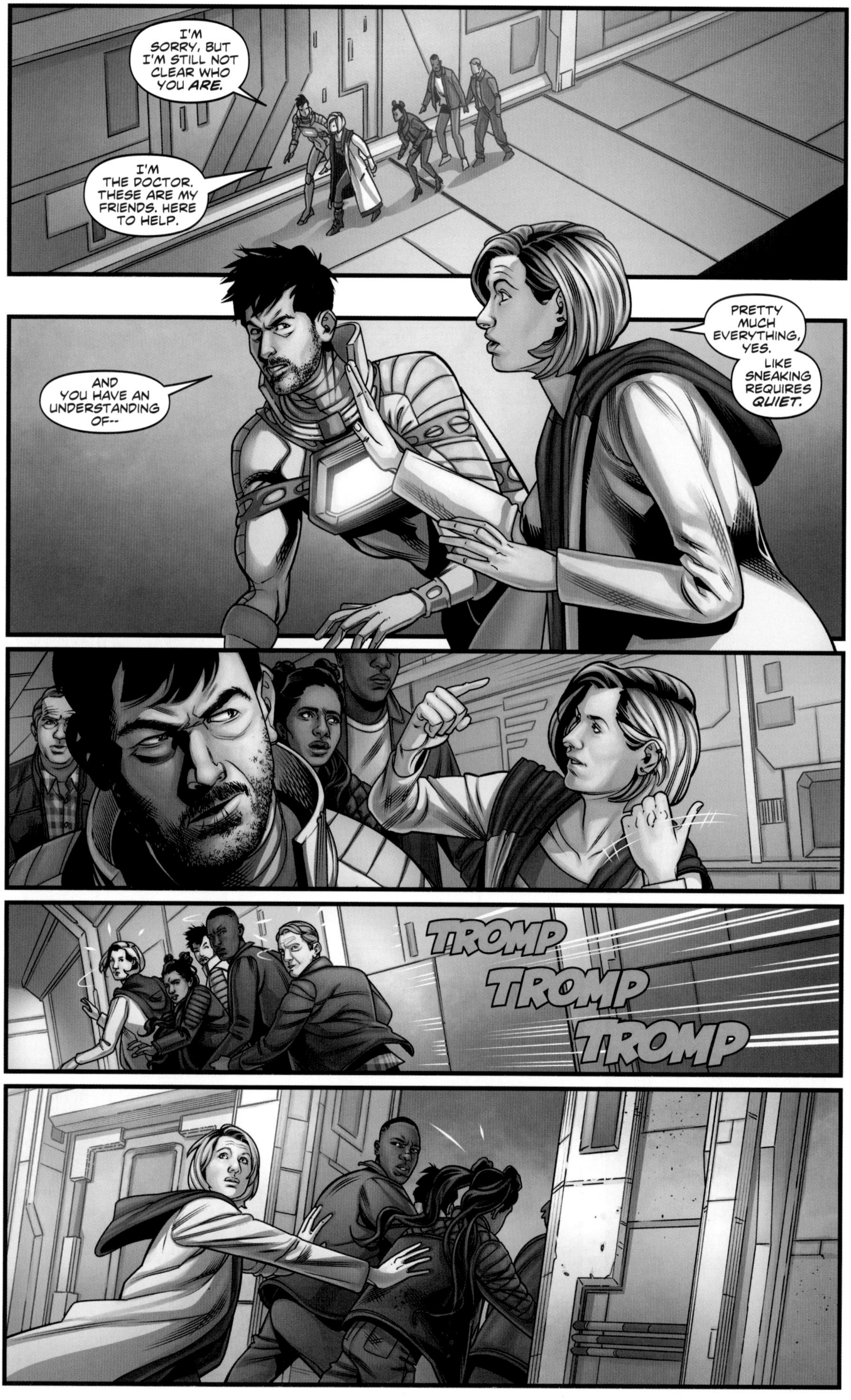
I'M SORRY, BUT I'M STILL NOT CLEAR WHO YOU ARE.
I'M THE DOCTOR. THESE ARE MY FRIENDS. HERE TO HELP.
AND YOU HAVE AN UNDERSTANDING OF--
PRETTY MUCH EVERYTHING, YES.
LIKE SNEAKING REQUIRES QUIET.
TROMP
TROMP
TROMP

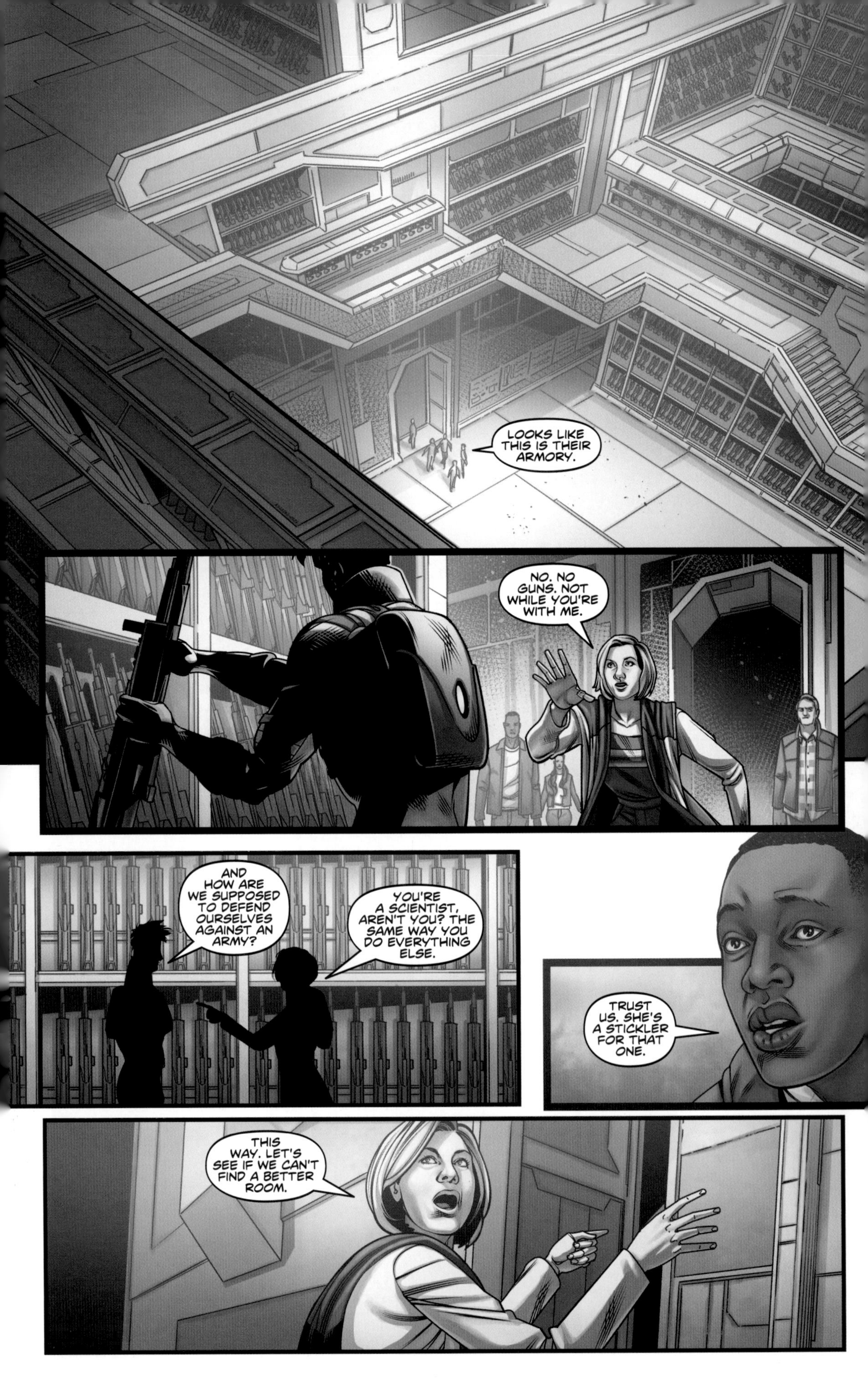
LOOKS LIKE THIS IS THEIR ARMORY.
NO. NO GUNS. NOT WHILE YOU'RE WITH ME.
AND HOW ARE WE SUPPOSED TO DEFEND OURSELVES AGAINST AN ARMY?
YOU'RE A SCIENTIST, AREN'T YOU? THE SAME WAY YOU DO EVERYTHING ELSE.
TRUST US. SHE'S A STICKLER FOR THAT ONE.
THIS WAY. LET'S SEE IF WE CAN'T FIND A BETTER ROOM.

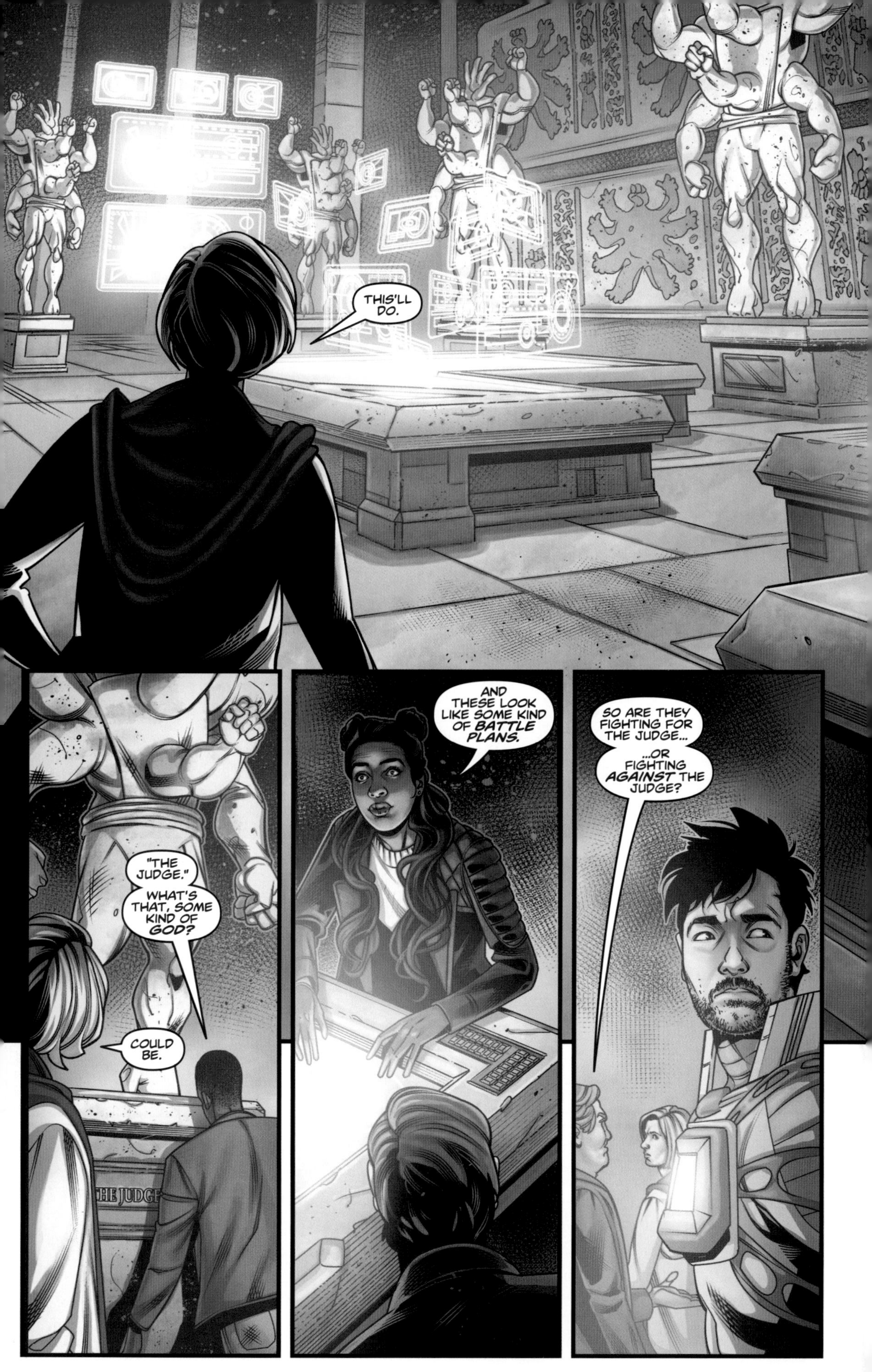
THIS'LL DO.
"THE JUDGE."
WHAT'S THAT, SOME KIND OF GOD?
COULD BE.
THE JUDGE
AND THESE LOOK LIKE SOME KIND OF BATTLE PLANS.
SO ARE THEY FIGHTING FOR THE JUDGE...
...OR FIGHTING AGAINST THE JUDGE?

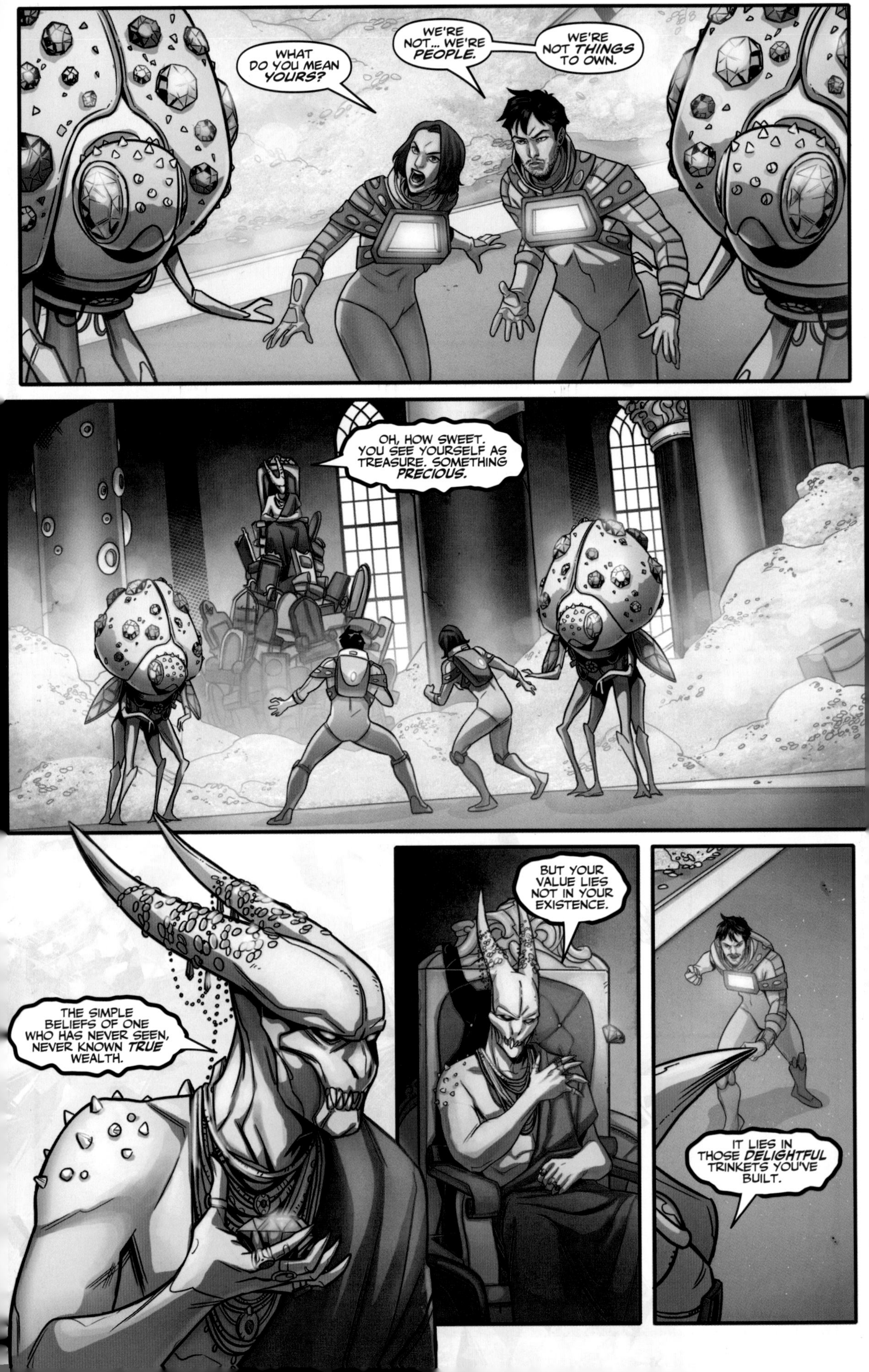
WHAT DO YOU MEAN *YOURS?*
WE'RE NOT... WE'RE *PEOPLE.*
WE'RE NOT *THINGS* TO OWN.
OH, HOW SWEET. YOU SEE YOURSELF AS TREASURE. SOMETHING *PRECIOUS.*
THE SIMPLE BELIEFS OF ONE WHO HAS NEVER SEEN, NEVER KNOWN *TRUE* WEALTH.
BUT YOUR VALUE LIES NOT IN YOUR EXISTENCE.
IT LIES IN THOSE *DELIGHTFUL* TRINKETS YOU'VE BUILT.

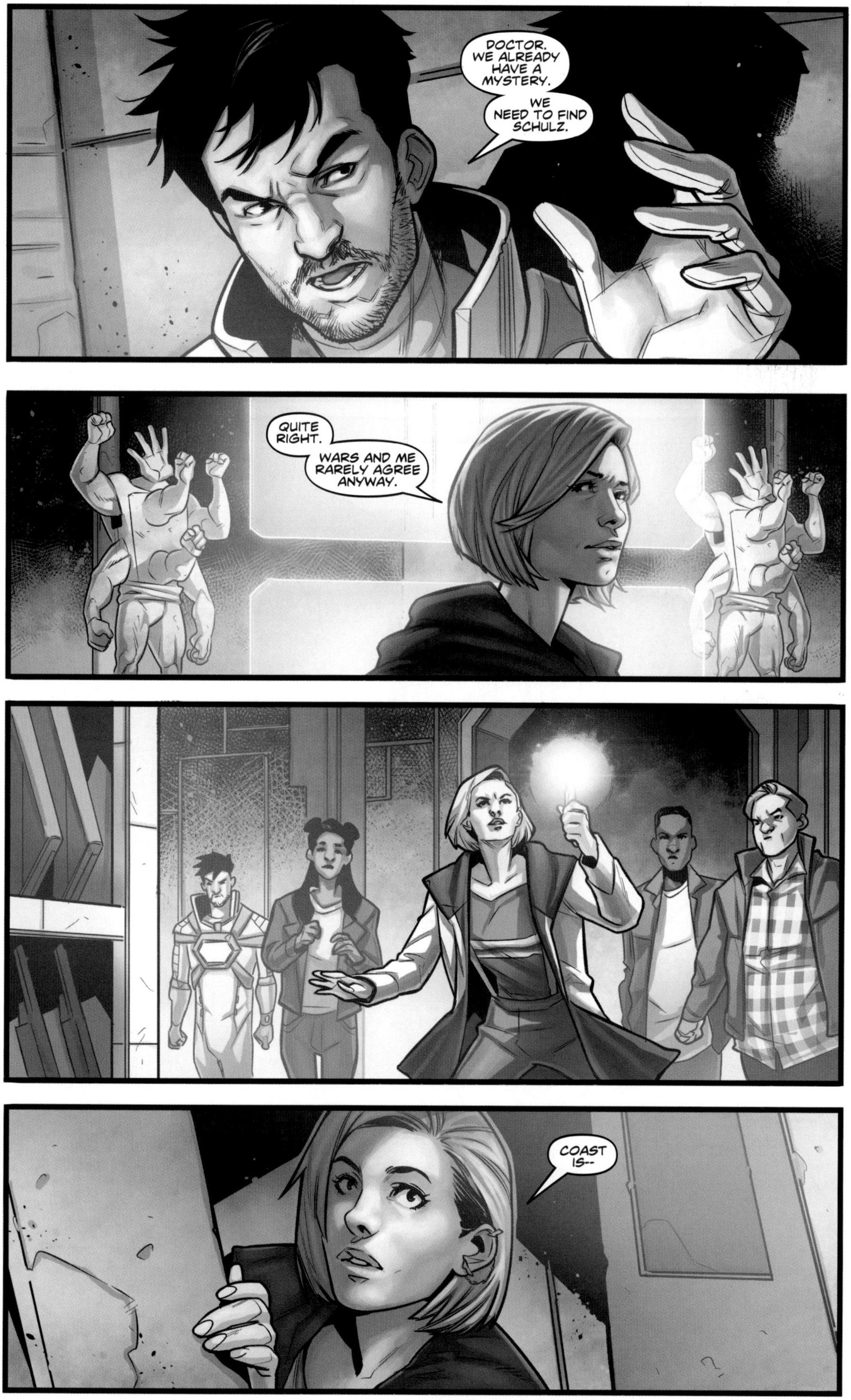
DOCTOR. WE ALREADY HAVE A MYSTERY.
WE NEED TO FIND SCHULZ.
QUITE RIGHT.
WARS AND ME RARELY AGREE ANYWAY.
COAST IS--

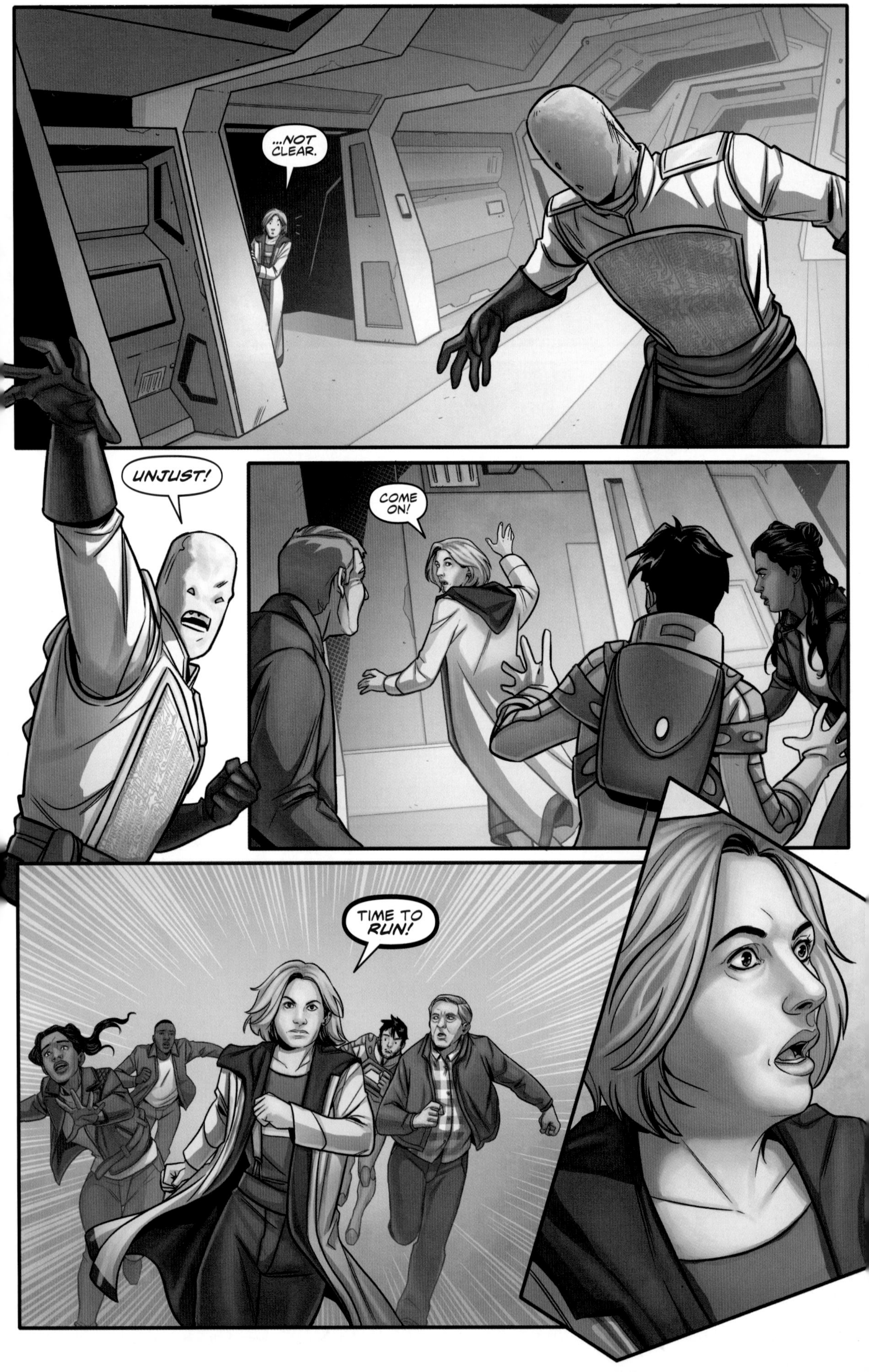

...NOT CLEAR.
UNJUST!
COME ON!
TIME TO RUN!

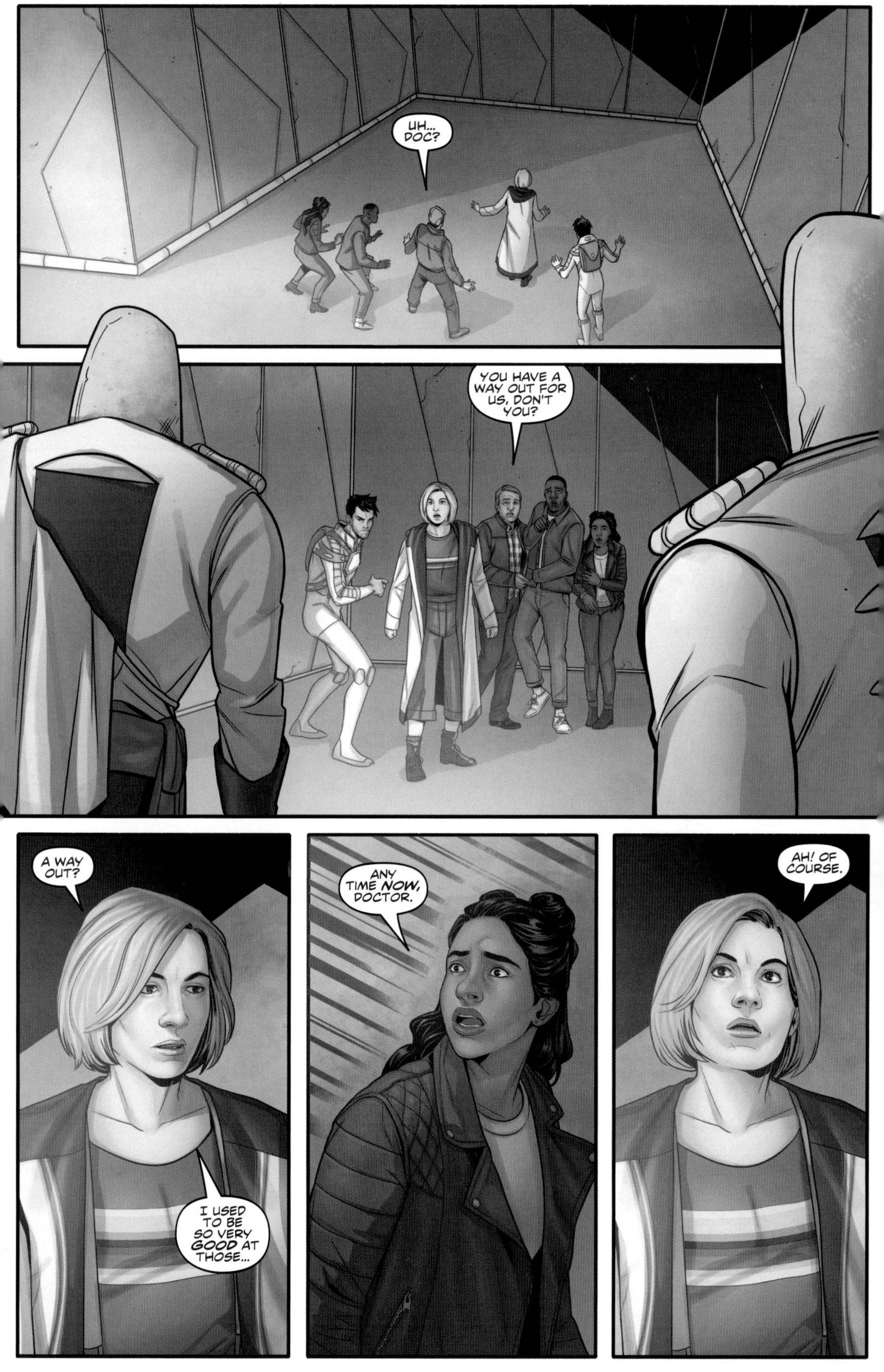
UH... DOC?
YOU HAVE A WAY OUT FOR US, DON'T YOU?
A WAY OUT?
I USED TO BE SO VERY GOOD AT THOSE...
ANY TIME NOW, DOCTOR.
AH! OF COURSE.

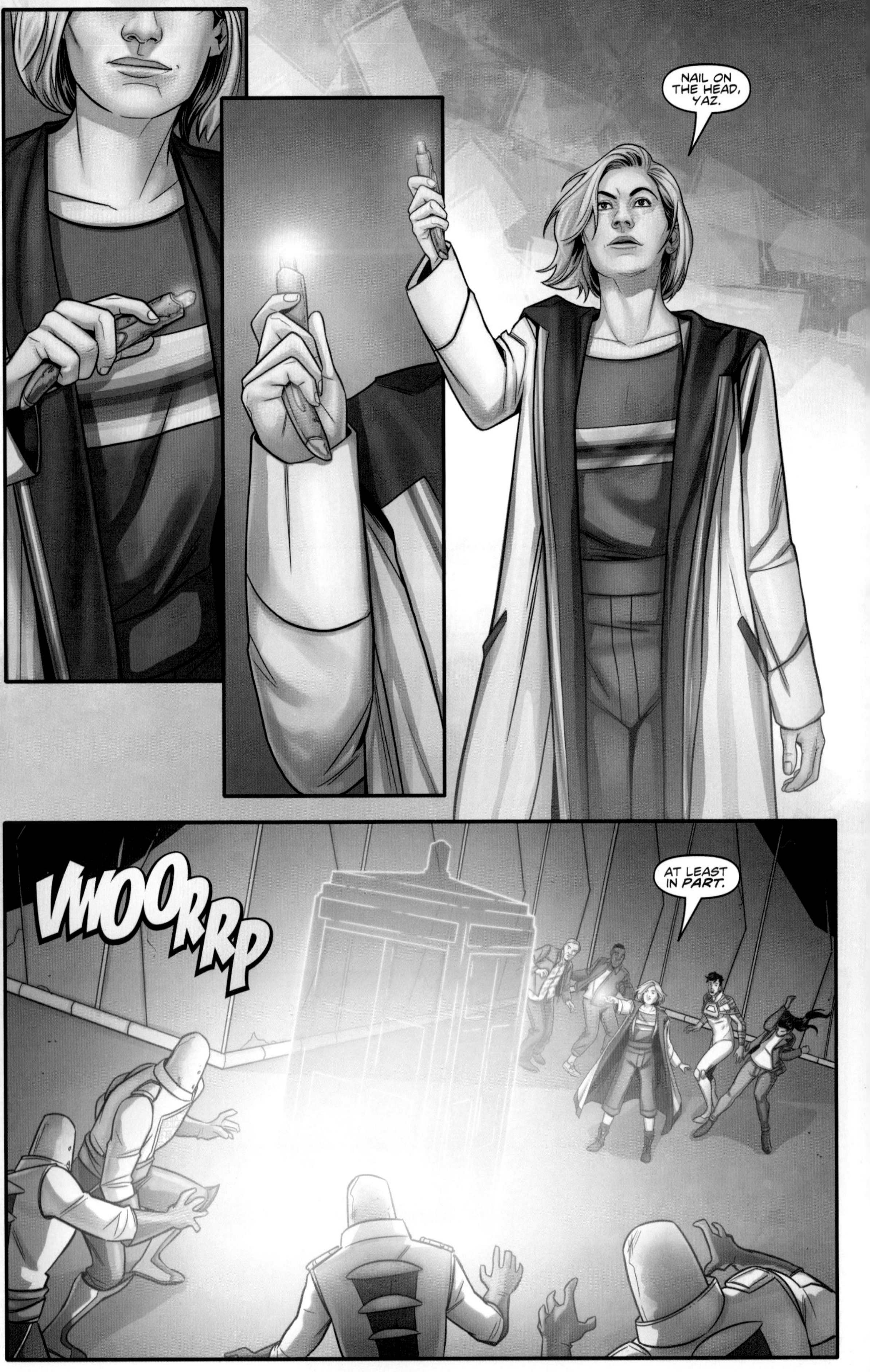
NAIL ON THE HEAD, YAZ.
VWOORRP
AT LEAST IN *PART*.

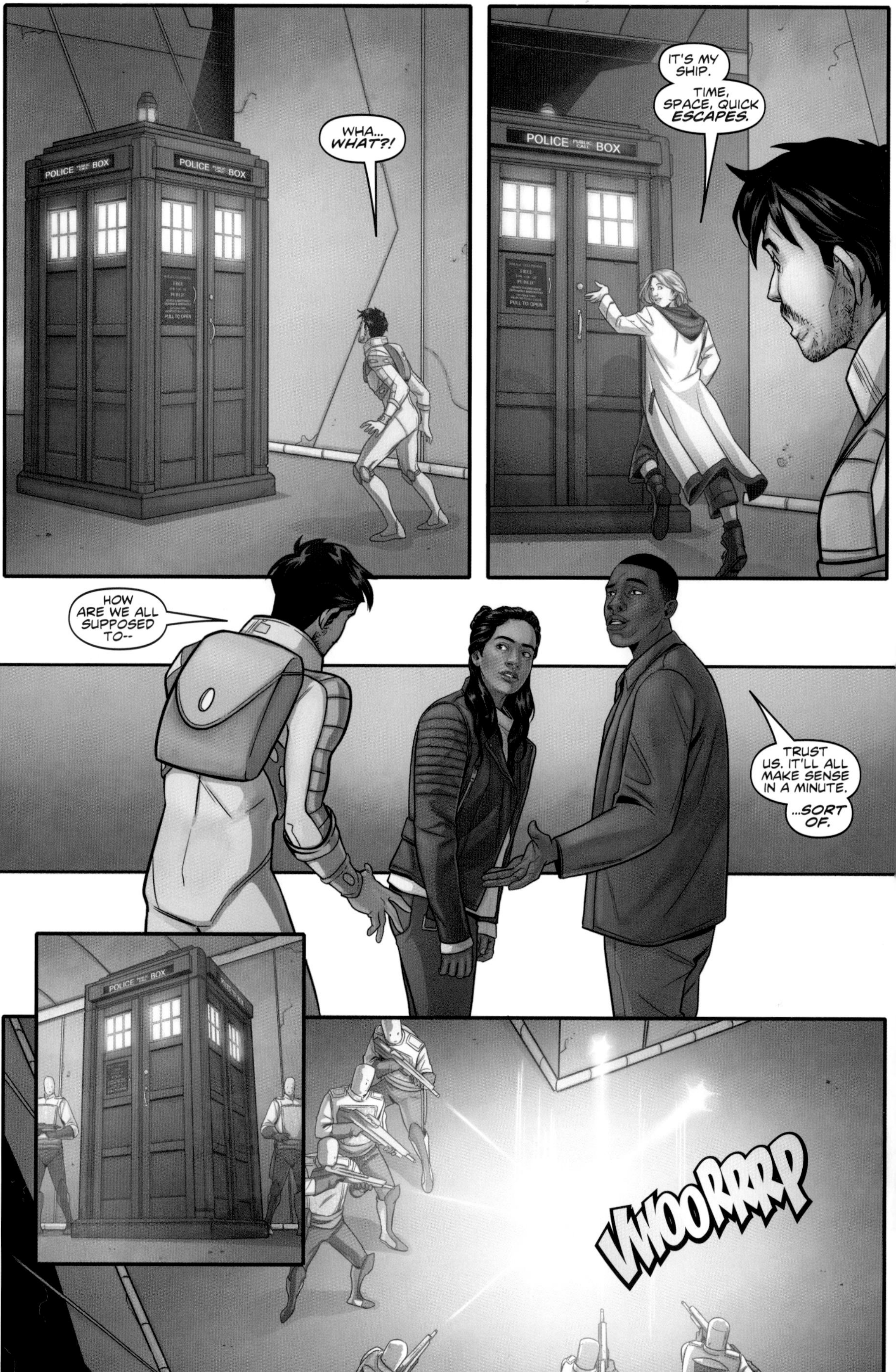
POLICE PUBLIC CALL BOX
WHA... WHAT?!
IT'S MY SHIP.
TIME, SPACE, QUICK ESCAPES.
HOW ARE WE ALL SUPPOSED TO--
TRUST US. IT'LL ALL MAKE SENSE IN A MINUTE.
...SORT OF.
VWOORRRP

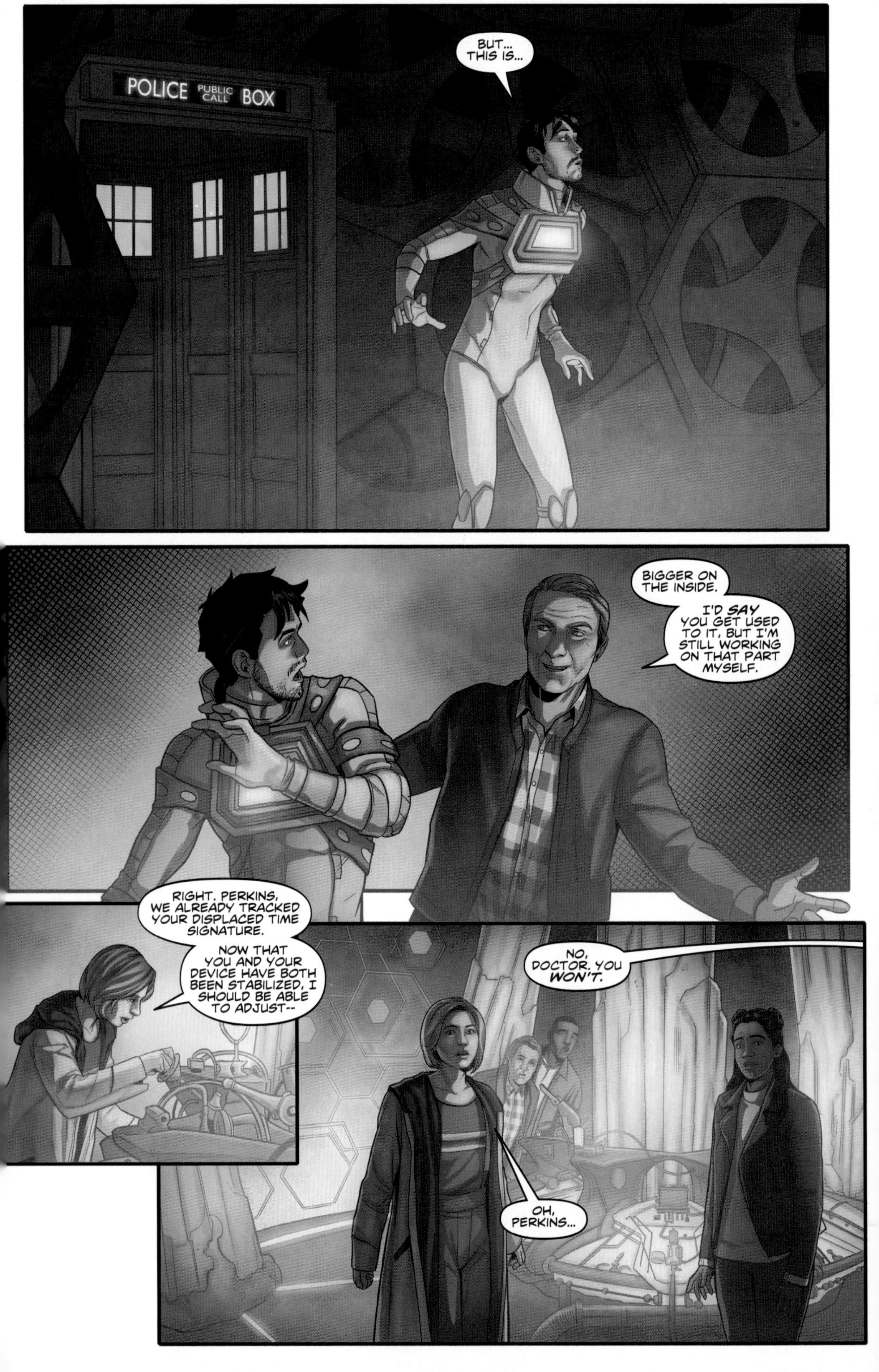
POLICE PUBLIC CALL BOX
BUT... THIS IS...
BIGGER ON THE INSIDE.
I'D SAY YOU GET USED TO IT, BUT I'M STILL WORKING ON THAT PART MYSELF.
RIGHT. PERKINS, WE ALREADY TRACKED YOUR DISPLACED TIME SIGNATURE.
NOW THAT YOU AND YOUR DEVICE HAVE BOTH BEEN STABILIZED, I SHOULD BE ABLE TO ADJUST--
NO, DOCTOR. YOU WON'T.
OH, PERKINS...

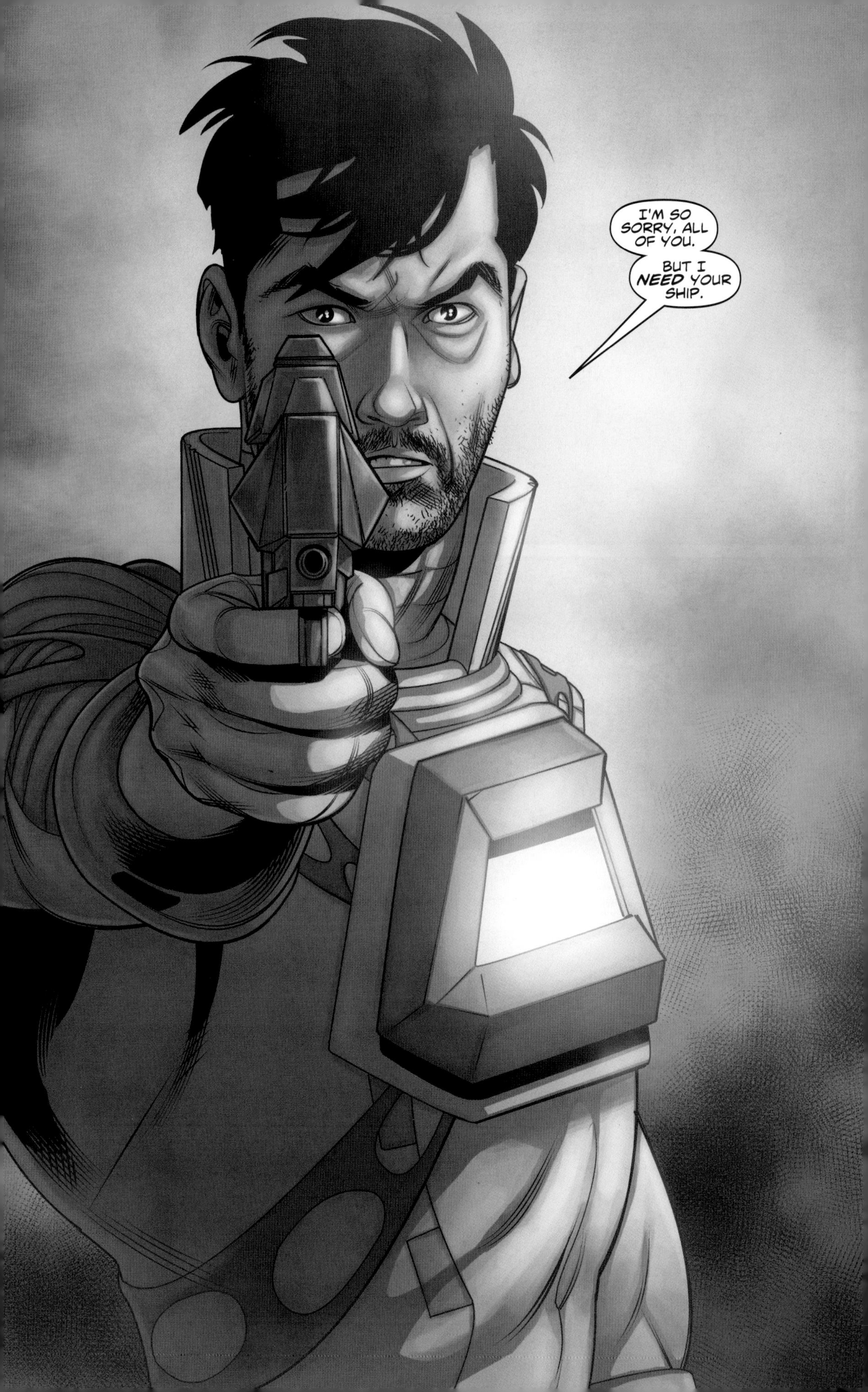
I'M SO SORRY, ALL OF YOU.
BUT I **NEED** YOUR SHIP.

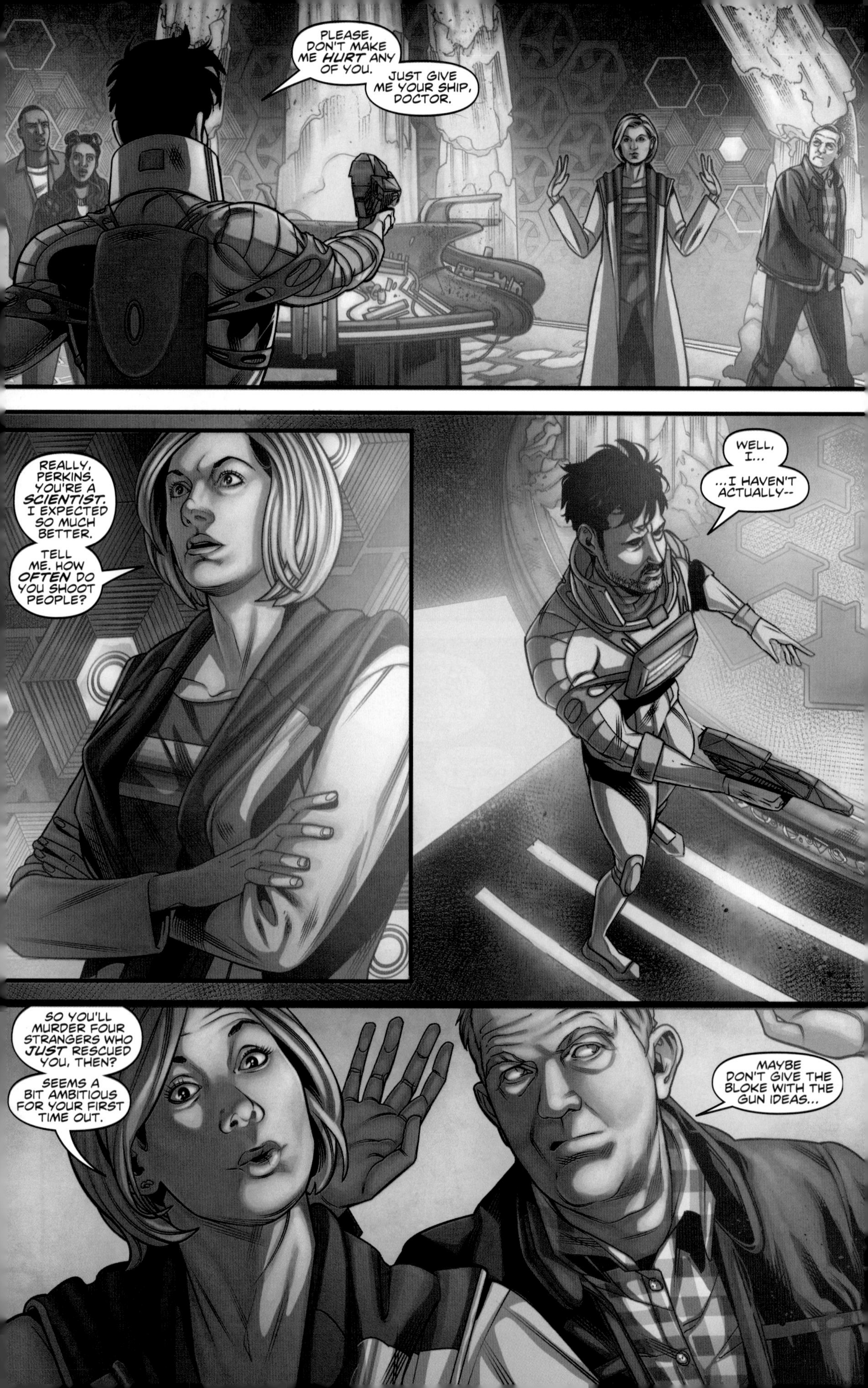
PLEASE, DON'T MAKE ME HURT ANY OF YOU.
JUST GIVE ME YOUR SHIP, DOCTOR.
REALLY, PERKINS. YOU'RE A SCIENTIST. I EXPECTED SO MUCH BETTER.
TELL ME. HOW OFTEN DO YOU SHOOT PEOPLE?
WELL, I...
...I HAVEN'T ACTUALLY--
SO YOU'LL MURDER FOUR STRANGERS WHO JUST RESCUED YOU, THEN?
SEEMS A BIT AMBITIOUS FOR YOUR FIRST TIME OUT.
MAYBE DON'T GIVE THE BLOKE WITH THE GUN IDEAS...

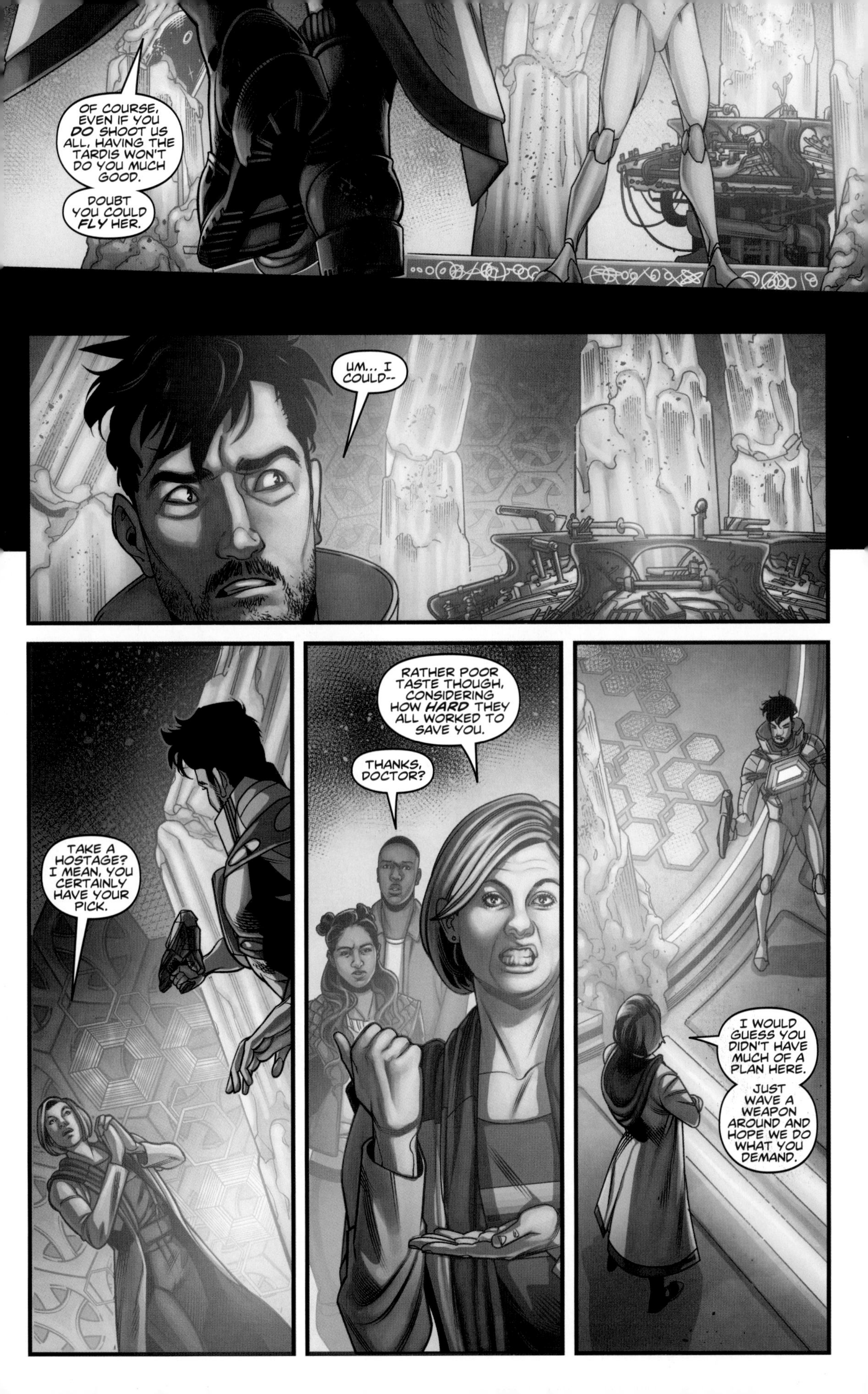
OF COURSE, EVEN IF YOU DO SHOOT US ALL, HAVING THE TARDIS WON'T DO YOU MUCH GOOD.
DOUBT YOU COULD FLY HER.
UM... I COULD--
TAKE A HOSTAGE? I MEAN, YOU CERTAINLY HAVE YOUR PICK.
RATHER POOR TASTE THOUGH, CONSIDERING HOW HARD THEY ALL WORKED TO SAVE YOU.
THANKS, DOCTOR?
I WOULD GUESS YOU DIDN'T HAVE MUCH OF A PLAN HERE.
JUST WAVE A WEAPON AROUND AND HOPE WE DO WHAT YOU DEMAND.

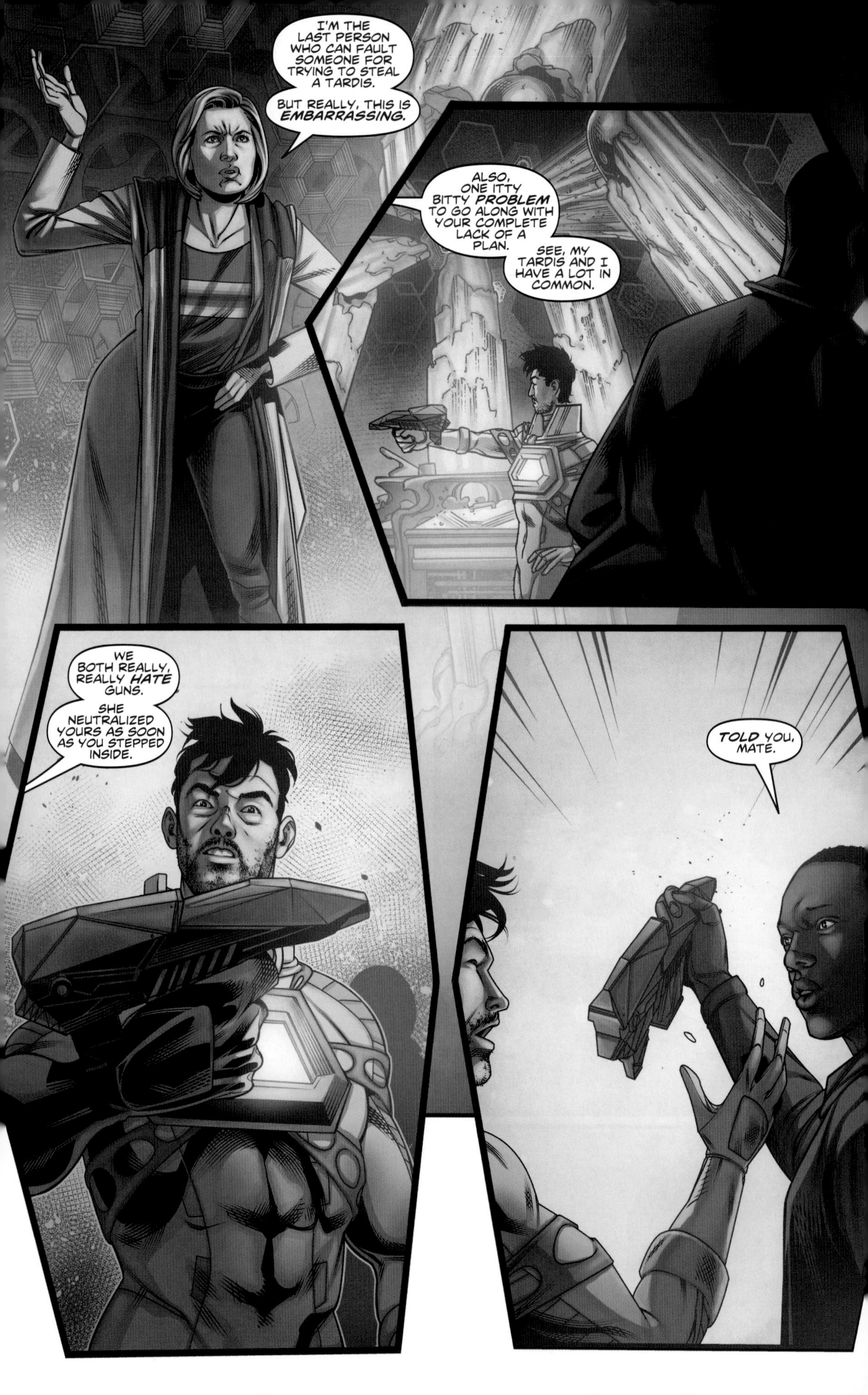

I'M THE LAST PERSON WHO CAN FAULT SOMEONE FOR TRYING TO STEAL A TARDIS.
BUT REALLY, THIS IS *EMBARRASSING.*
ALSO, ONE ITTY BITTY **PROBLEM** TO GO ALONG WITH YOUR COMPLETE LACK OF A PLAN.
SEE, MY TARDIS AND I HAVE A LOT IN COMMON.
WE BOTH REALLY, REALLY *HATE* GUNS.
SHE NEUTRALIZED YOURS AS SOON AS YOU STEPPED INSIDE.
TOLD YOU, MATE.

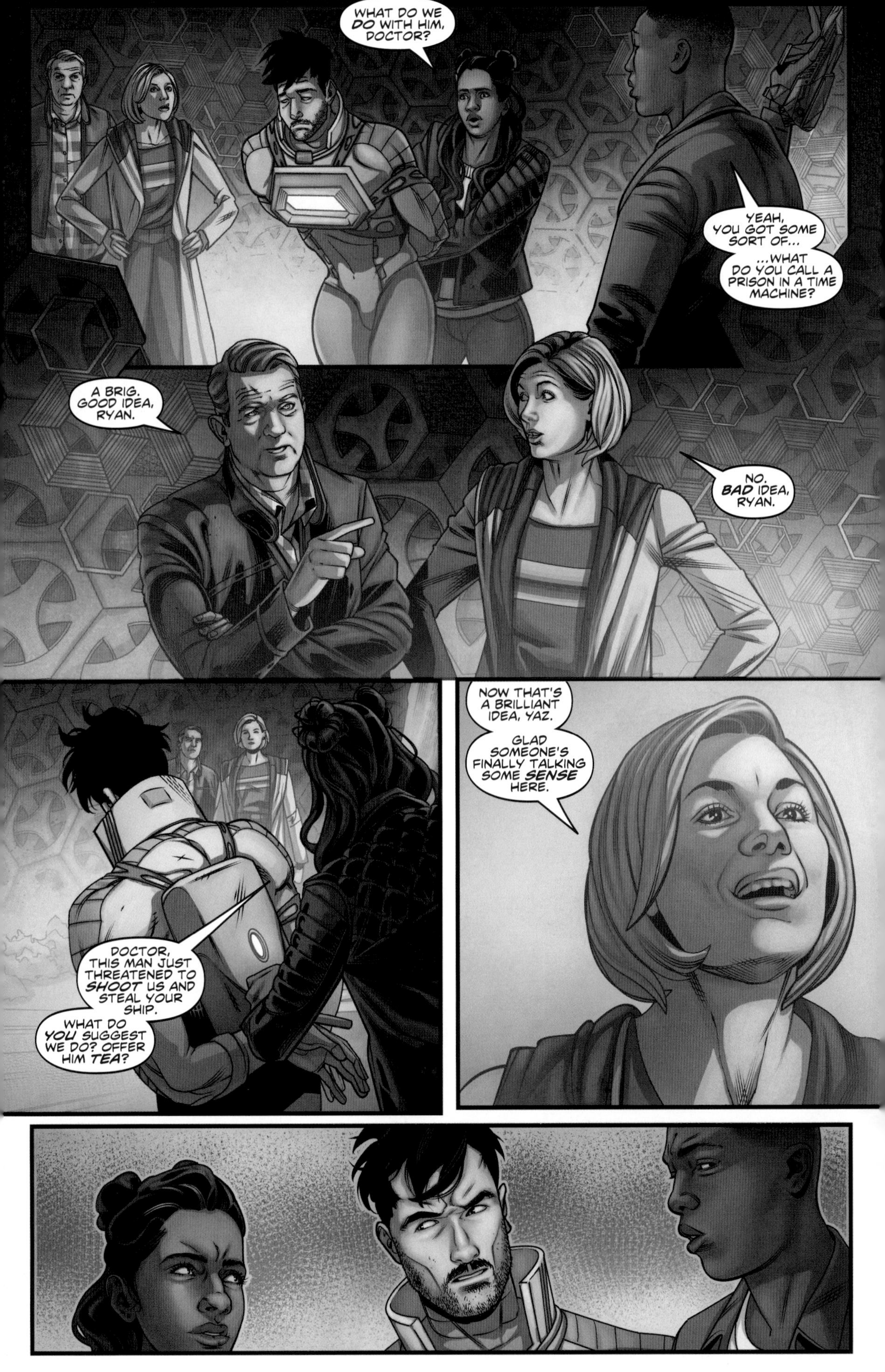
WHAT DO WE DO WITH HIM, DOCTOR?
YEAH, YOU GOT SOME SORT OF...
...WHAT DO YOU CALL A PRISON IN A TIME MACHINE?
A BRIG. GOOD IDEA, RYAN.
NO. BAD IDEA, RYAN.
DOCTOR, THIS MAN JUST THREATENED TO SHOOT US AND STEAL YOUR SHIP.
WHAT DO YOU SUGGEST WE DO? OFFER HIM TEA?
NOW THAT'S A BRILLIANT IDEA, YAZ.
GLAD SOMEONE'S FINALLY TALKING SOME SENSE HERE.

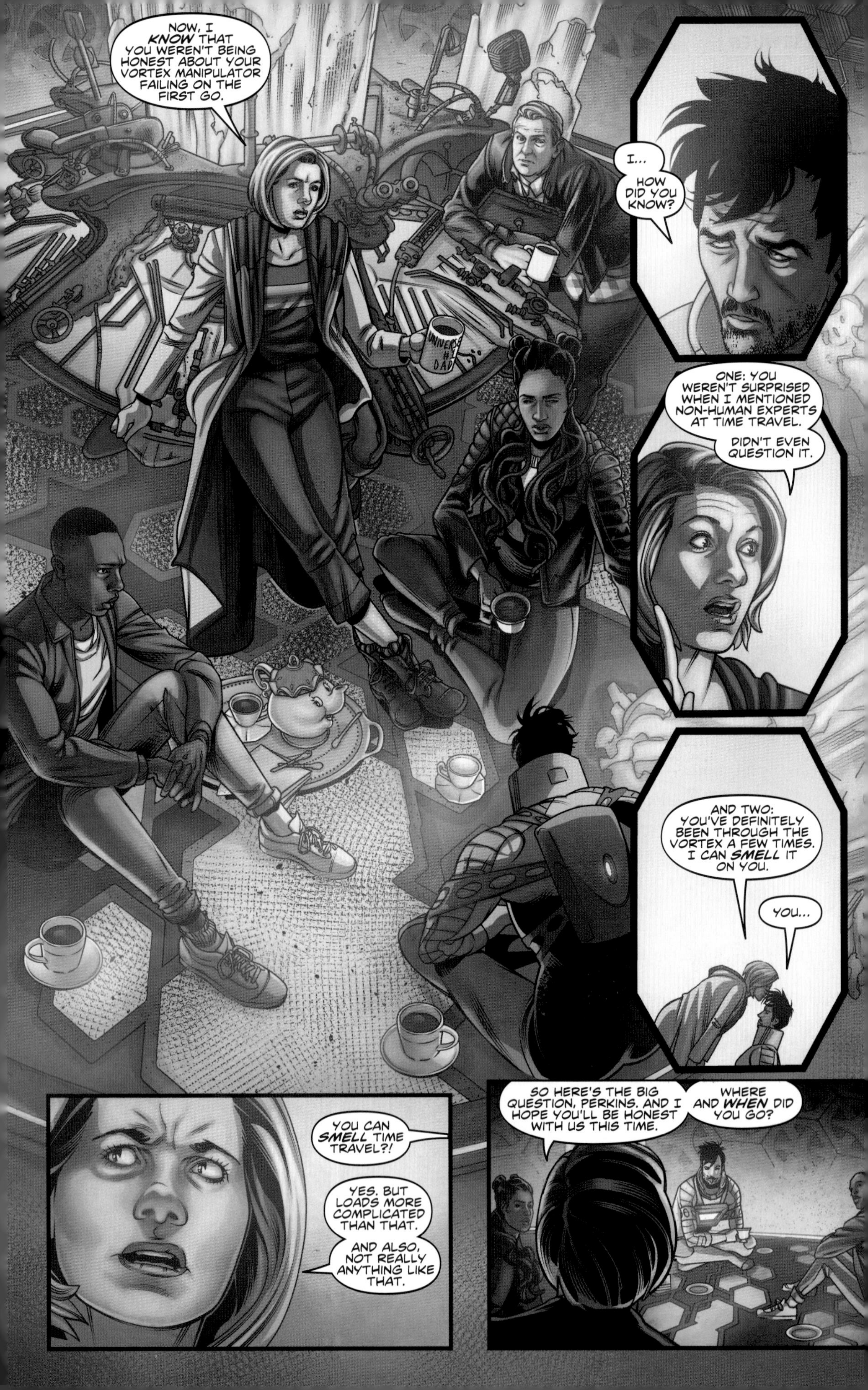
NOW, I KNOW THAT YOU WEREN'T BEING HONEST ABOUT YOUR VORTEX MANIPULATOR FAILING ON THE FIRST GO.
I... HOW DID YOU KNOW?
ONE: YOU WEREN'T SURPRISED WHEN I MENTIONED NON-HUMAN EXPERTS AT TIME TRAVEL.
DIDN'T EVEN QUESTION IT.
AND TWO: YOU'VE DEFINITELY BEEN THROUGH THE VORTEX A FEW TIMES. I CAN SMELL IT ON YOU.
YOU...
UNIVERSE'S #1 DAD
YOU CAN SMELL TIME TRAVEL?!
YES. BUT LOADS MORE COMPLICATED THAN THAT.
AND ALSO, NOT REALLY ANYTHING LIKE THAT.
SO HERE'S THE BIG QUESTION, PERKINS. AND I HOPE YOU'LL BE HONEST WITH US THIS TIME.
WHERE AND WHEN DID YOU GO?

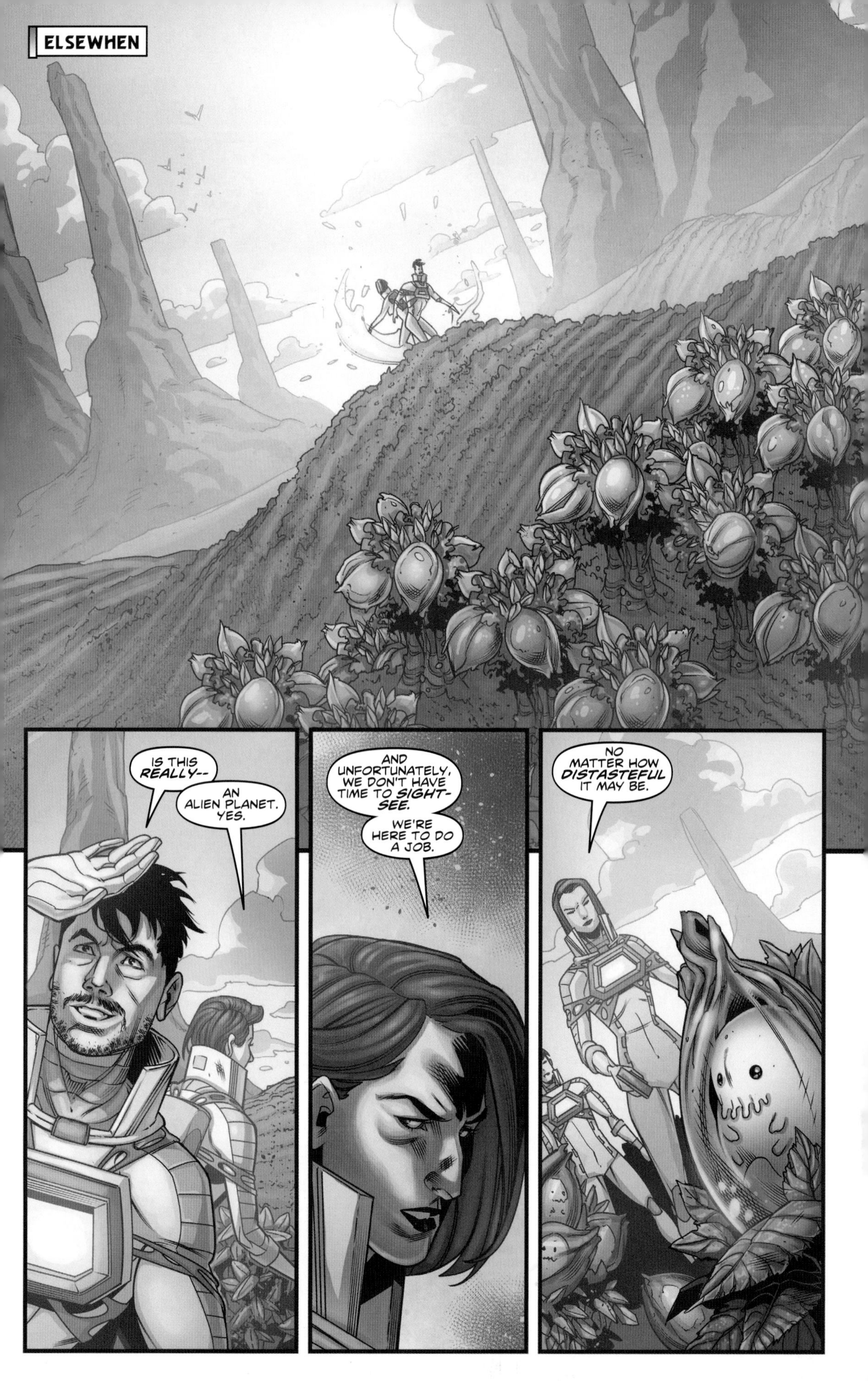
ELSEWHEN
IS THIS REALLY--
AN ALIEN PLANET. YES.
AND UNFORTUNATELY, WE DON'T HAVE TIME TO SIGHT-SEE.
WE'RE HERE TO DO A JOB.
NO MATTER HOW DISTASTEFUL IT MAY BE.

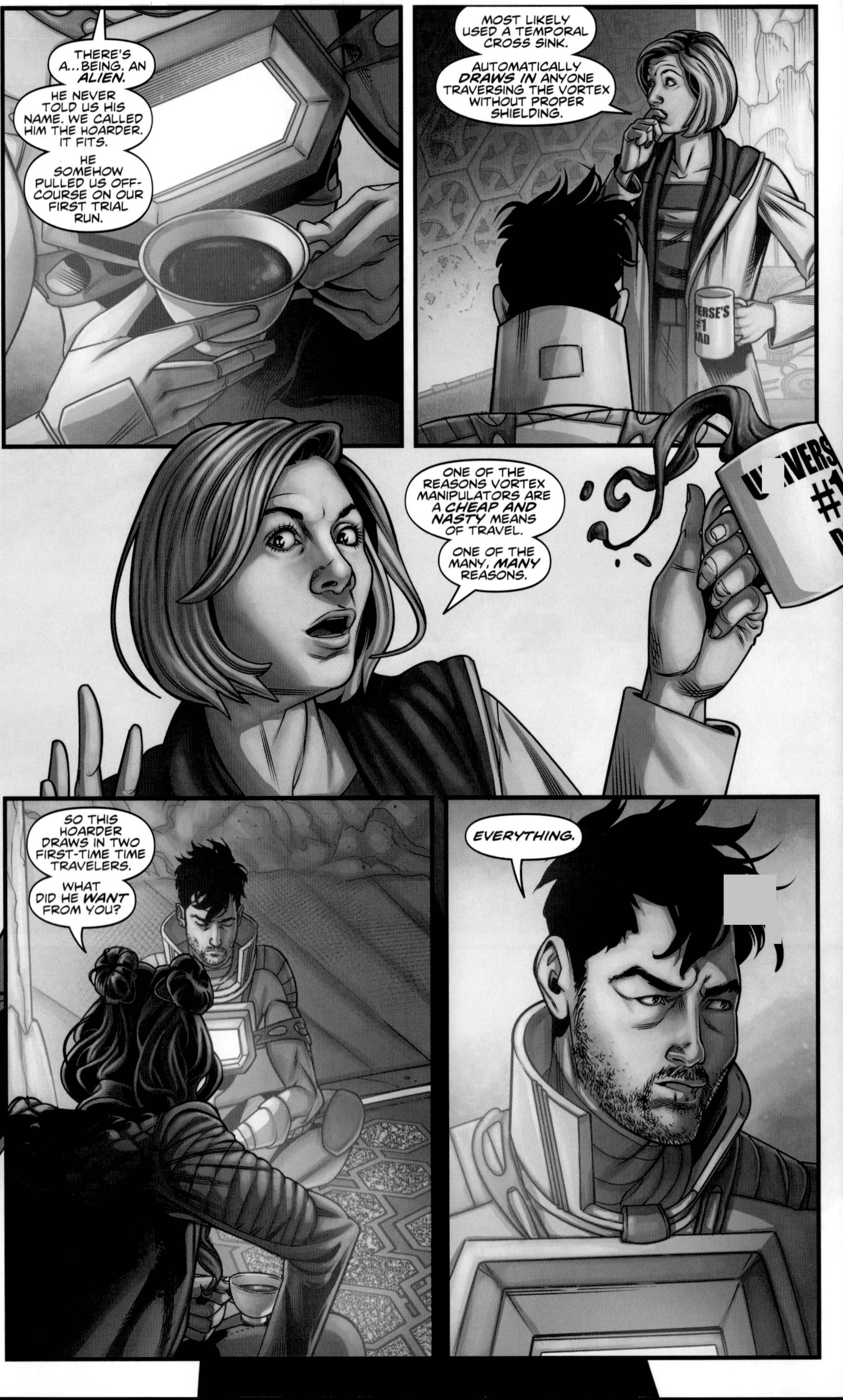

THERE'S A...BEING. AN *ALIEN.*
HE NEVER TOLD US HIS NAME. WE CALLED HIM THE HOARDER. IT FITS.
HE SOMEHOW PULLED US OFF-COURSE ON OUR FIRST TRIAL RUN.
MOST LIKELY USED A TEMPORAL CROSS SINK.
AUTOMATICALLY *DRAWS IN* ANYONE TRAVERSING THE VORTEX WITHOUT PROPER SHIELDING.
ONE OF THE REASONS VORTEX MANIPULATORS ARE A *CHEAP AND NASTY* MEANS OF TRAVEL.
ONE OF THE MANY, *MANY* REASONS.
SO THIS HOARDER DRAWS IN TWO FIRST-TIME TIME TRAVELERS.
WHAT DID HE *WANT* FROM YOU?
EVERYTHING.

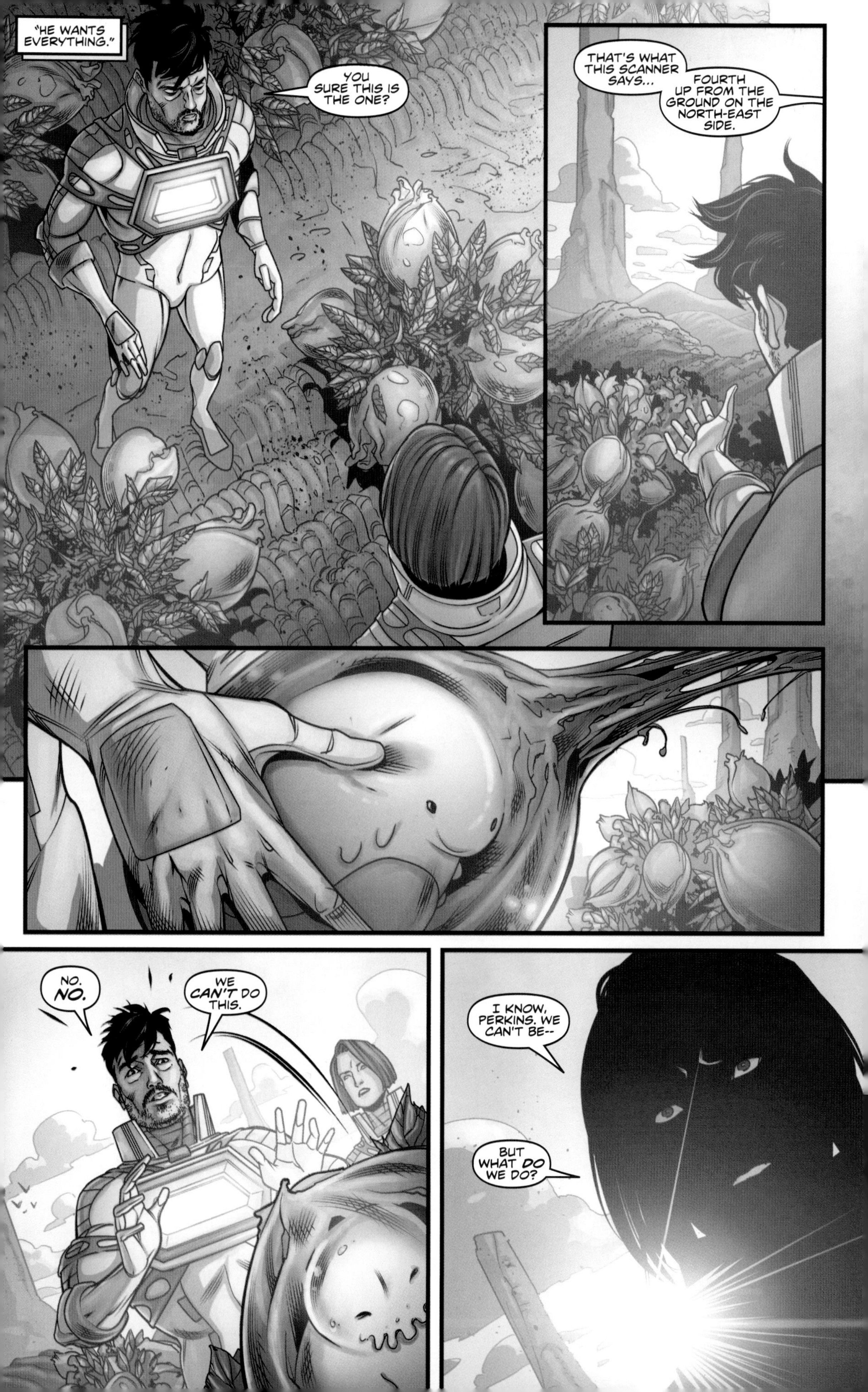
"HE WANTS EVERYTHING."
YOU SURE THIS IS THE ONE?
THAT'S WHAT THIS SCANNER SAYS...
FOURTH UP FROM THE GROUND ON THE NORTH-EAST SIDE.
NO. NO.
WE CAN'T DO THIS.
I KNOW, PERKINS. WE CAN'T BE--
BUT WHAT DO WE DO?

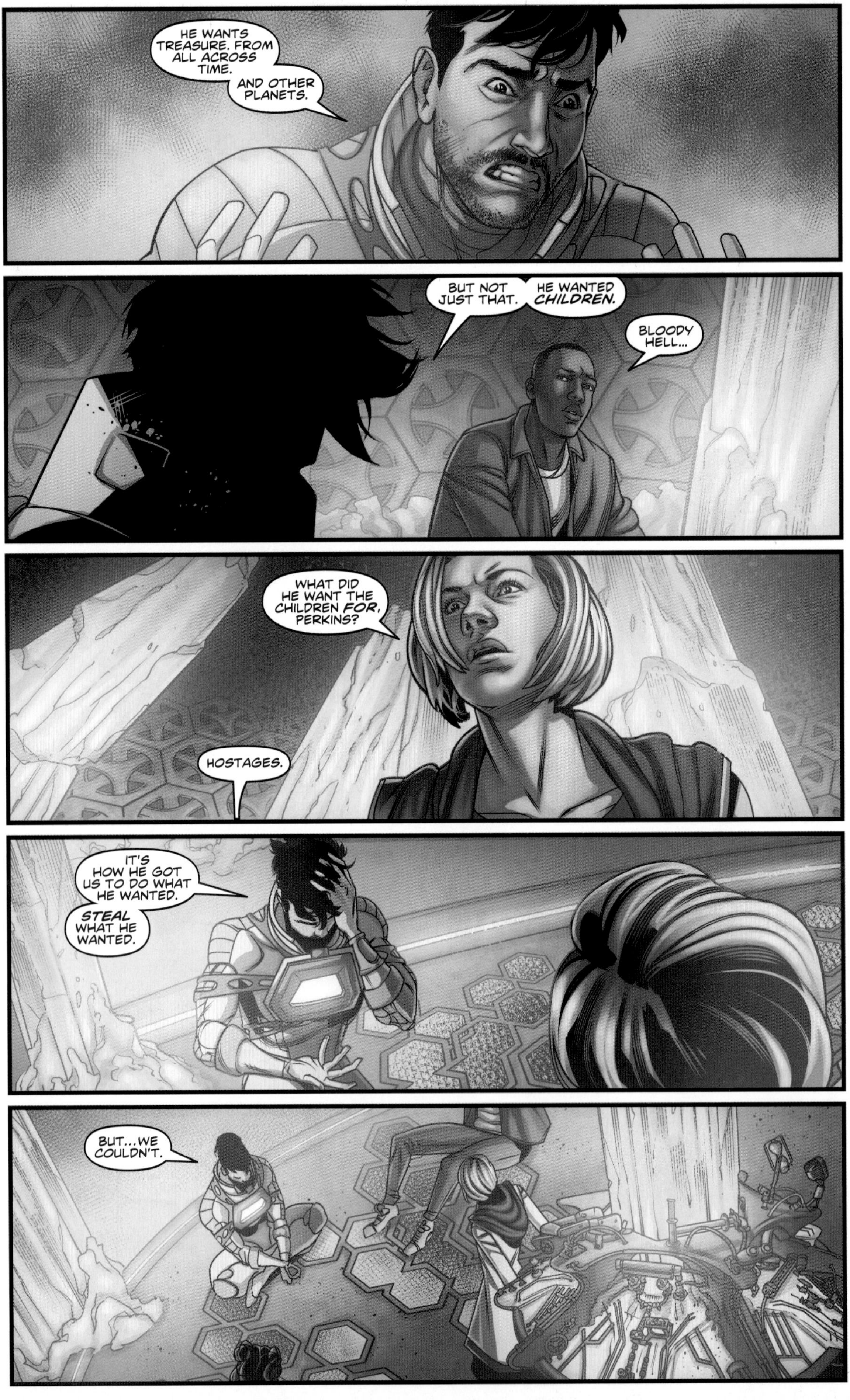
HE WANTS TREASURE. FROM ALL ACROSS TIME.
AND OTHER PLANETS.
BUT NOT JUST THAT.
HE WANTED *CHILDREN.*
BLOODY HELL...
WHAT DID HE WANT THE CHILDREN *FOR,* PERKINS?
HOSTAGES.
IT'S HOW HE GOT US TO DO WHAT HE WANTED.
STEAL WHAT HE WANTED.
BUT...WE COULDN'T.

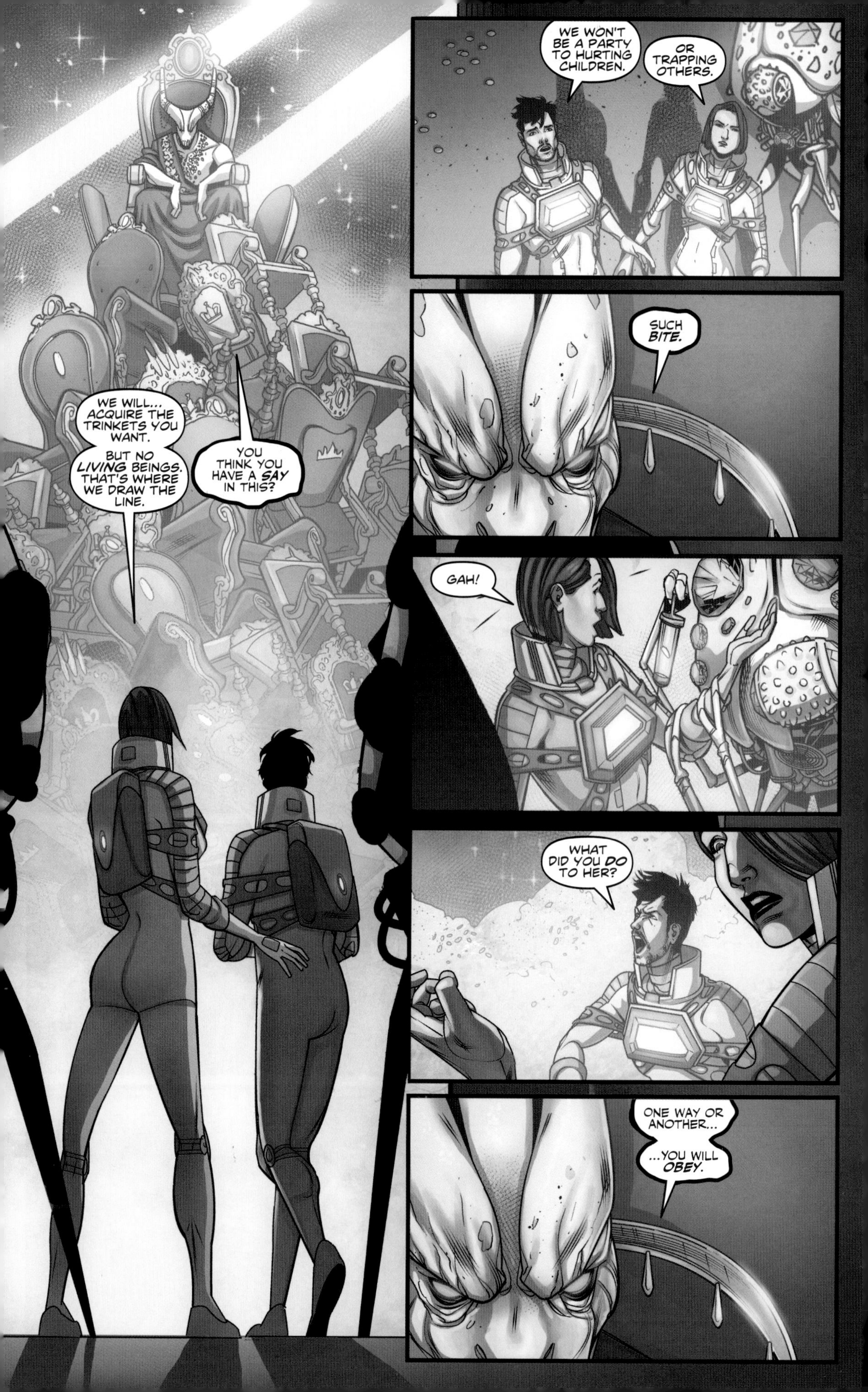
WE WILL... ACQUIRE THE TRINKETS YOU WANT.
BUT NO LIVING BEINGS. THAT'S WHERE WE DRAW THE LINE.
YOU THINK YOU HAVE A SAY IN THIS?
WE WON'T BE A PARTY TO HURTING CHILDREN.
OR TRAPPING OTHERS.
SUCH BITE.
GAH!
WHAT DID YOU DO TO HER?
ONE WAY OR ANOTHER...
...YOU WILL OBEY.

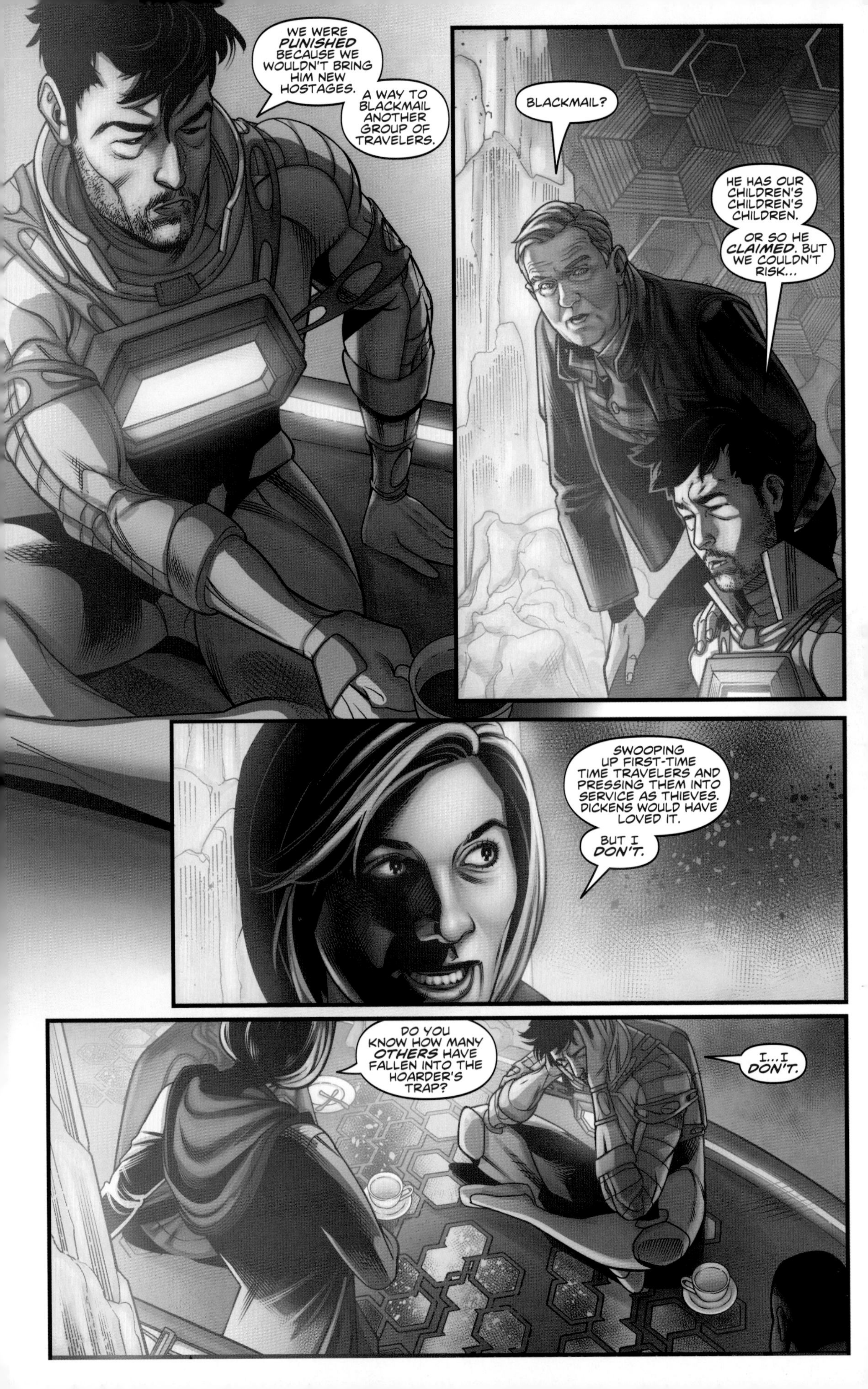
WE WERE PUNISHED BECAUSE WE WOULDN'T BRING HIM NEW HOSTAGES.
A WAY TO BLACKMAIL ANOTHER GROUP OF TRAVELERS.
BLACKMAIL?
HE HAS OUR CHILDREN'S CHILDREN'S CHILDREN.
OR SO HE CLAIMED. BUT WE COULDN'T RISK...
SWOOPING UP FIRST-TIME TIME TRAVELERS AND PRESSING THEM INTO SERVICE AS THIEVES. DICKENS WOULD HAVE LOVED IT.
BUT I DON'T.
DO YOU KNOW HOW MANY OTHERS HAVE FALLEN INTO THE HOARDER'S TRAP?
I...I DON'T.

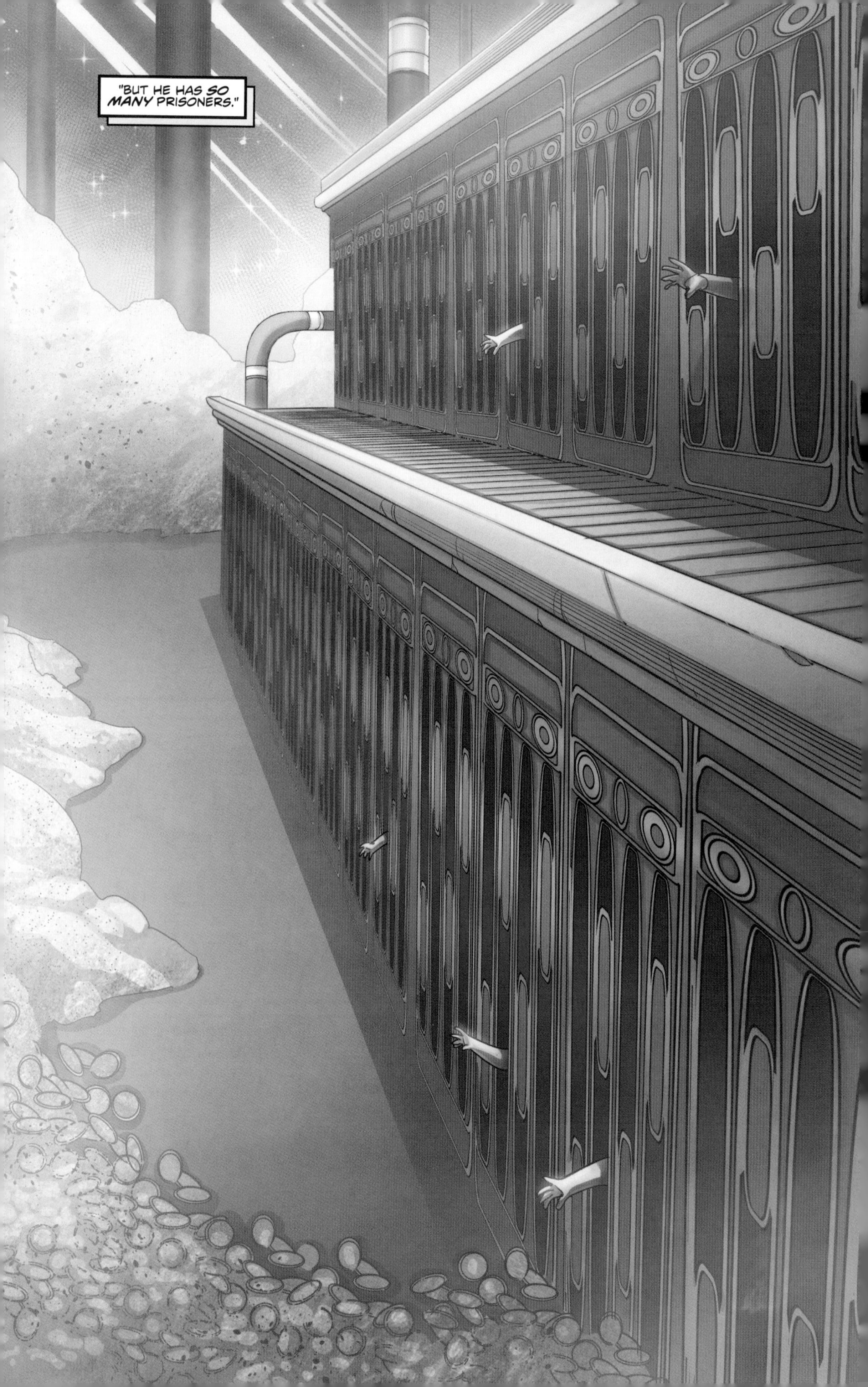
"BUT HE HAS SO MANY PRISONERS."

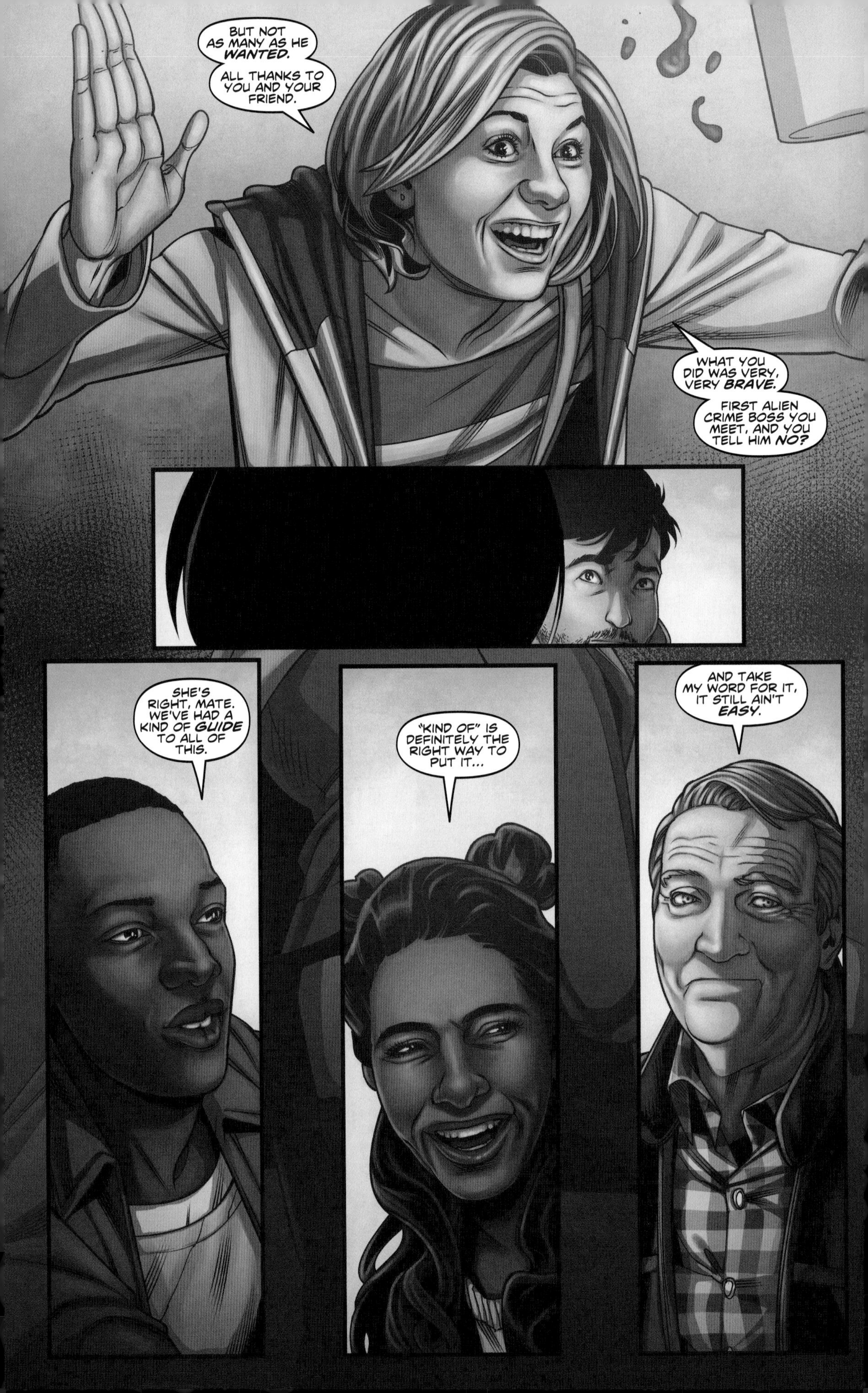
BUT NOT AS MANY AS HE *WANTED.*
ALL THANKS TO YOU AND YOUR FRIEND.
WHAT YOU DID WAS VERY, VERY *BRAVE.*
FIRST ALIEN CRIME BOSS YOU MEET, AND YOU TELL HIM *NO?*
SHE'S RIGHT, MATE. WE'VE HAD A KIND OF *GUIDE* TO ALL OF THIS.
"KIND OF" IS DEFINITELY THE RIGHT WAY TO PUT IT...
AND TAKE MY WORD FOR IT, IT STILL AIN'T *EASY.*

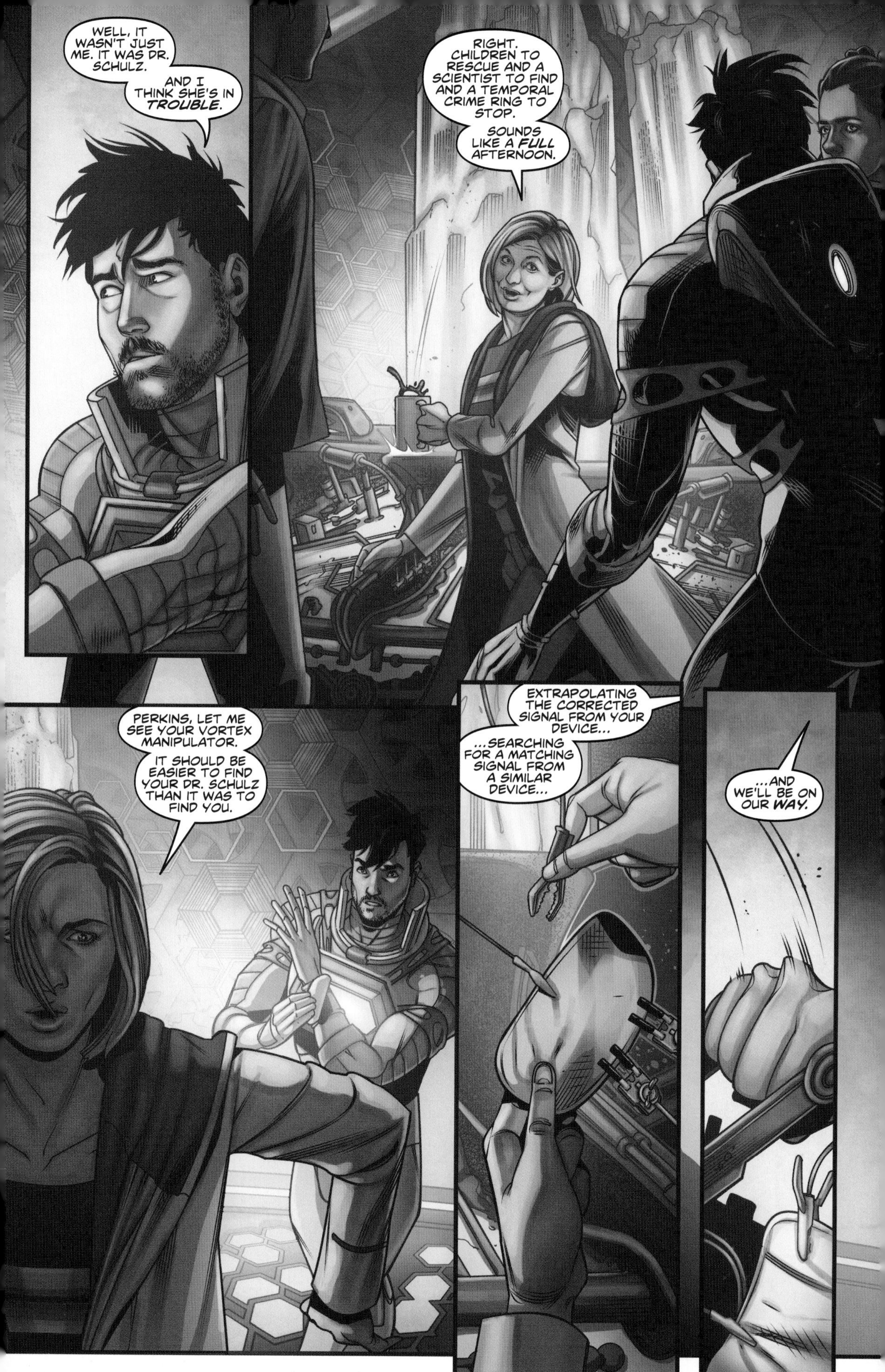
WELL, IT WASN'T JUST ME. IT WAS DR. SCHULZ.
AND I THINK SHE'S IN *TROUBLE*.
RIGHT. CHILDREN TO RESCUE AND A SCIENTIST TO FIND AND A TEMPORAL CRIME RING TO STOP.
SOUNDS LIKE A *FULL* AFTERNOON.
PERKINS, LET ME SEE YOUR VORTEX MANIPULATOR.
IT SHOULD BE *EASIER* TO FIND YOUR DR. SCHULZ THAN IT WAS TO FIND YOU.
EXTRAPOLATING THE CORRECTED SIGNAL FROM YOUR DEVICE...
...SEARCHING FOR A MATCHING SIGNAL FROM A SIMILAR DEVICE...
...AND WE'LL BE ON OUR *WAY*.

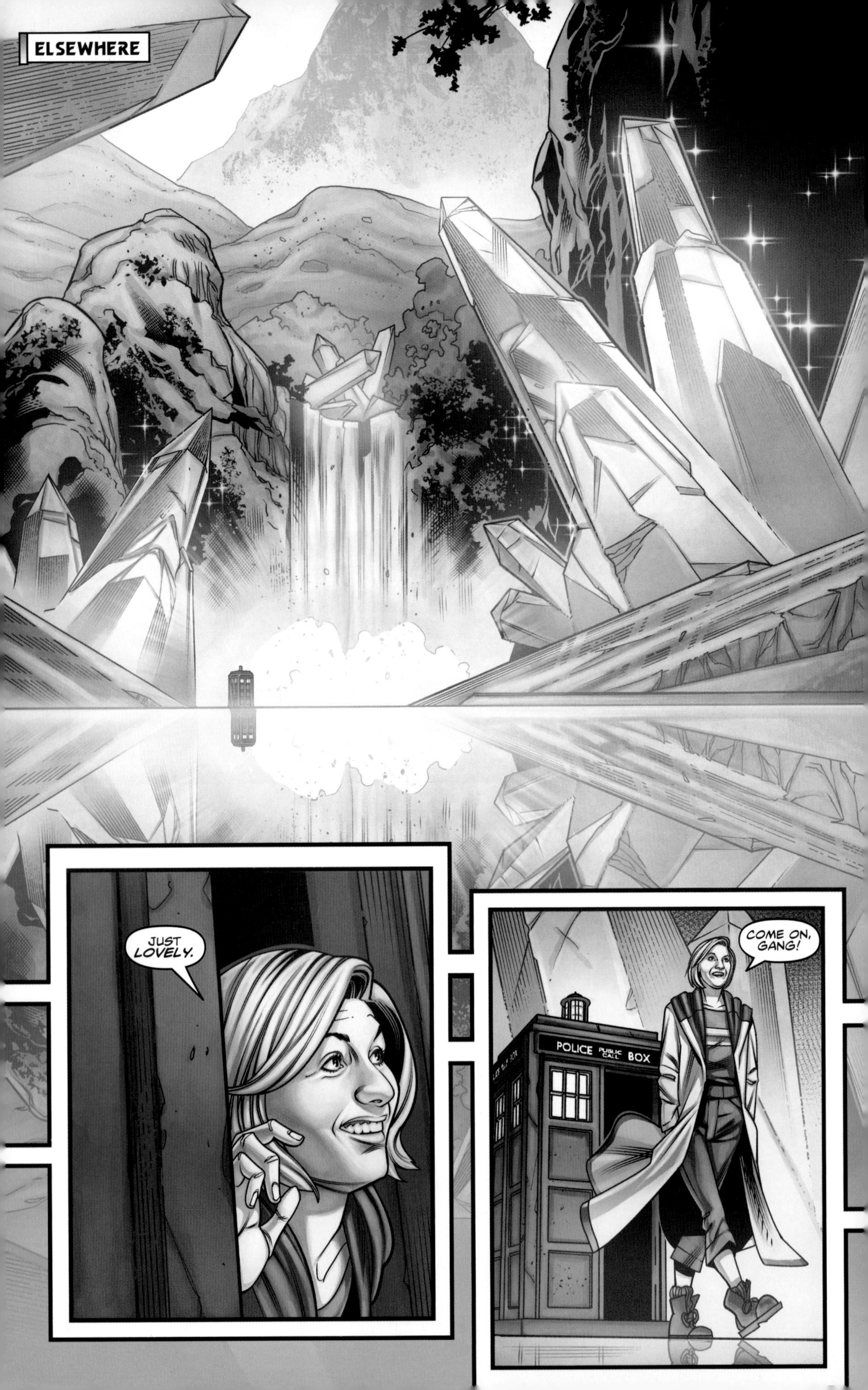
ELSEWHERE
JUST LOVELY.
COME ON, GANG!
POLICE PUBLIC CALL BOX

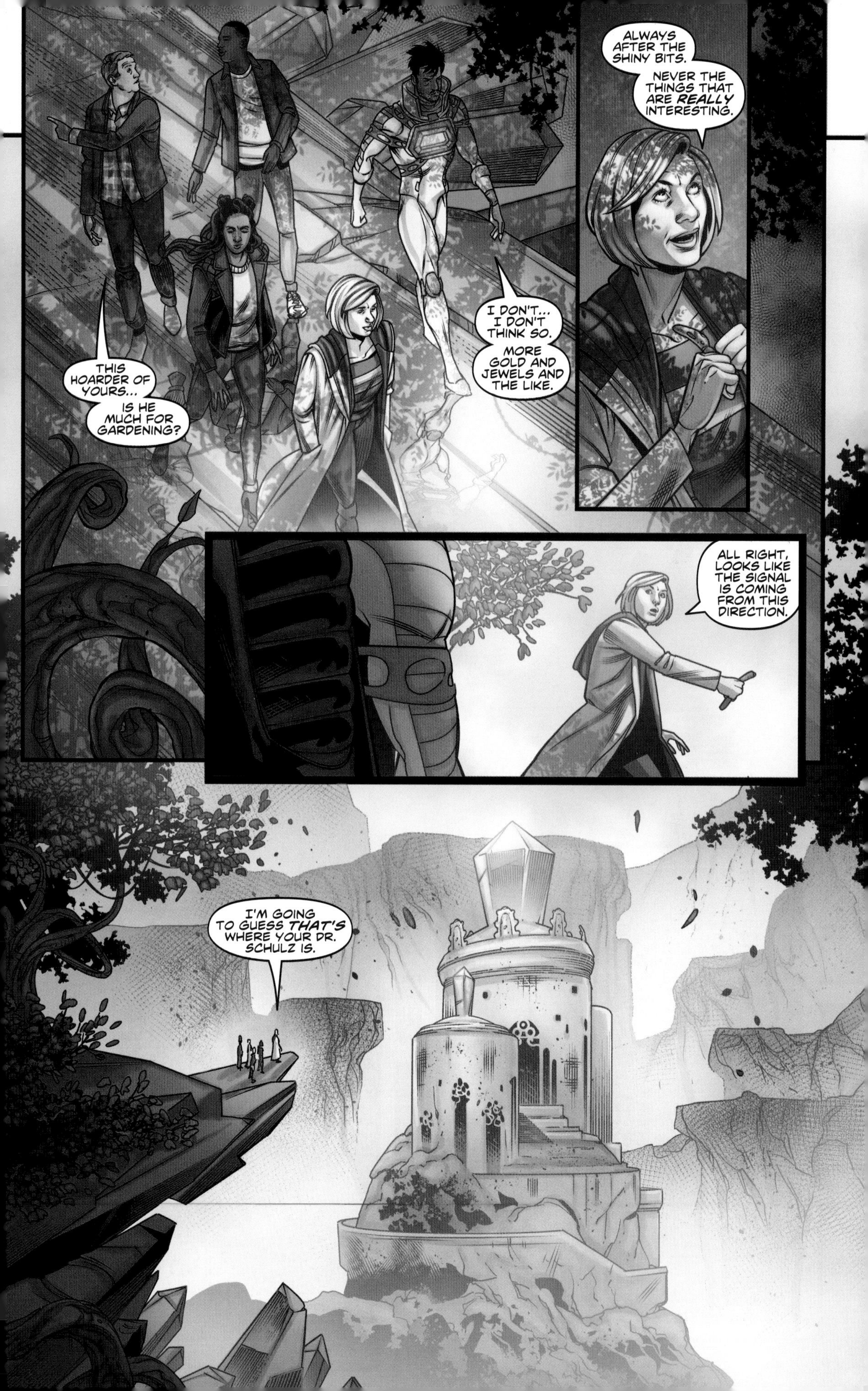
THIS HOARDER OF YOURS... IS HE MUCH FOR GARDENING?
I DON'T... I DON'T THINK SO. MORE GOLD AND JEWELS AND THE LIKE.
ALWAYS AFTER THE SHINY BITS. NEVER THE THINGS THAT ARE *REALLY* INTERESTING.
ALL RIGHT, LOOKS LIKE THE SIGNAL IS COMING FROM THIS DIRECTION.
I'M GOING TO GUESS *THAT'S* WHERE YOUR DR. SCHULZ IS.

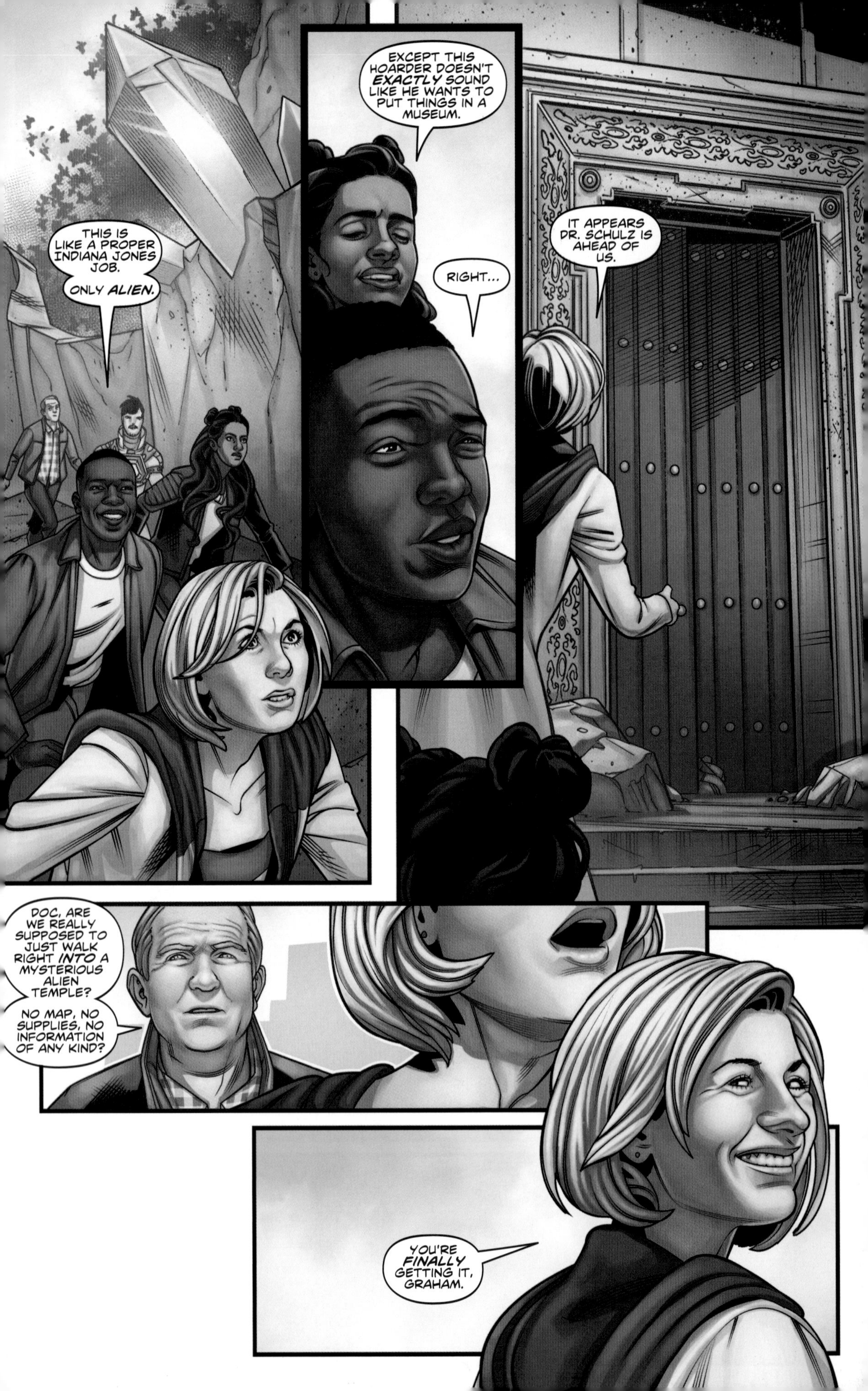
THIS IS LIKE A PROPER INDIANA JONES JOB.
ONLY ALIEN.
EXCEPT THIS HOARDER DOESN'T EXACTLY SOUND LIKE HE WANTS TO PUT THINGS IN A MUSEUM.
RIGHT...
IT APPEARS DR. SCHULZ IS AHEAD OF US.
DOC, ARE WE REALLY SUPPOSED TO JUST WALK RIGHT INTO A MYSTERIOUS ALIEN TEMPLE?
NO MAP, NO SUPPLIES, NO INFORMATION OF ANY KIND?
YOU'RE FINALLY GETTING IT, GRAHAM.

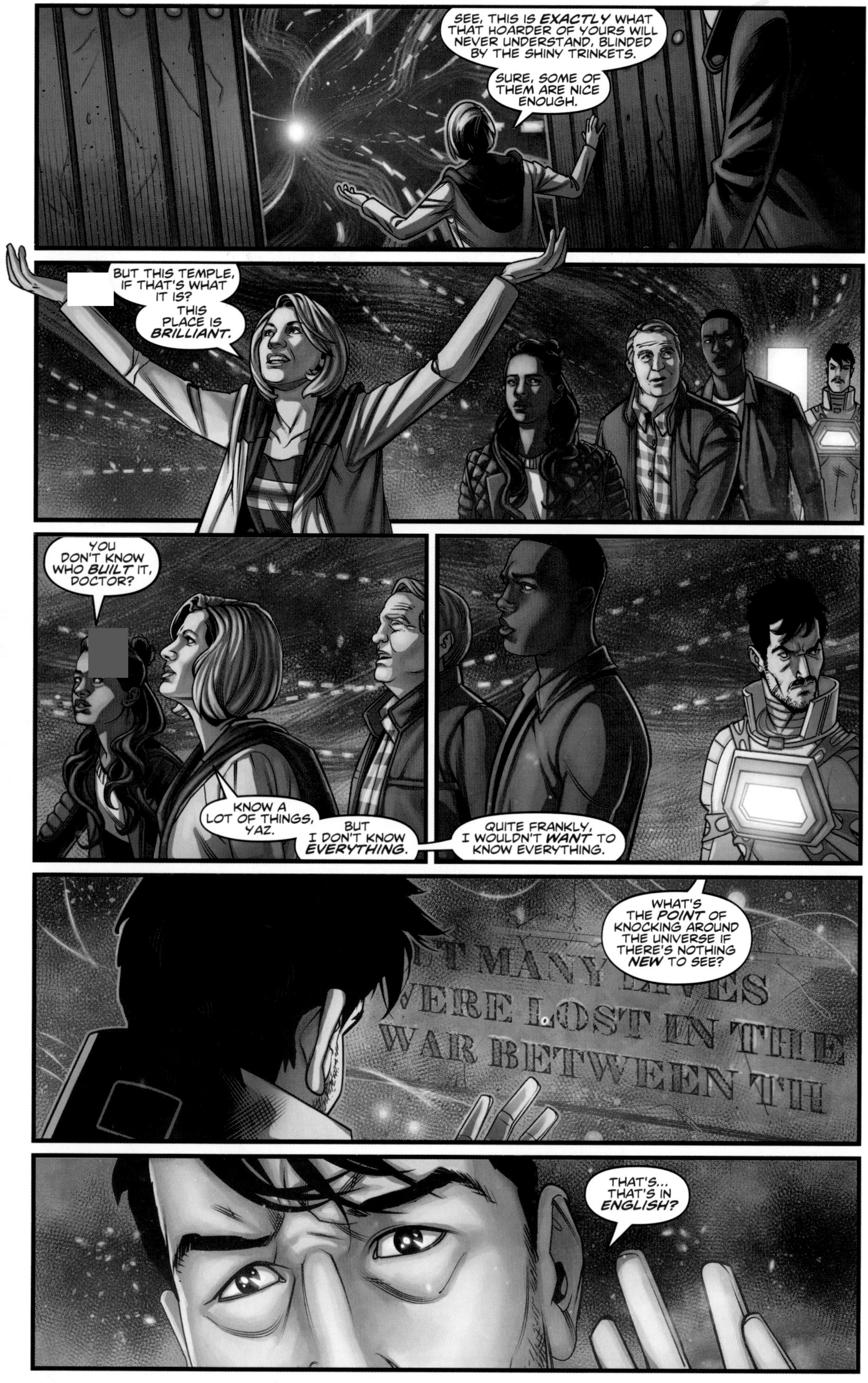
SEE, THIS IS EXACTLY WHAT THAT HOARDER OF YOURS WILL NEVER UNDERSTAND, BLINDED BY THE SHINY TRINKETS.
SURE, SOME OF THEM ARE NICE ENOUGH.
BUT THIS TEMPLE, IF THAT'S WHAT IT IS?
THIS PLACE IS BRILLIANT.
YOU DON'T KNOW WHO BUILT IT, DOCTOR?
KNOW A LOT OF THINGS, YAZ.
BUT I DON'T KNOW EVERYTHING.
QUITE FRANKLY, I WOULDN'T WANT TO KNOW EVERYTHING.
WHAT'S THE POINT OF KNOCKING AROUND THE UNIVERSE IF THERE'S NOTHING NEW TO SEE?
T MANY LIVES
VERE LOST IN THE
WAR BETWEEN TH
THAT'S... THAT'S IN ENGLISH?

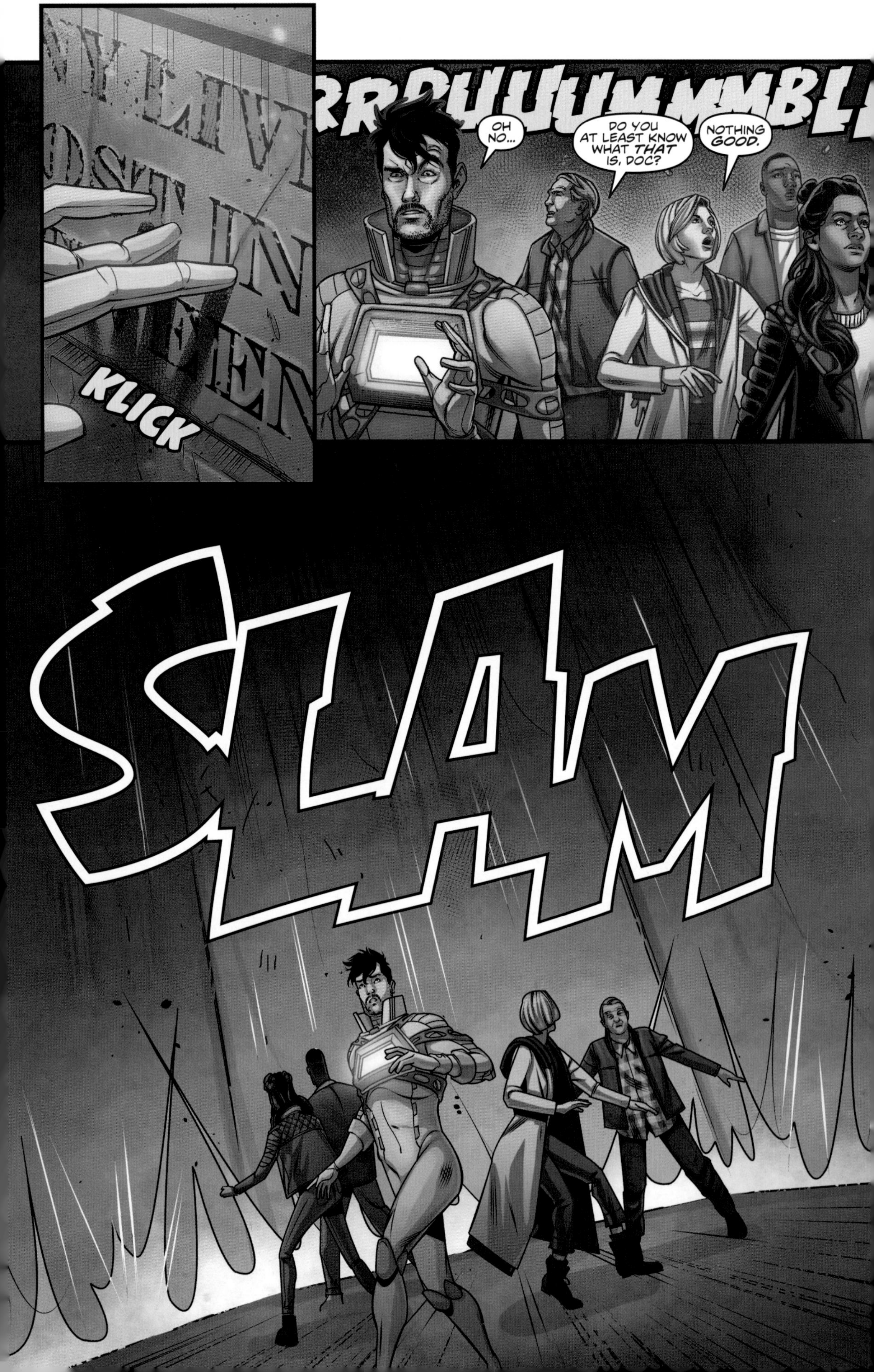
KLICK
RRRUUUMMMBLE
OH NO...
DO YOU AT LEAST KNOW WHAT *THAT* IS, DOC?
NOTHING *GOOD.*
SLAM

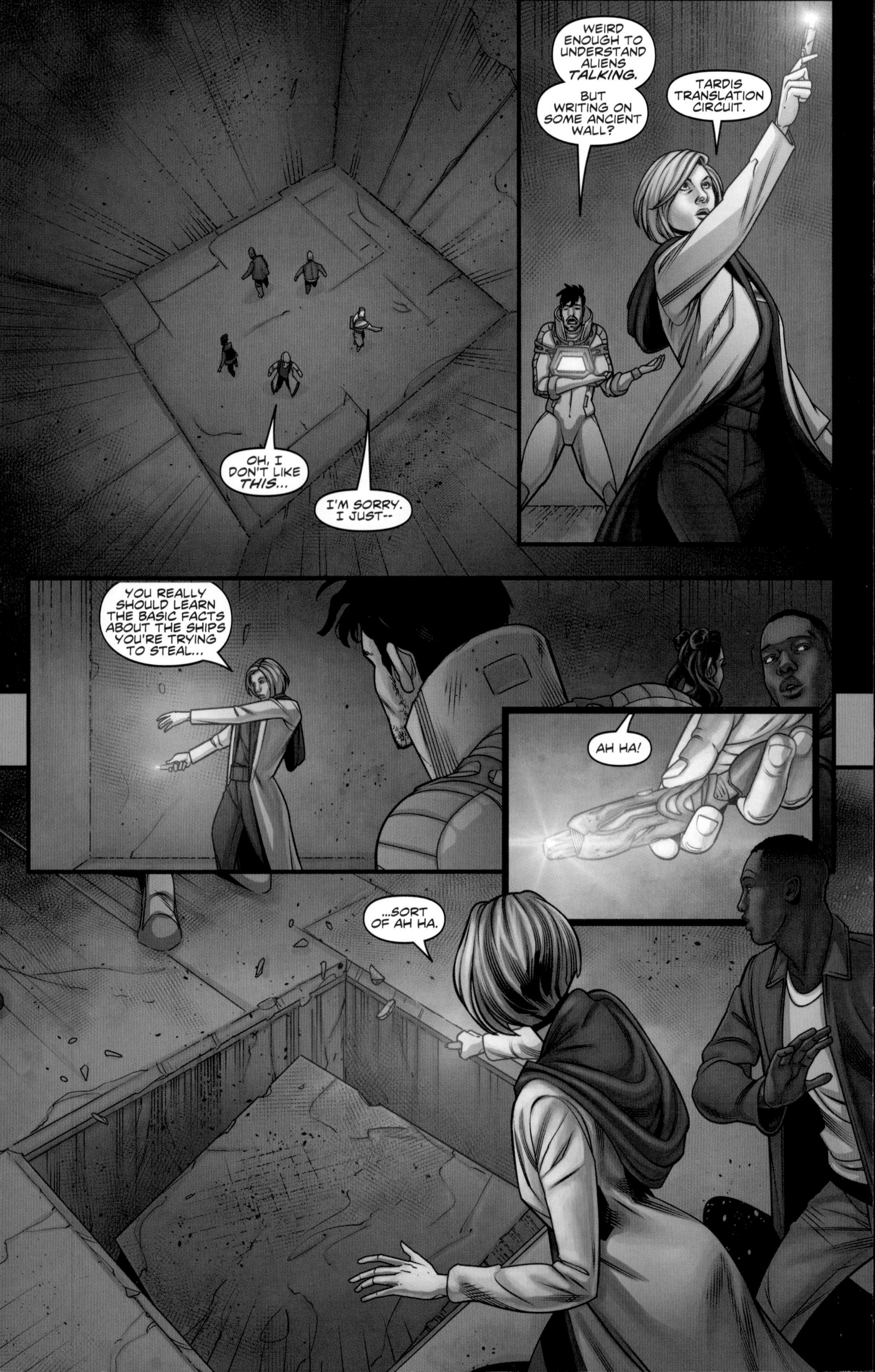
OH, I DON'T LIKE THIS...
I'M SORRY. I JUST--
WEIRD ENOUGH TO UNDERSTAND ALIENS TALKING.
BUT WRITING ON SOME ANCIENT WALL?
TARDIS TRANSLATION CIRCUIT.
YOU REALLY SHOULD LEARN THE BASIC FACTS ABOUT THE SHIPS YOU'RE TRYING TO STEAL...
AH HA!
...SORT OF AH HA.

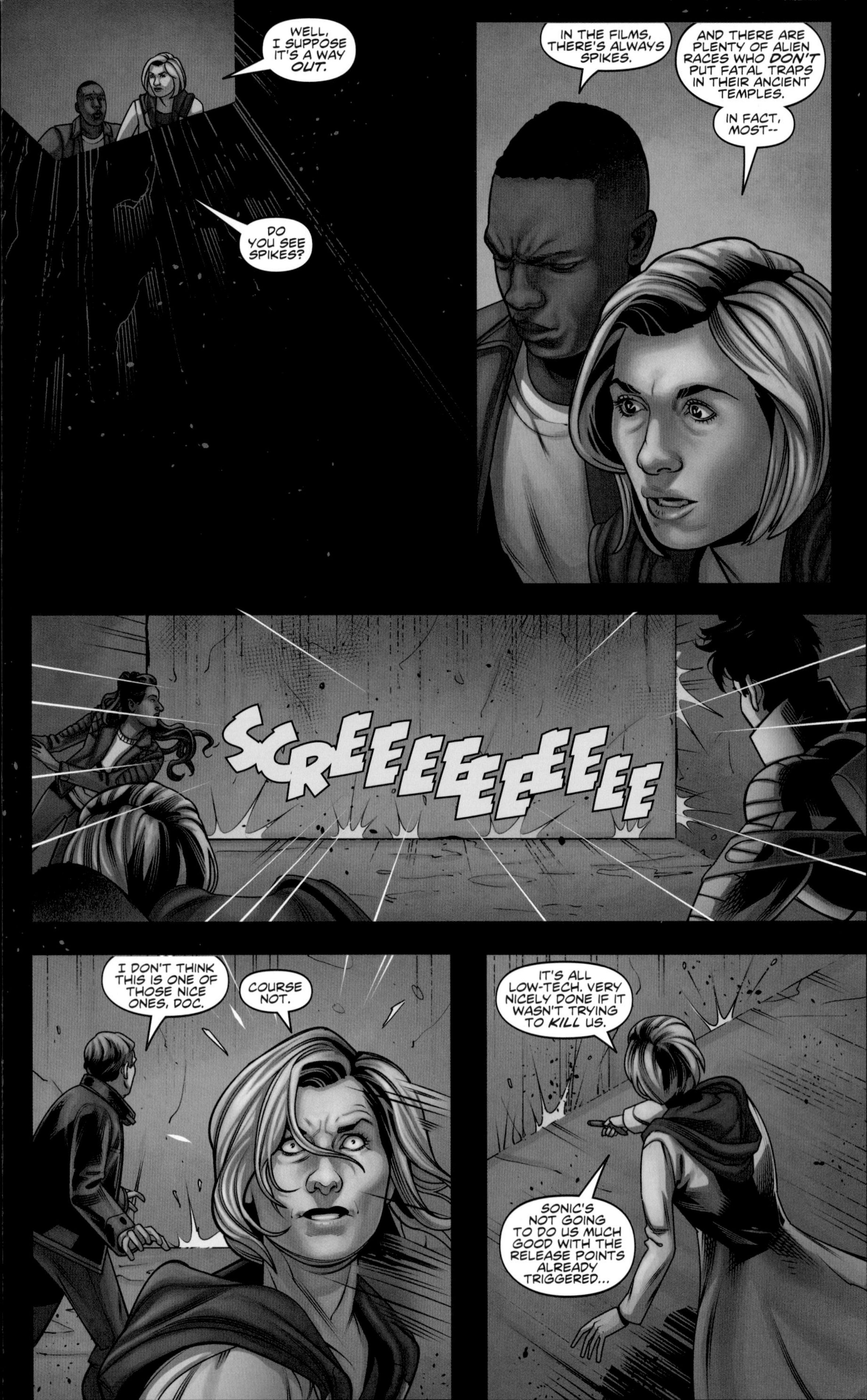
WELL, I SUPPOSE IT'S A WAY OUT.
DO YOU SEE SPIKES?
IN THE FILMS, THERE'S ALWAYS SPIKES.
AND THERE ARE PLENTY OF ALIEN RACES WHO DON'T PUT FATAL TRAPS IN THEIR ANCIENT TEMPLES.
IN FACT, MOST--
SCREEEEEEEEEEE
I DON'T THINK THIS IS ONE OF THOSE NICE ONES, DOC.
COURSE NOT.
IT'S ALL LOW-TECH. VERY NICELY DONE IF IT WASN'T TRYING TO KILL US.
SONIC'S NOT GOING TO DO US MUCH GOOD WITH THE RELEASE POINTS ALREADY TRIGGERED...

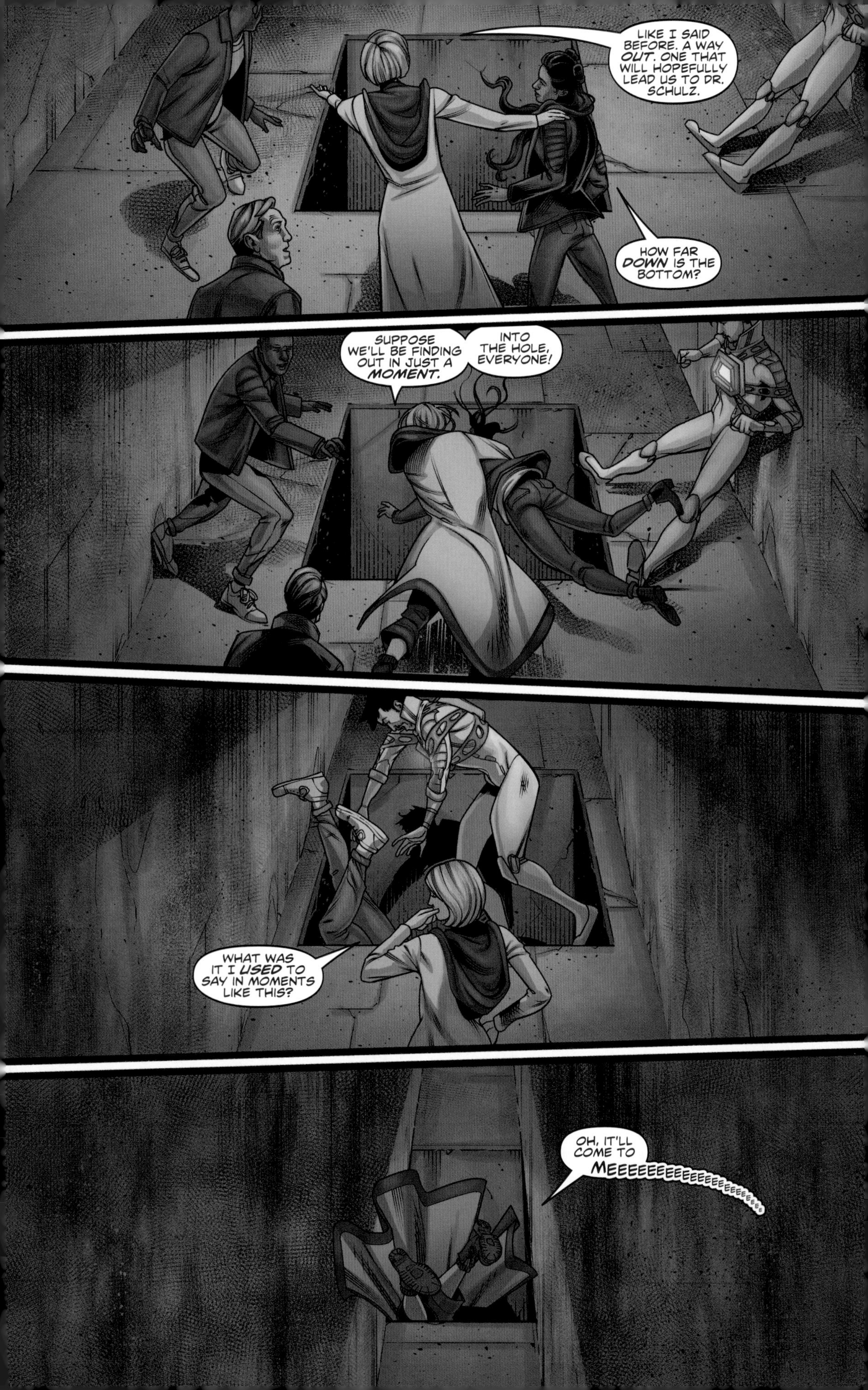
LIKE I SAID BEFORE. A WAY OUT. ONE THAT WILL HOPEFULLY LEAD US TO DR. SCHULZ.
HOW FAR DOWN IS THE BOTTOM?
SUPPOSE WE'LL BE FINDING OUT IN JUST A MOMENT.
INTO THE HOLE, EVERYONE!
WHAT WAS IT I USED TO SAY IN MOMENTS LIKE THIS?
OH, IT'LL COME TO MEEEEEEEEEEEEEEEEEEEEEE

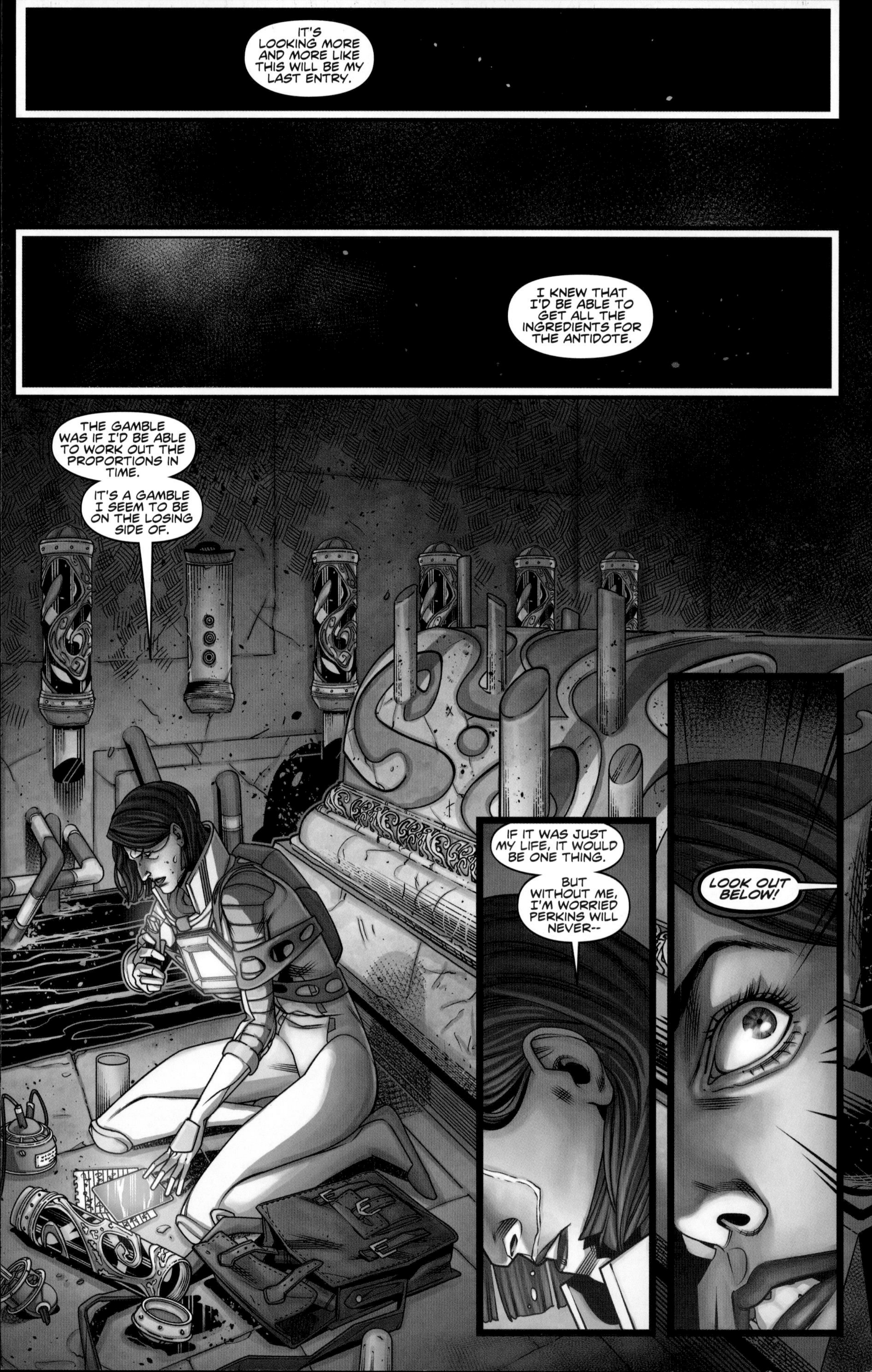
IT'S LOOKING MORE AND MORE LIKE THIS WILL BE MY LAST ENTRY.
I KNEW THAT I'D BE ABLE TO GET ALL THE INGREDIENTS FOR THE ANTIDOTE.
THE GAMBLE WAS IF I'D BE ABLE TO WORK OUT THE PROPORTIONS IN TIME.
IT'S A GAMBLE I SEEM TO BE ON THE LOSING SIDE OF.
IF IT WAS JUST MY LIFE, IT WOULD BE ONE THING.
BUT WITHOUT ME, I'M WORRIED PERKINS WILL NEVER--
LOOK OUT BELOW!

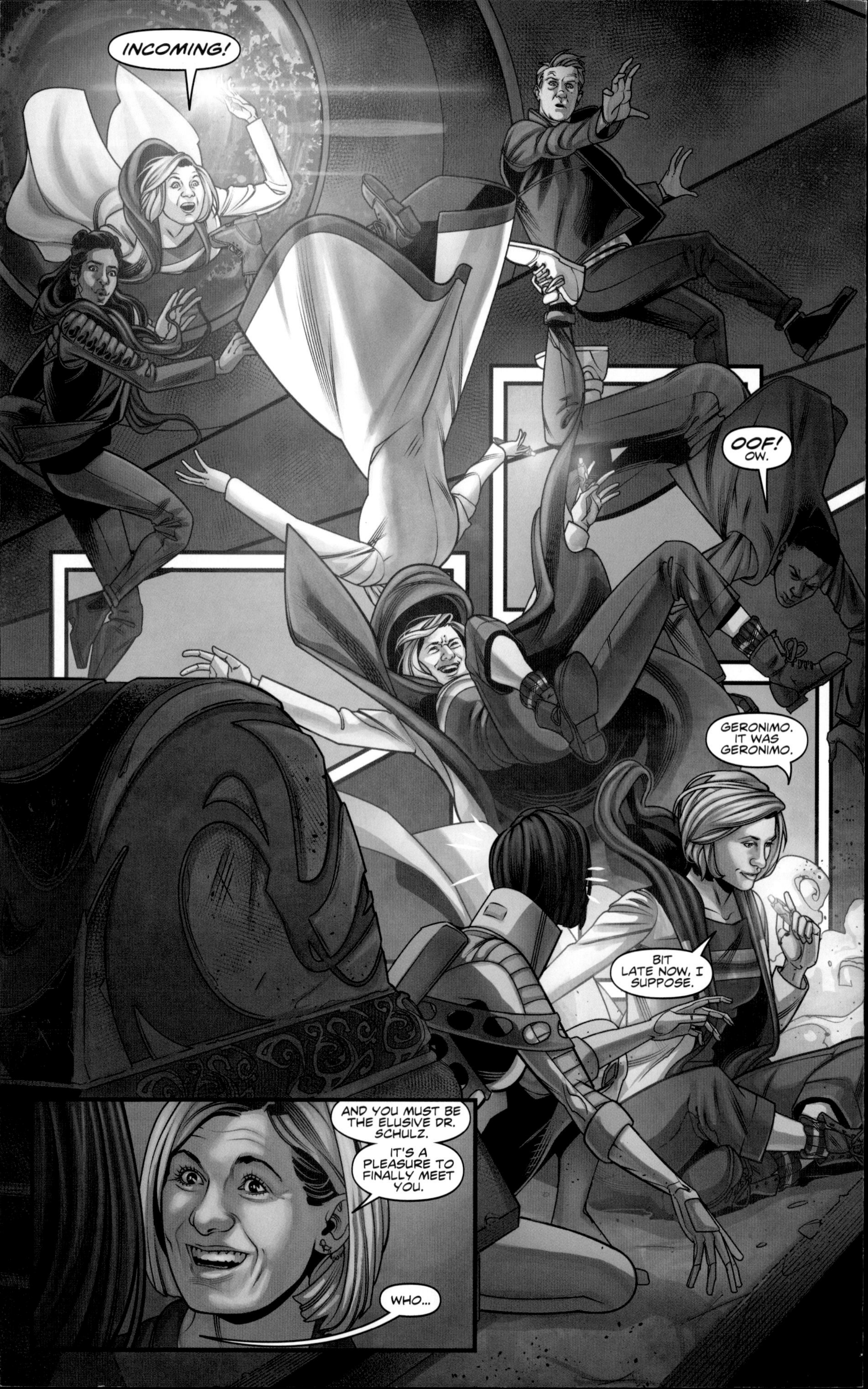
INCOMING!
OOF! OW.
GERONIMO. IT WAS GERONIMO.
BIT LATE NOW, I SUPPOSE.
AND YOU MUST BE THE ELUSIVE DR. SCHULZ.
IT'S A PLEASURE TO FINALLY MEET YOU.
WHO...

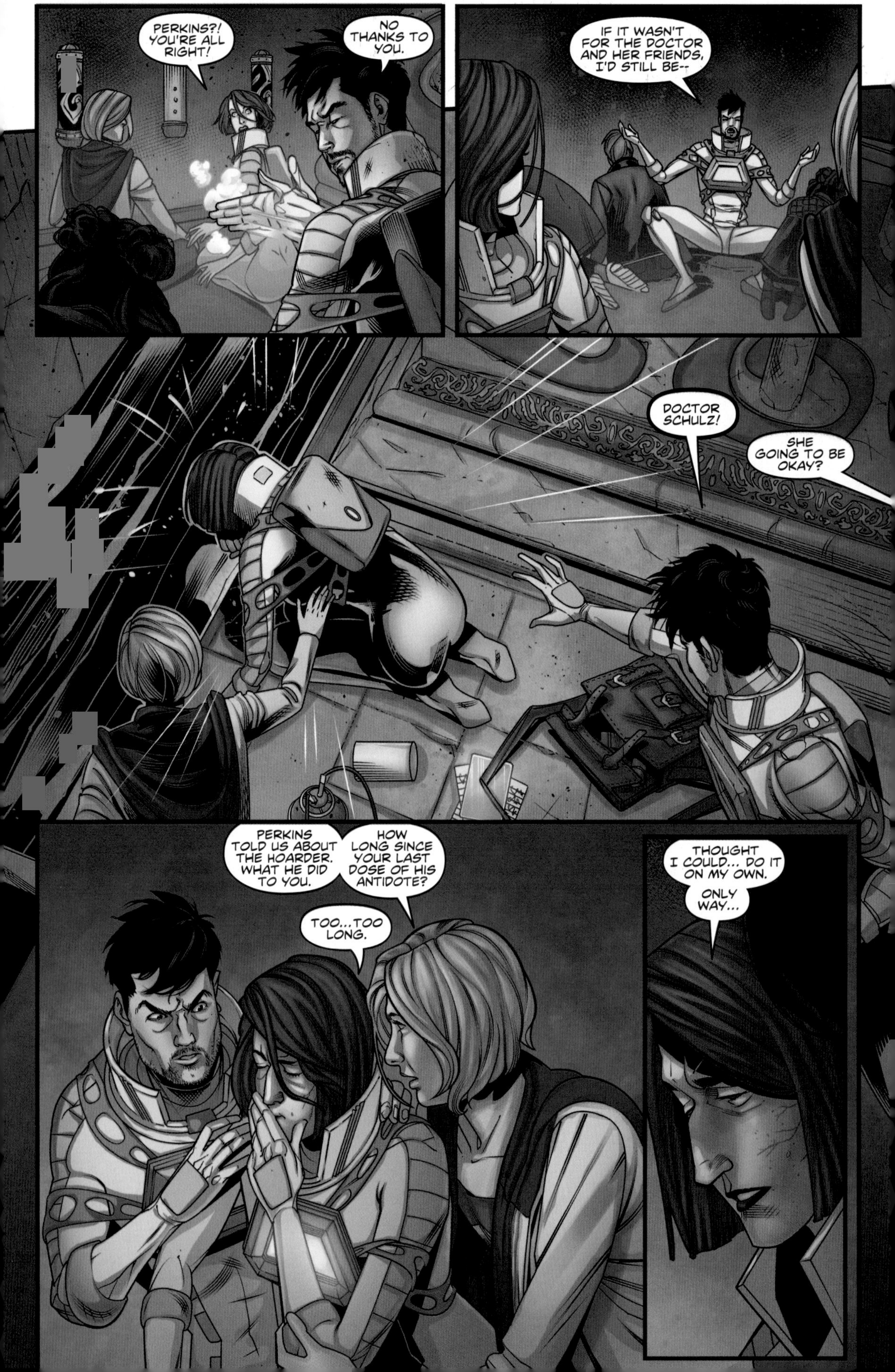
PERKINS?! YOU'RE ALL RIGHT!
NO THANKS TO YOU.
IF IT WASN'T FOR THE DOCTOR AND HER FRIENDS, I'D STILL BE--
DOCTOR SCHULZ!
SHE GOING TO BE OKAY?
PERKINS TOLD US ABOUT THE HOARDER. WHAT HE DID TO YOU.
HOW LONG SINCE YOUR LAST DOSE OF HIS ANTIDOTE?
TOO...TOO LONG.
THOUGHT I COULD... DO IT ON MY OWN.
ONLY WAY...

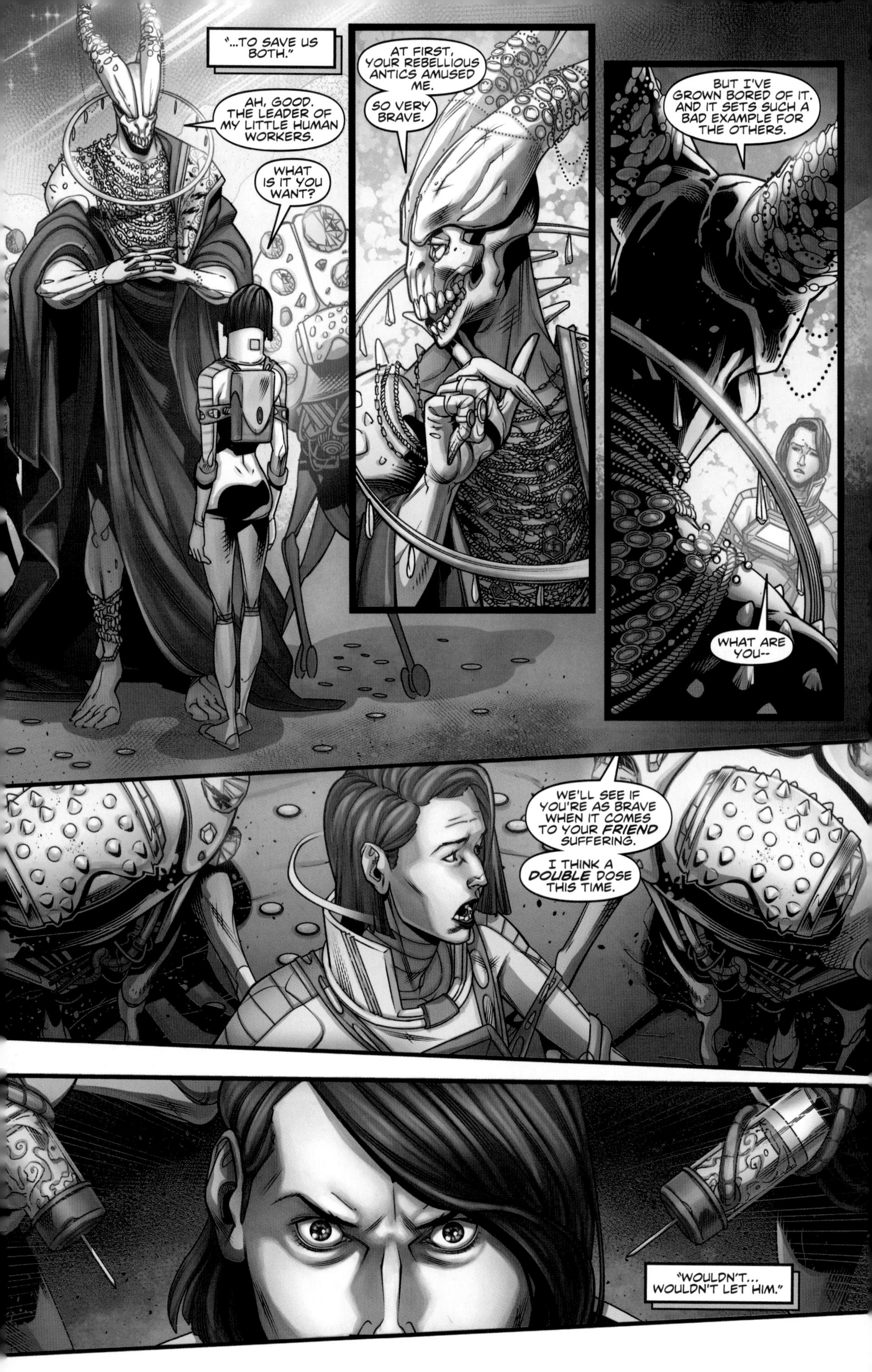
"...TO SAVE US BOTH."
AH, GOOD. THE LEADER OF MY LITTLE HUMAN WORKERS.
WHAT IS IT YOU WANT?
AT FIRST, YOUR REBELLIOUS ANTICS AMUSED ME.
SO VERY BRAVE.
BUT I'VE GROWN BORED OF IT. AND IT SETS SUCH A BAD EXAMPLE FOR THE OTHERS.
WHAT ARE YOU--
WE'LL SEE IF YOU'RE AS BRAVE WHEN IT COMES TO YOUR FRIEND SUFFERING.
I THINK A DOUBLE DOSE THIS TIME.
"WOULDN'T... WOULDN'T LET HIM."

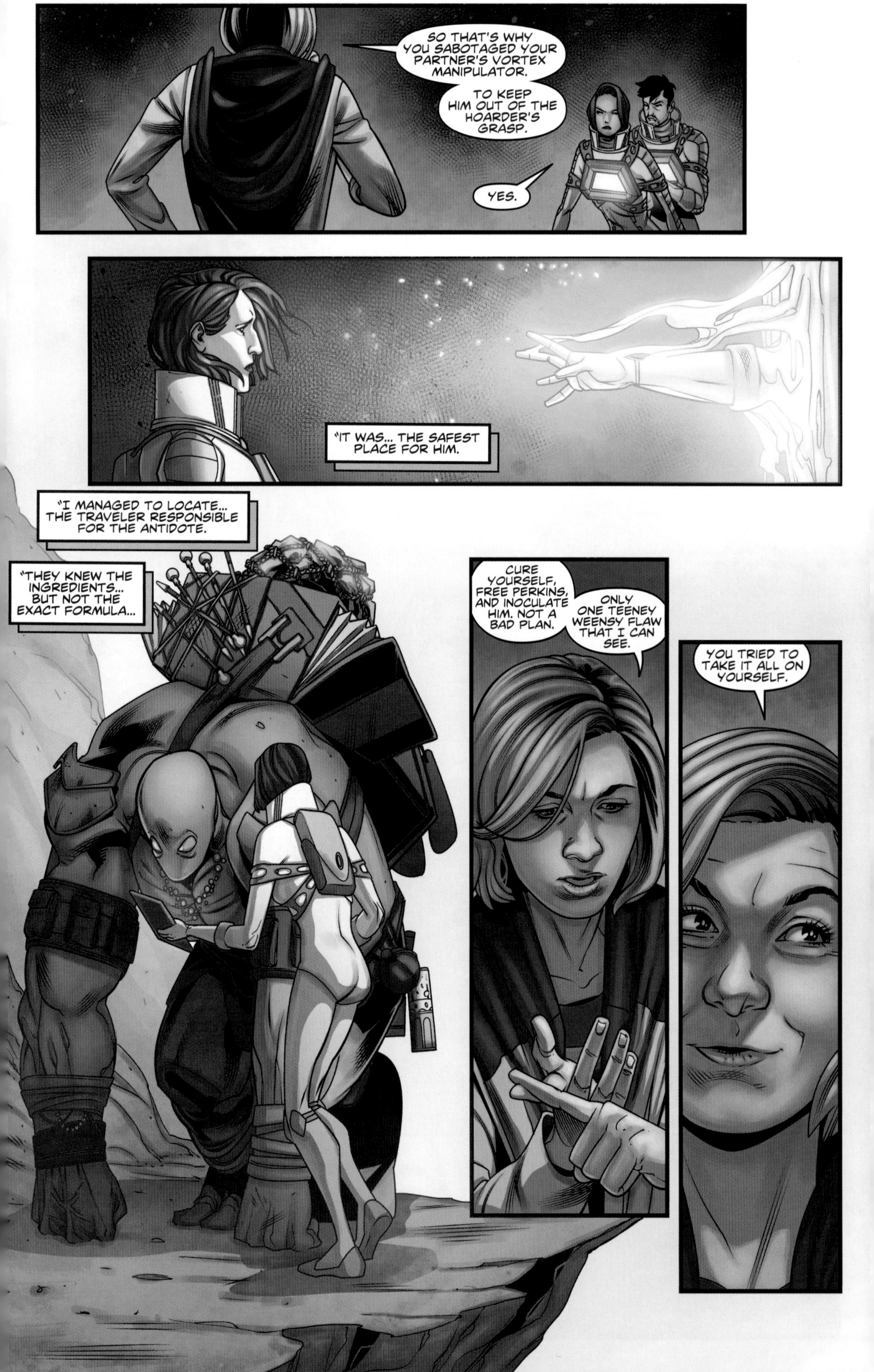
SO THAT'S WHY YOU SABOTAGED YOUR PARTNER'S VORTEX MANIPULATOR.
TO KEEP HIM OUT OF THE HOARDER'S GRASP.
YES.
"IT WAS... THE SAFEST PLACE FOR HIM.
"I MANAGED TO LOCATE... THE TRAVELER RESPONSIBLE FOR THE ANTIDOTE.
"THEY KNEW THE INGREDIENTS... BUT NOT THE EXACT FORMULA...
CURE YOURSELF, FREE PERKINS, AND INOCULATE HIM. NOT A BAD PLAN.
ONLY ONE TEENEY WEENSY FLAW THAT I CAN SEE.
YOU TRIED TO TAKE IT ALL ON YOURSELF.

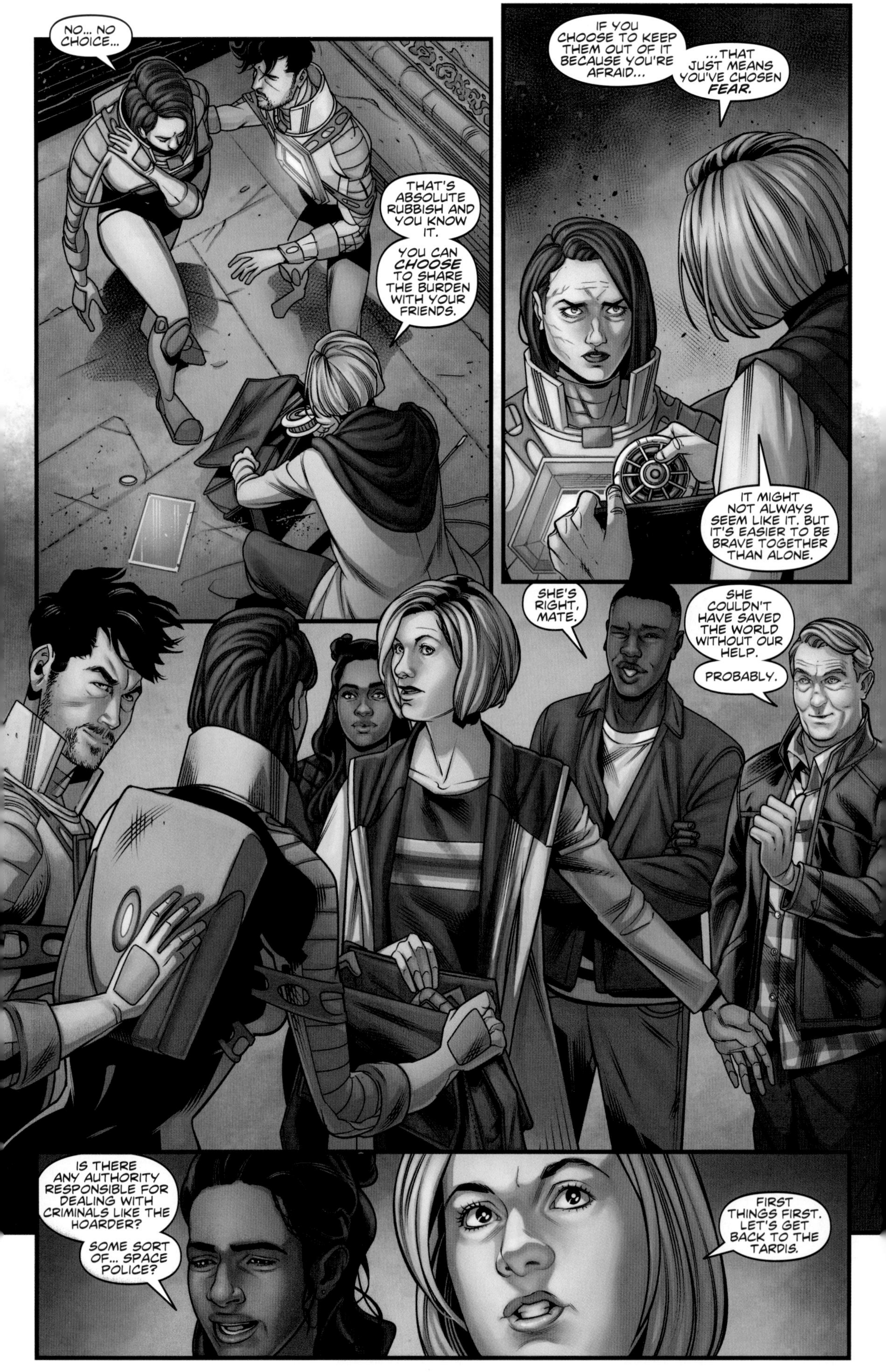
NO... NO CHOICE...
THAT'S ABSOLUTE RUBBISH AND YOU KNOW IT.
YOU CAN CHOOSE TO SHARE THE BURDEN WITH YOUR FRIENDS.
IF YOU CHOOSE TO KEEP THEM OUT OF IT BECAUSE YOU'RE AFRAID...
...THAT JUST MEANS YOU'VE CHOSEN FEAR.
IT MIGHT NOT ALWAYS SEEM LIKE IT. BUT IT'S EASIER TO BE BRAVE TOGETHER THAN ALONE.
SHE'S RIGHT, MATE.
SHE COULDN'T HAVE SAVED THE WORLD WITHOUT OUR HELP.
PROBABLY.
IS THERE ANY AUTHORITY RESPONSIBLE FOR DEALING WITH CRIMINALS LIKE THE HOARDER?
SOME SORT OF... SPACE POLICE?
FIRST THINGS FIRST. LET'S GET BACK TO THE TARDIS.

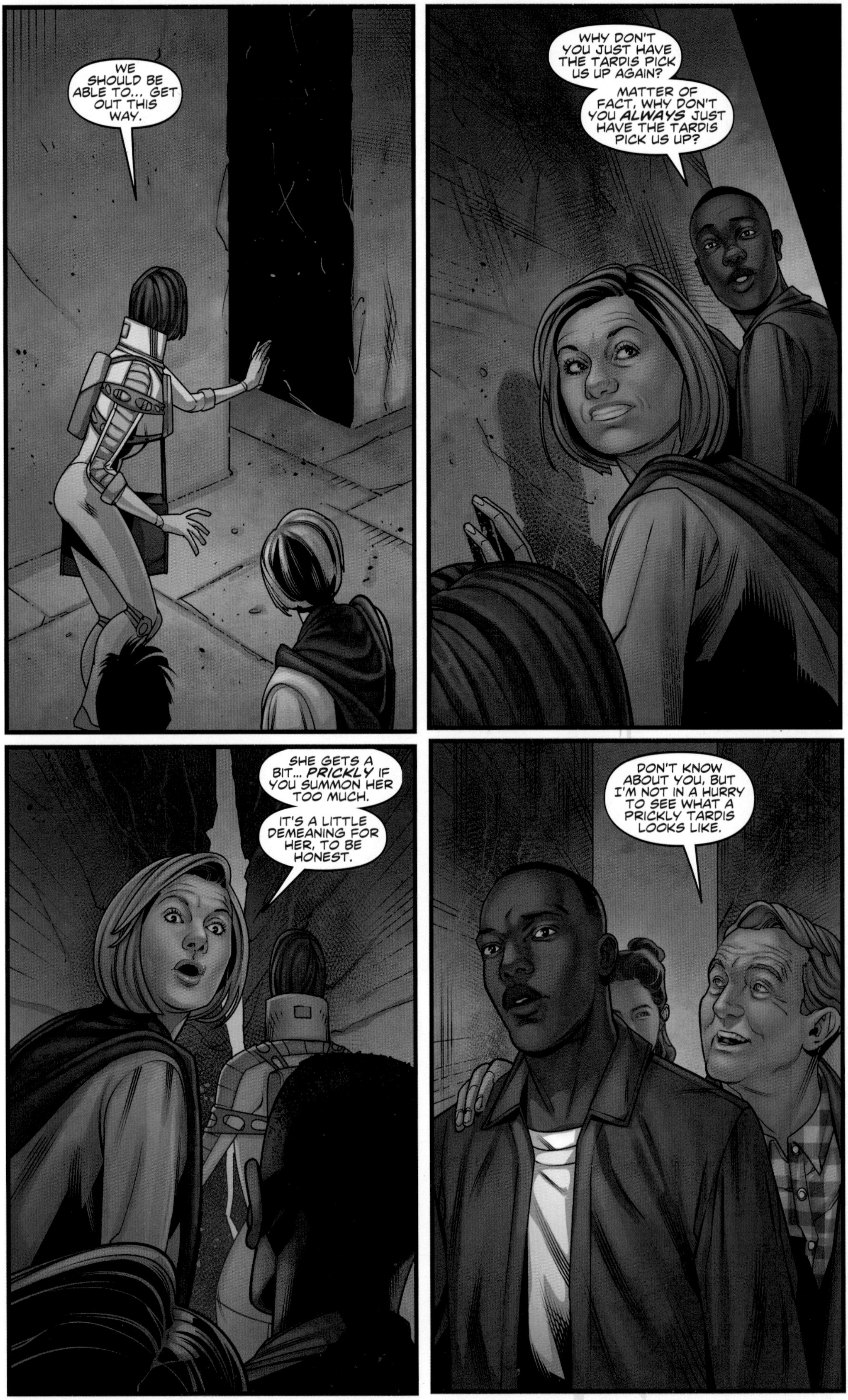
WE SHOULD BE ABLE TO... GET OUT THIS WAY.
WHY DON'T YOU JUST HAVE THE TARDIS PICK US UP AGAIN?
MATTER OF FACT, WHY DON'T YOU *ALWAYS* JUST HAVE THE TARDIS PICK US UP?
SHE GETS A BIT... *PRICKLY* IF YOU SUMMON HER TOO MUCH.
IT'S A LITTLE DEMEANING FOR HER, TO BE HONEST.
DON'T KNOW ABOUT YOU, BUT I'M NOT IN A HURRY TO SEE WHAT A PRICKLY TARDIS LOOKS LIKE.

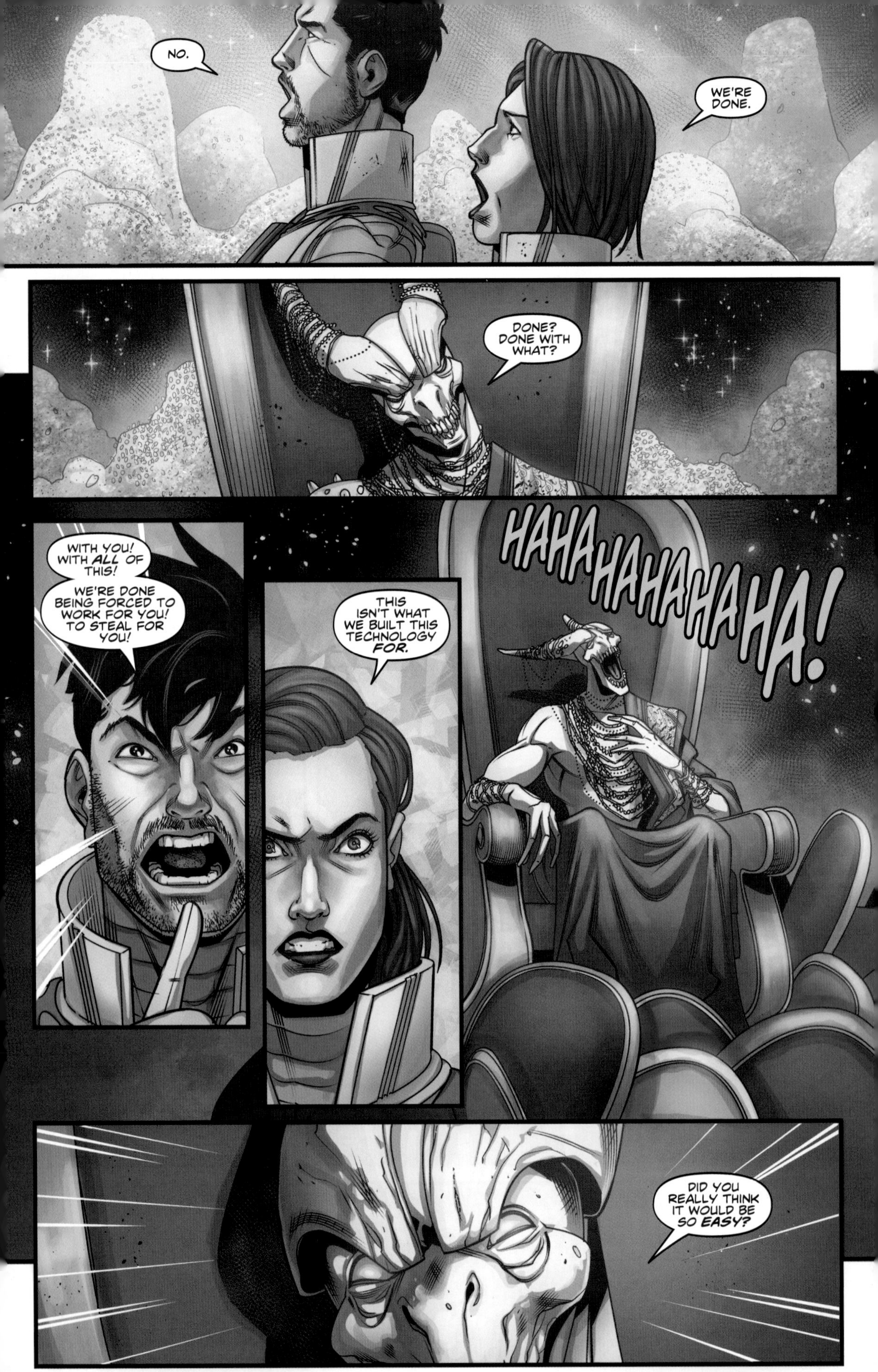
NO.
WE'RE DONE.
DONE? DONE WITH WHAT?
WITH YOU! WITH ALL OF THIS!
WE'RE DONE BEING FORCED TO WORK FOR YOU! TO STEAL FOR YOU!
THIS ISN'T WHAT WE BUILT THIS TECHNOLOGY FOR.
HAHAHAHAHAHAHAHA!
DID YOU REALLY THINK IT WOULD BE SO EASY?

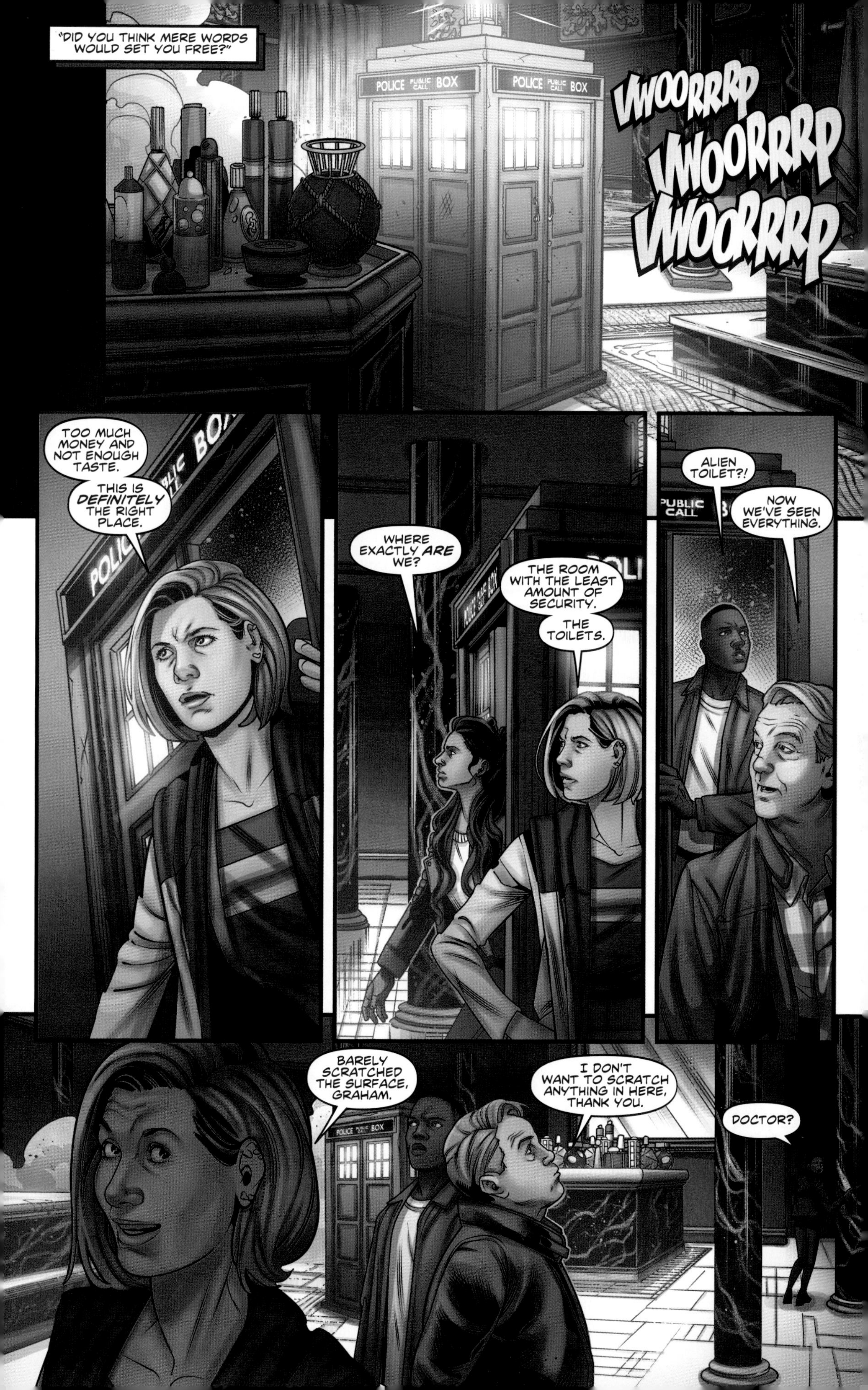
"DID YOU THINK MERE WORDS WOULD SET YOU FREE?"
POLICE PUBLIC CALL BOX
VWOORRRP
VWOORRRP
VWOORRRP
TOO MUCH MONEY AND NOT ENOUGH TASTE.
THIS IS *DEFINITELY* THE RIGHT PLACE.
WHERE EXACTLY *ARE* WE?
THE ROOM WITH THE LEAST AMOUNT OF SECURITY.
THE TOILETS.
ALIEN TOILET?!
NOW WE'VE SEEN EVERYTHING.
BARELY SCRATCHED THE SURFACE, GRAHAM.
I DON'T WANT TO SCRATCH ANYTHING IN HERE, THANK YOU.
DOCTOR?

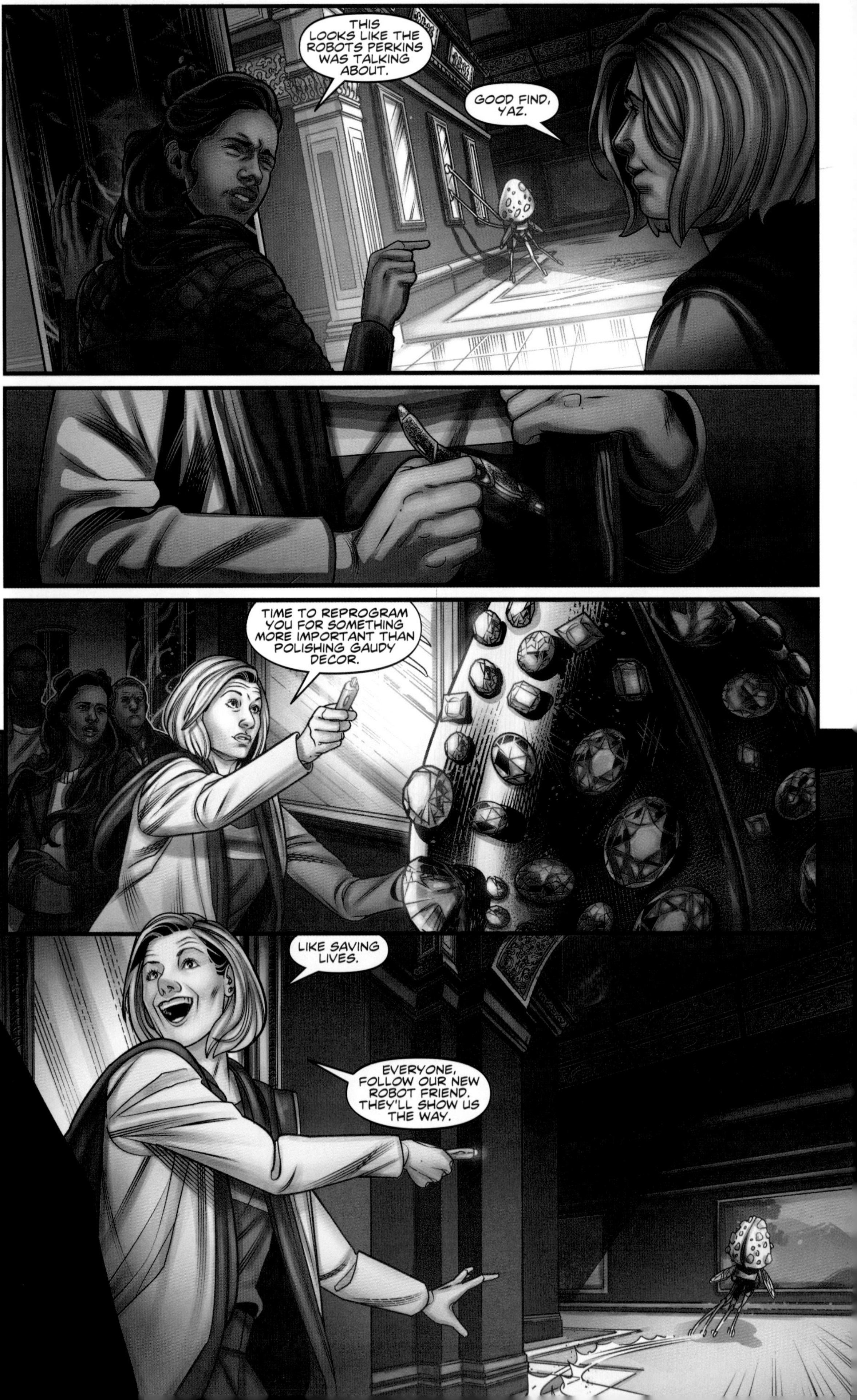
THIS LOOKS LIKE THE ROBOTS PERKINS WAS TALKING ABOUT.
GOOD FIND, YAZ.
TIME TO REPROGRAM YOU FOR SOMETHING MORE IMPORTANT THAN POLISHING GAUDY DECOR.
LIKE SAVING LIVES.
EVERYONE, FOLLOW OUR NEW ROBOT FRIEND. THEY'LL SHOW US THE WAY.

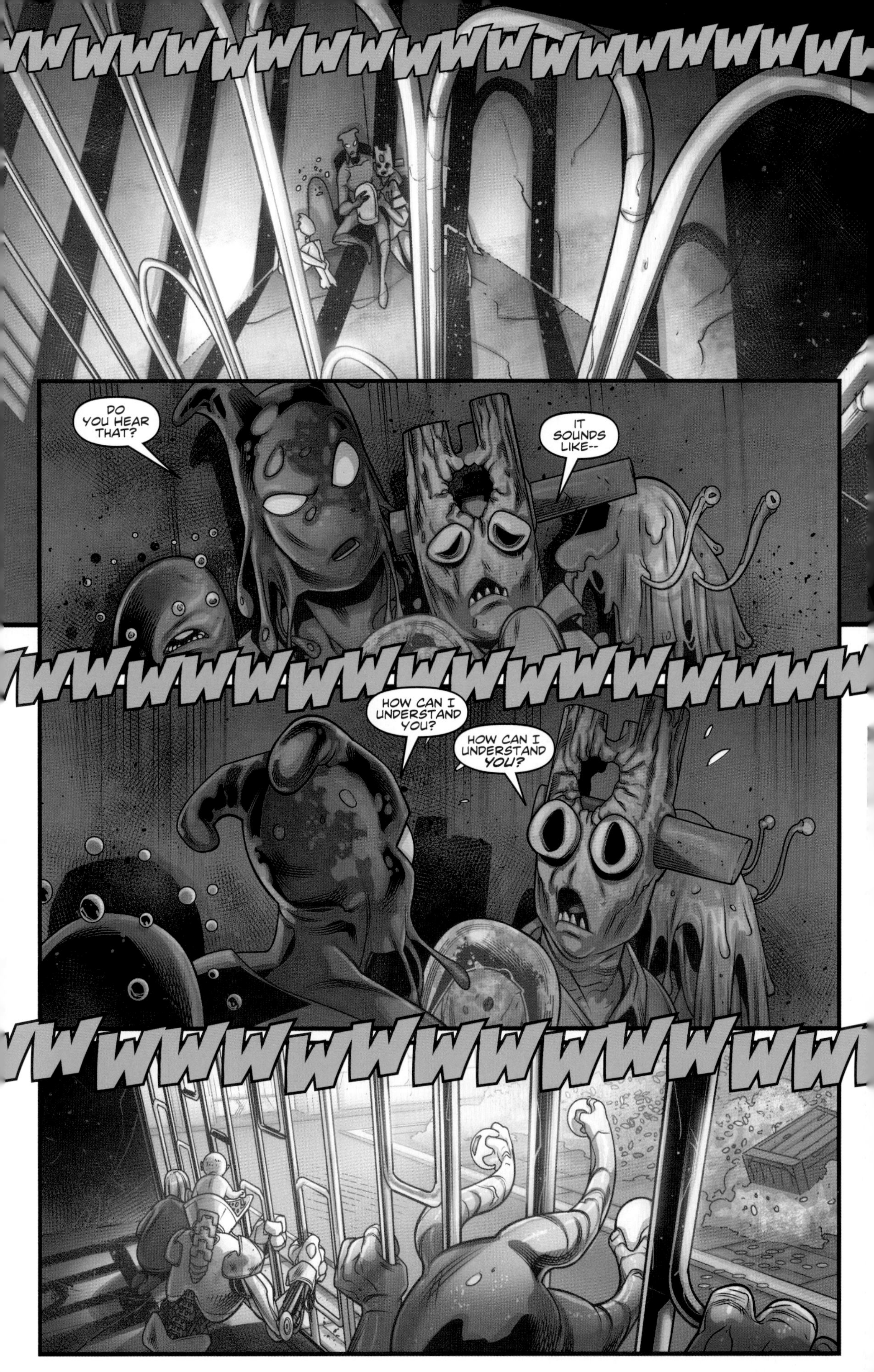
WWWWWWWWWWWWWWWWWWWWW
DO YOU HEAR THAT?
IT SOUNDS LIKE--
WWWWWWWWWWWWWWWWWWWW
HOW CAN I UNDERSTAND YOU?
HOW CAN I UNDERSTAND *YOU*?
WWWWWWWWWWWWWWWWWWWW

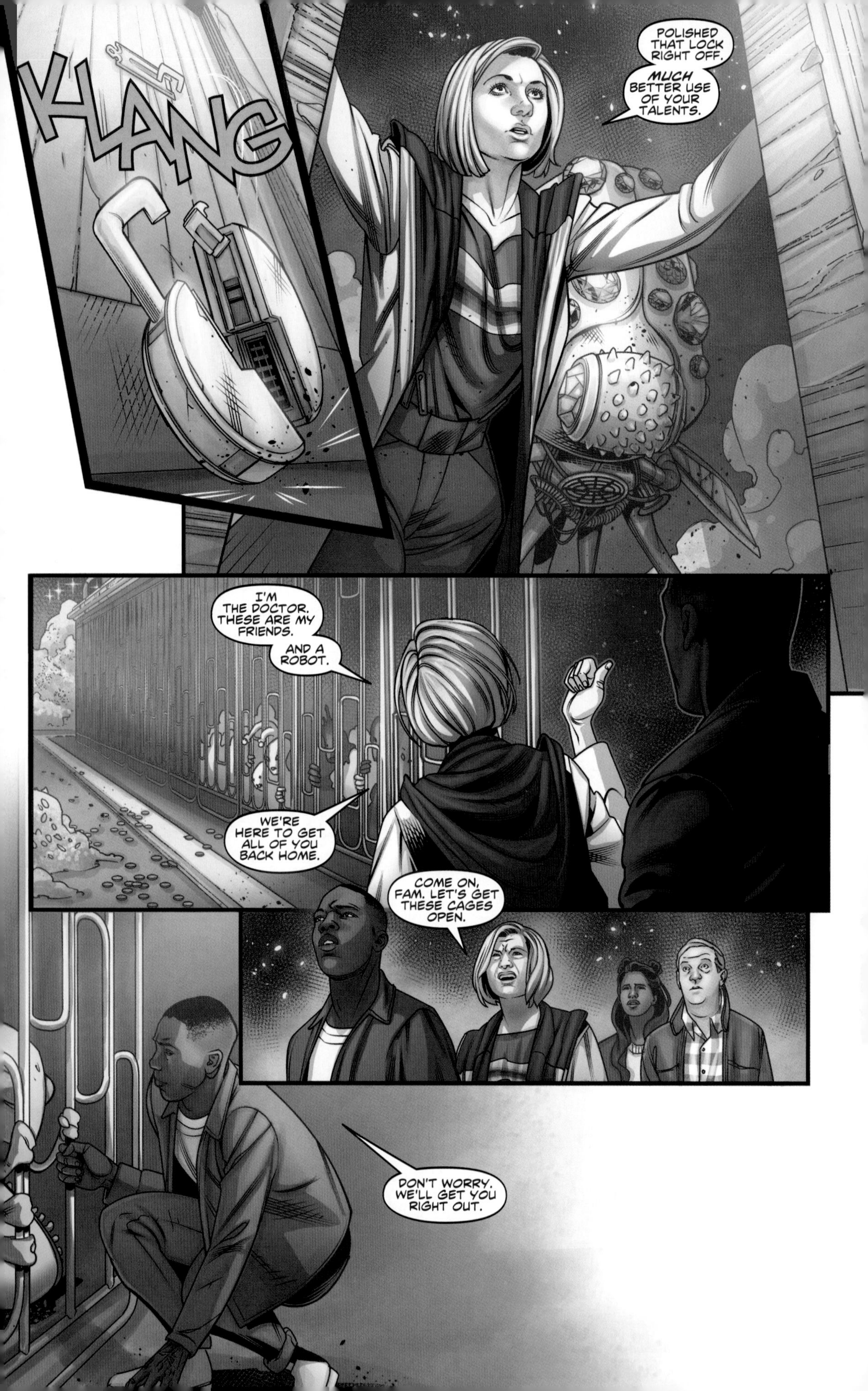
KLANG
POLISHED THAT LOCK RIGHT OFF.
MUCH BETTER USE OF YOUR TALENTS.
I'M THE DOCTOR. THESE ARE MY FRIENDS.
AND A ROBOT.
WE'RE HERE TO GET ALL OF YOU BACK HOME.
COME ON, FAM. LET'S GET THESE CAGES OPEN.
DON'T WORRY. WE'LL GET YOU RIGHT OUT.

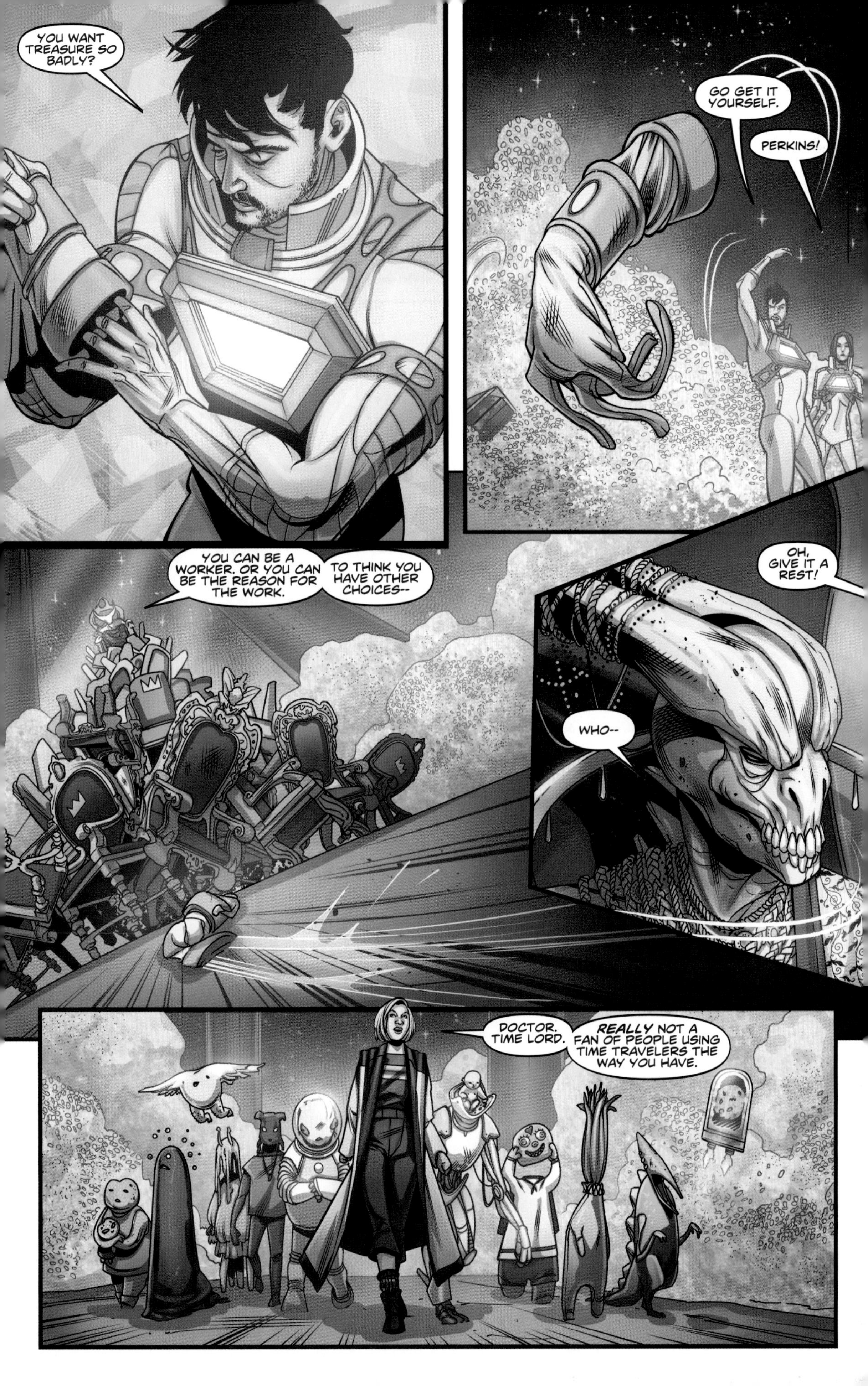
YOU WANT TREASURE SO BADLY?
GO GET IT YOURSELF.
PERKINS!
YOU CAN BE A WORKER. OR YOU CAN BE THE REASON FOR THE WORK.
TO THINK YOU HAVE OTHER CHOICES--
OH, GIVE IT A REST!
WHO--
DOCTOR. TIME LORD.
REALLY NOT A FAN OF PEOPLE USING TIME TRAVELERS THE WAY YOU HAVE.

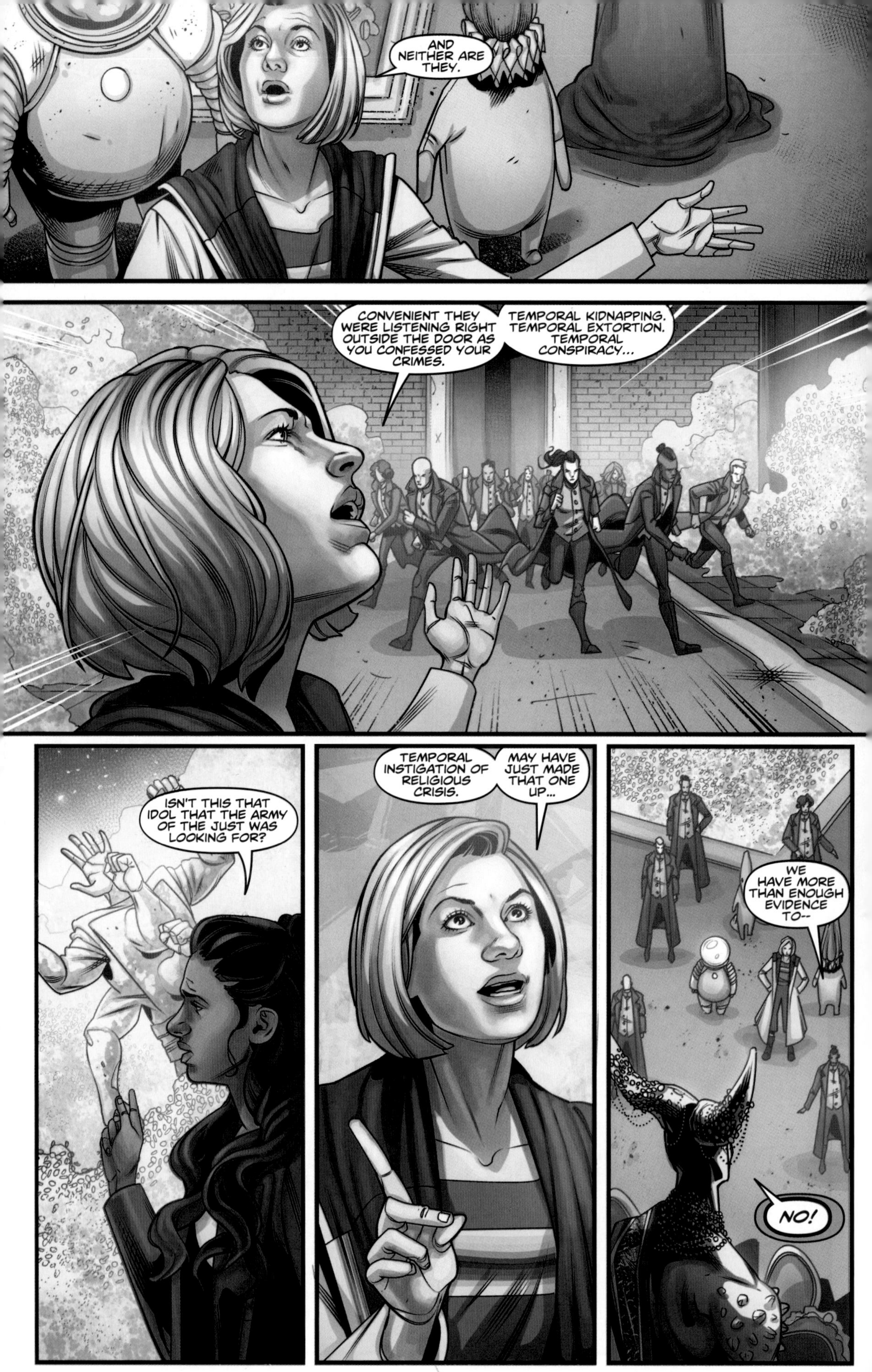
AND NEITHER ARE THEY.
CONVENIENT THEY WERE LISTENING RIGHT OUTSIDE THE DOOR AS YOU CONFESSED YOUR CRIMES.
TEMPORAL KIDNAPPING. TEMPORAL EXTORTION. TEMPORAL CONSPIRACY...
ISN'T THIS THAT IDOL THAT THE ARMY OF THE JUST WAS LOOKING FOR?
TEMPORAL INSTIGATION OF RELIGIOUS CRISIS.
MAY HAVE JUST MADE THAT ONE UP...
WE HAVE MORE THAN ENOUGH EVIDENCE TO--
NO!

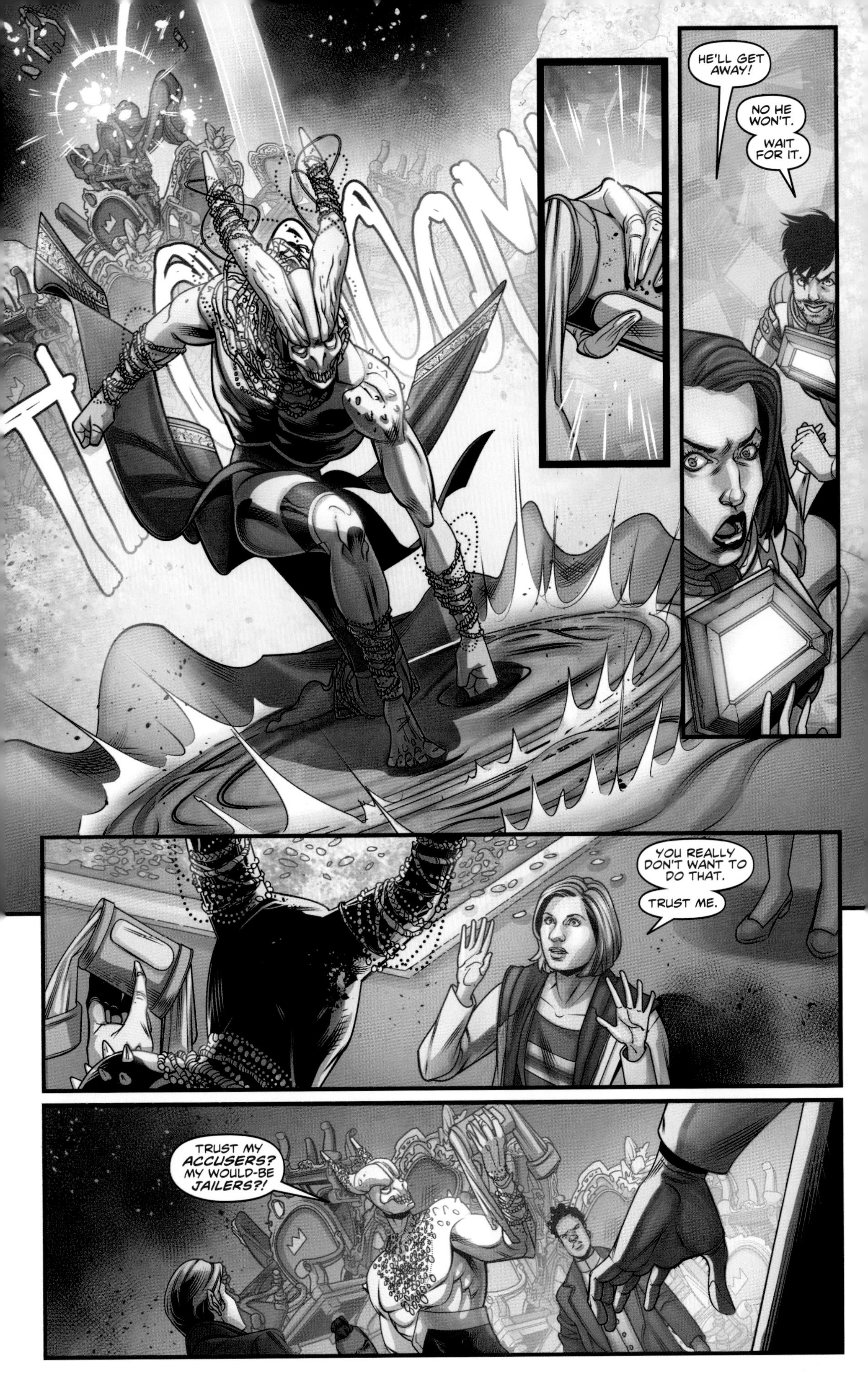
THOOOM
HE'LL GET AWAY!
NO HE WON'T.
WAIT FOR IT.
YOU REALLY DON'T WANT TO DO THAT.
TRUST ME.
TRUST MY ACCUSERS? MY WOULD-BE JAILERS?!

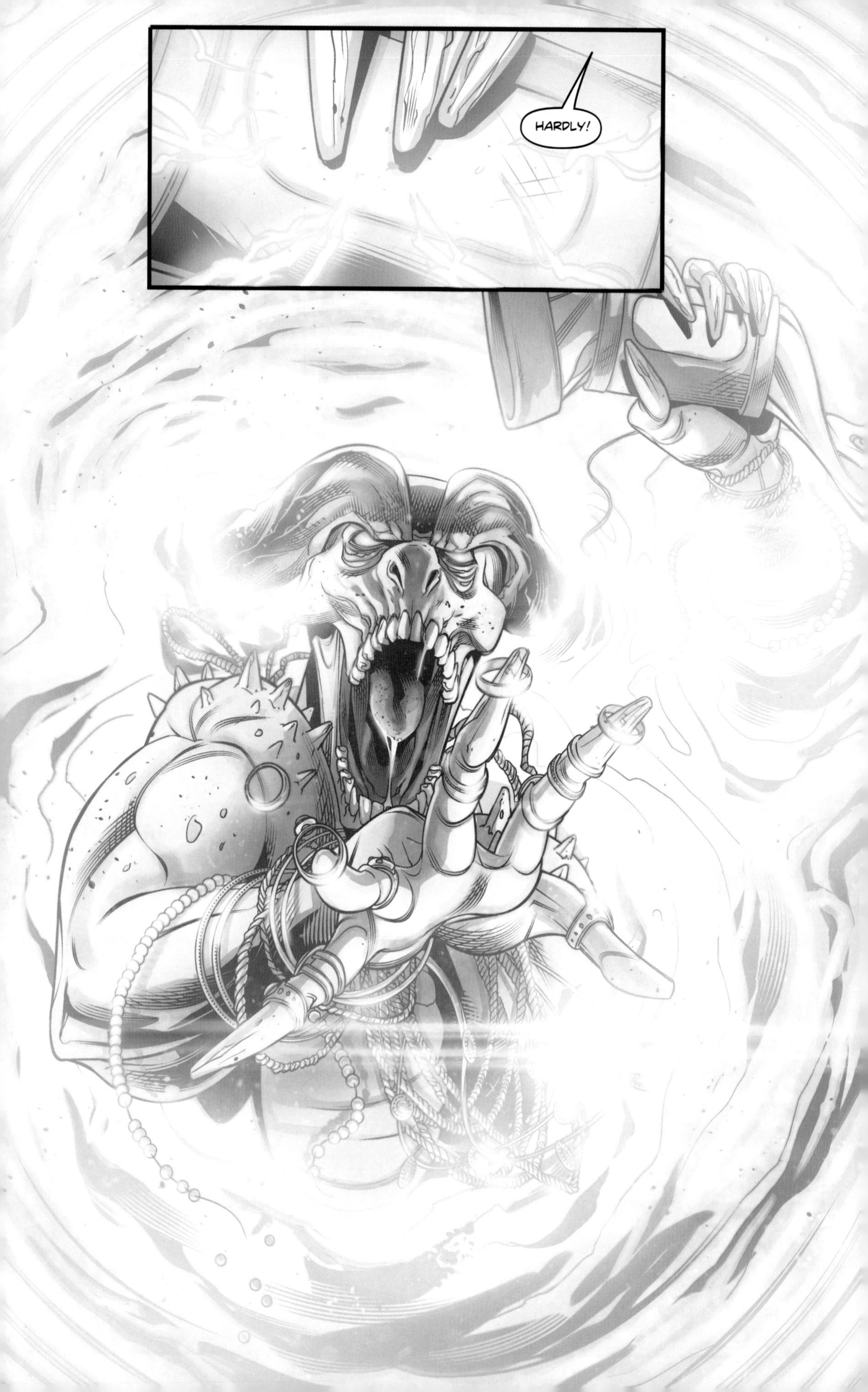
HARDLY!

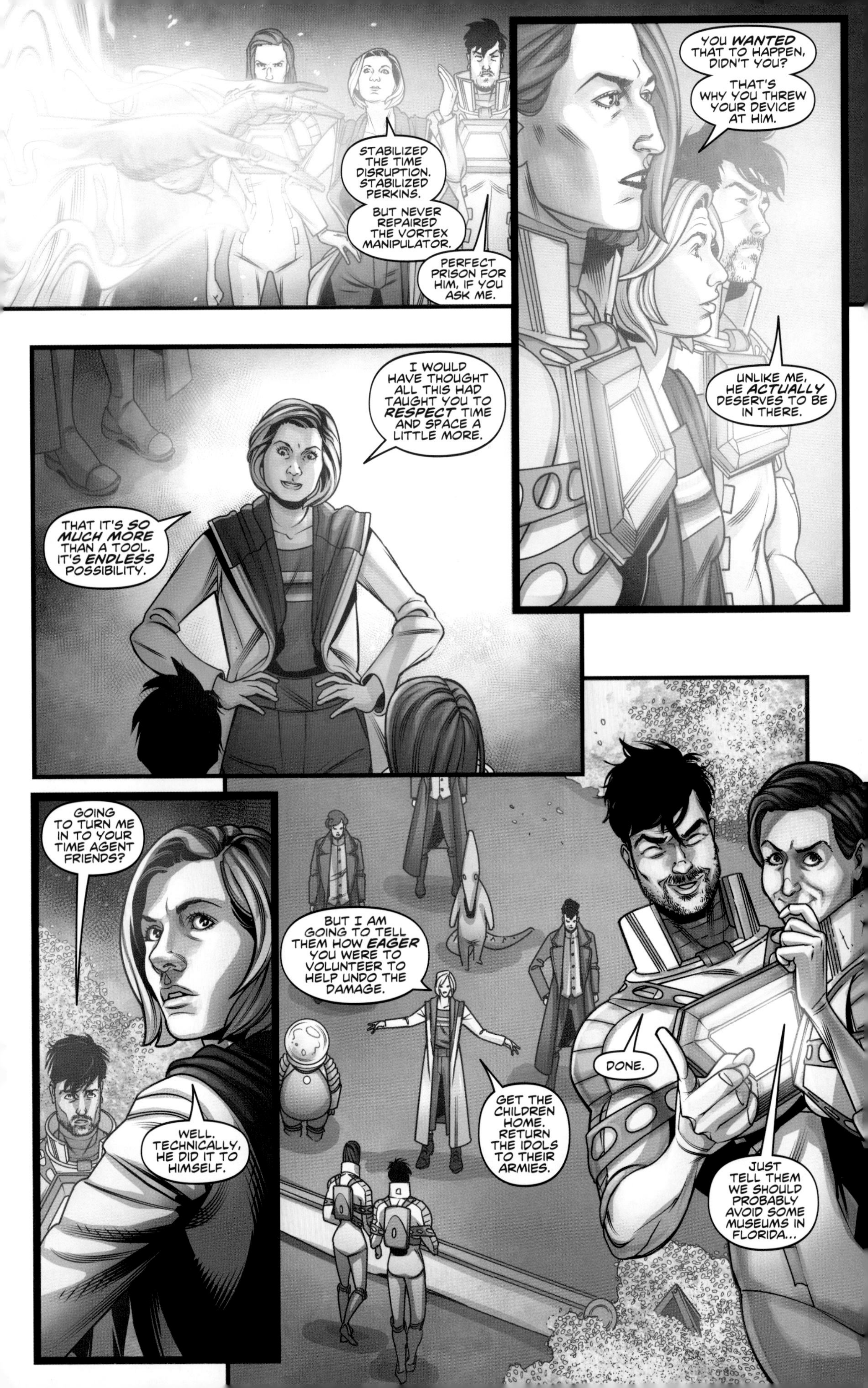
STABILIZED THE TIME DISRUPTION. STABILIZED PERKINS.
BUT NEVER REPAIRED THE VORTEX MANIPULATOR.
PERFECT PRISON FOR HIM, IF YOU ASK ME.
YOU WANTED THAT TO HAPPEN, DIDN'T YOU?
THAT'S WHY YOU THREW YOUR DEVICE AT HIM.
UNLIKE ME, HE ACTUALLY DESERVES TO BE IN THERE.
I WOULD HAVE THOUGHT ALL THIS HAD TAUGHT YOU TO RESPECT TIME AND SPACE A LITTLE MORE.
THAT IT'S SO MUCH MORE THAN A TOOL. IT'S ENDLESS POSSIBILITY.
GOING TO TURN ME IN TO YOUR TIME AGENT FRIENDS?
WELL. TECHNICALLY, HE DID IT TO HIMSELF.
BUT I AM GOING TO TELL THEM HOW EAGER YOU WERE TO VOLUNTEER TO HELP UNDO THE DAMAGE.
GET THE CHILDREN HOME. RETURN THE IDOLS TO THEIR ARMIES.
DONE.
JUST TELL THEM WE SHOULD PROBABLY AVOID SOME MUSEUMS IN FLORIDA...

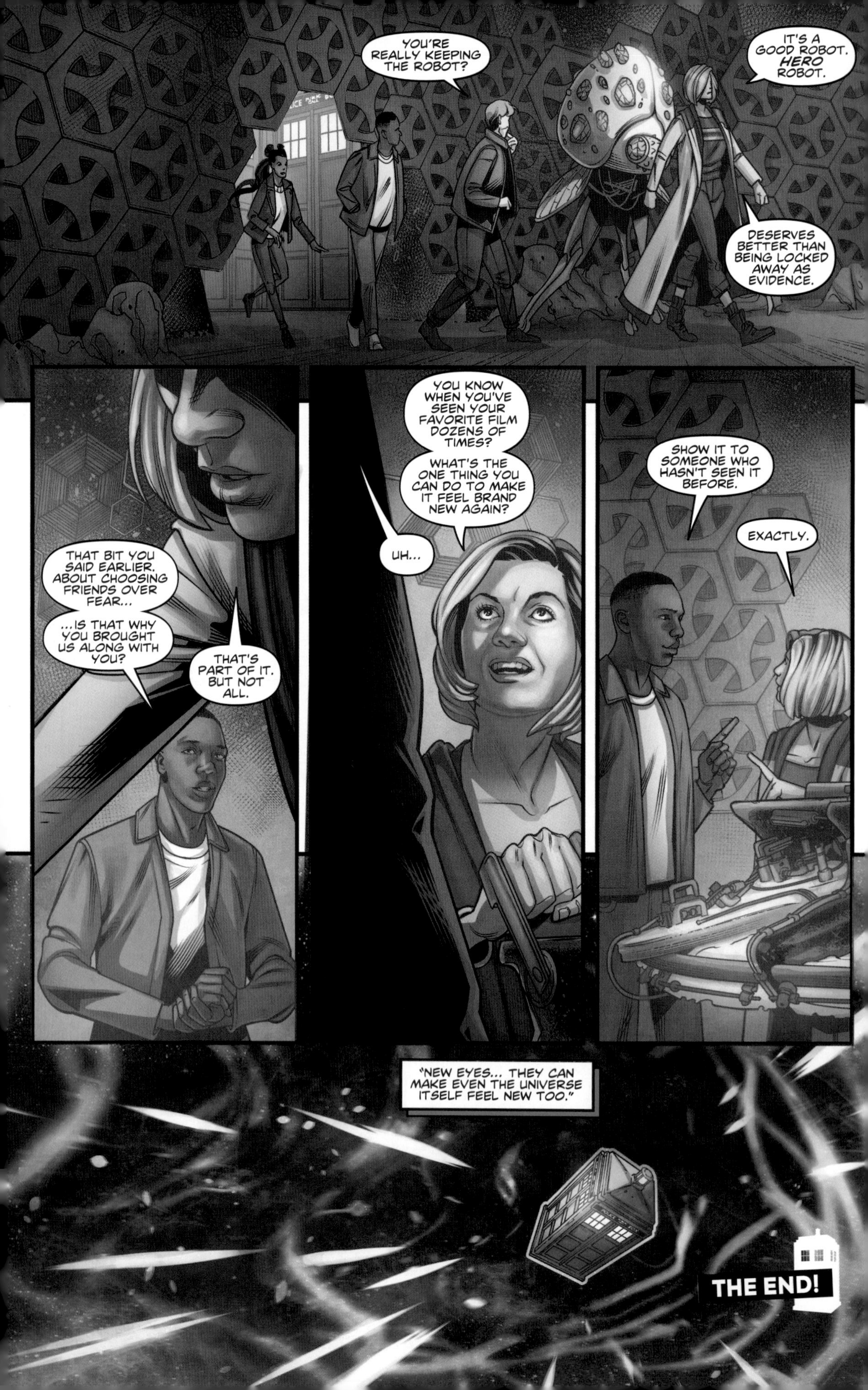
YOU'RE REALLY KEEPING THE ROBOT?
IT'S A GOOD ROBOT. HERO ROBOT.
DESERVES BETTER THAN BEING LOCKED AWAY AS EVIDENCE.
THAT BIT YOU SAID EARLIER. ABOUT CHOOSING FRIENDS OVER FEAR...
...IS THAT WHY YOU BROUGHT US ALONG WITH YOU?
THAT'S PART OF IT. BUT NOT ALL.
YOU KNOW WHEN YOU'VE SEEN YOUR FAVORITE FILM DOZENS OF TIMES?
WHAT'S THE ONE THING YOU CAN DO TO MAKE IT FEEL BRAND NEW AGAIN?
UH...
SHOW IT TO SOMEONE WHO HASN'T SEEN IT BEFORE.
EXACTLY.
"NEW EYES... THEY CAN MAKE EVEN THE UNIVERSE ITSELF FEEL NEW TOO."
THE END!

BBC

DOCTOR WHO

THE THIRTEENTH DOCTOR

Covers Gallery

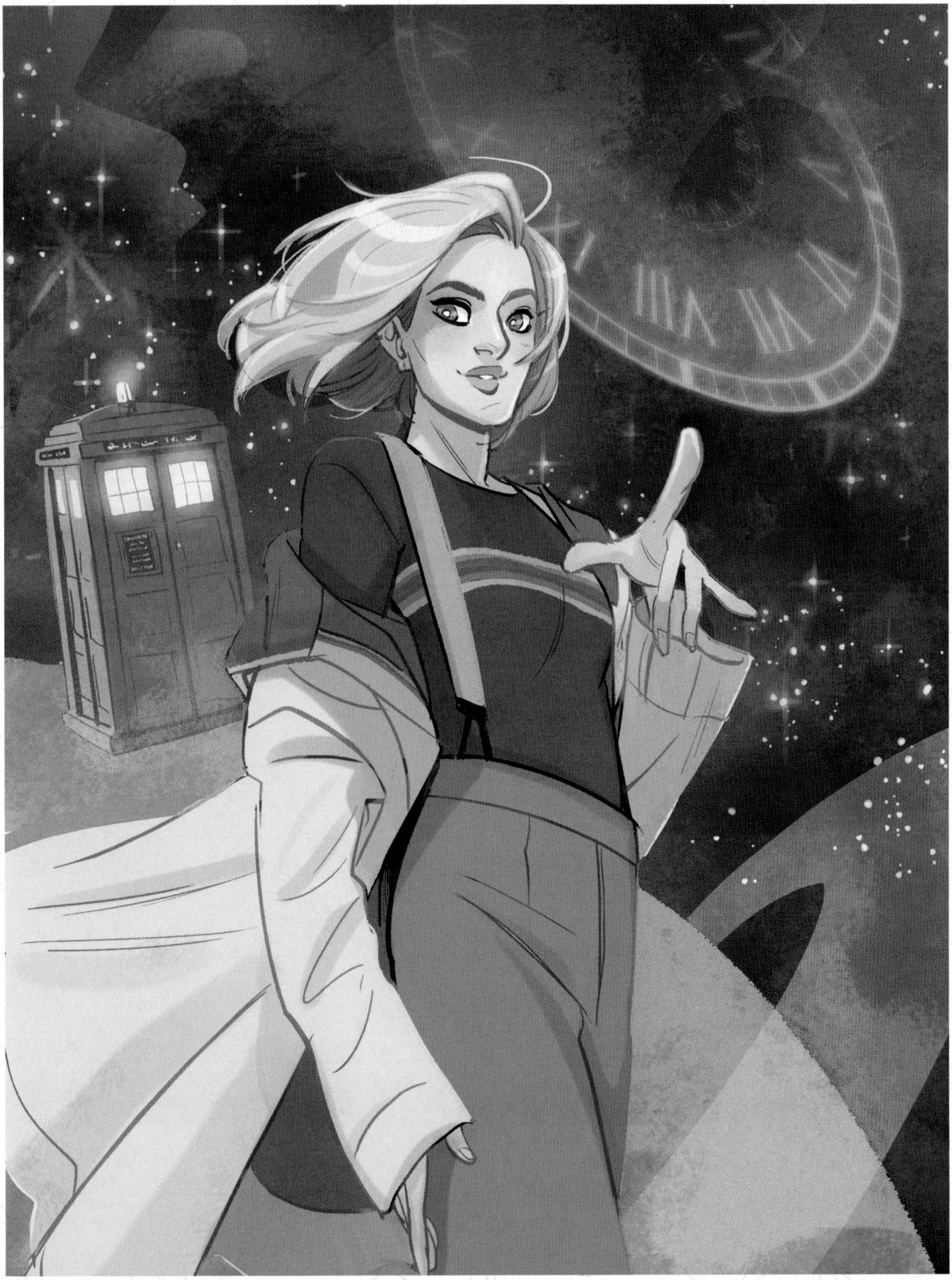

ISSUE #1 COVER A • BABS TARR

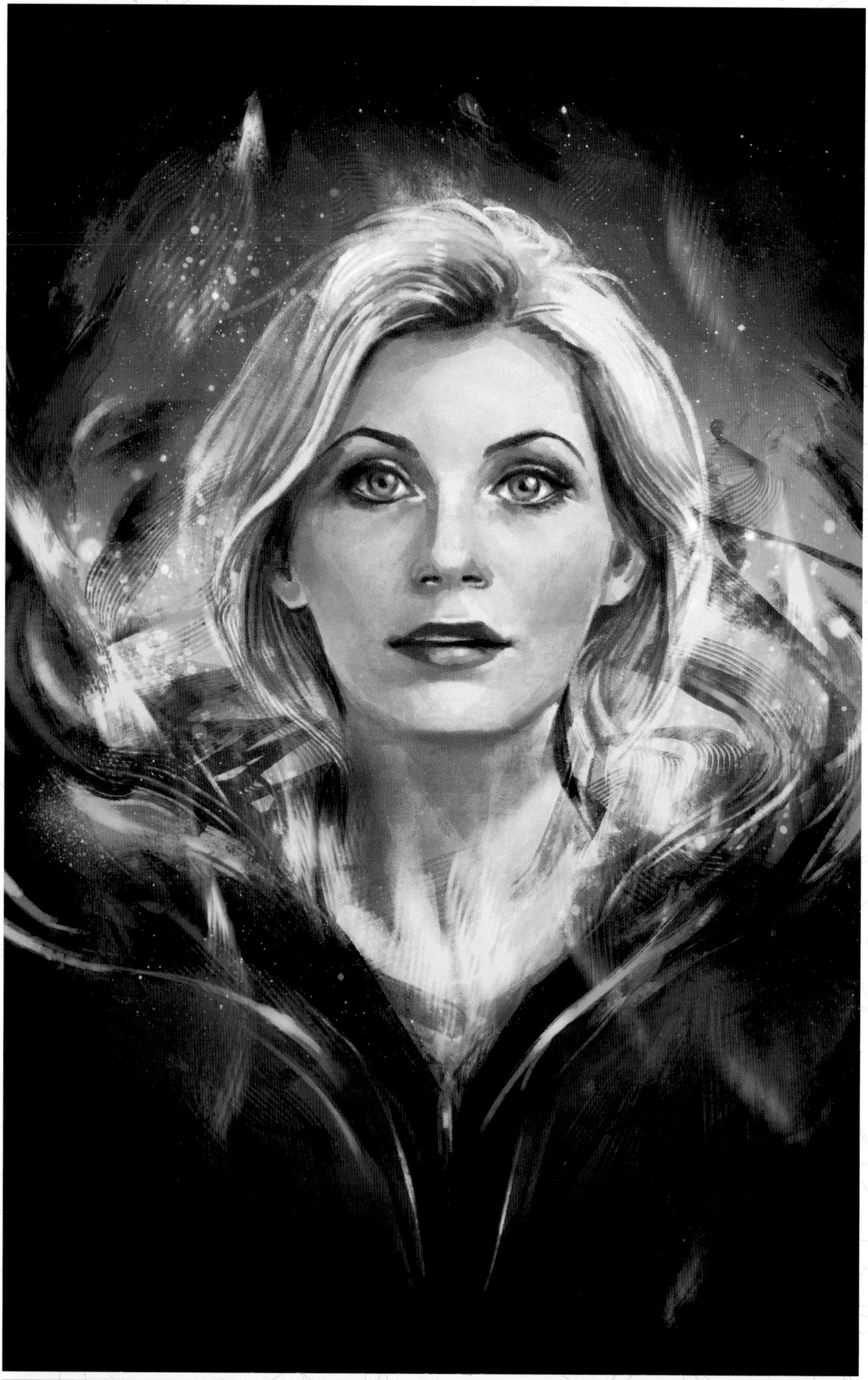

ISSUE #1 COVER C • ALICE X. ZHANG

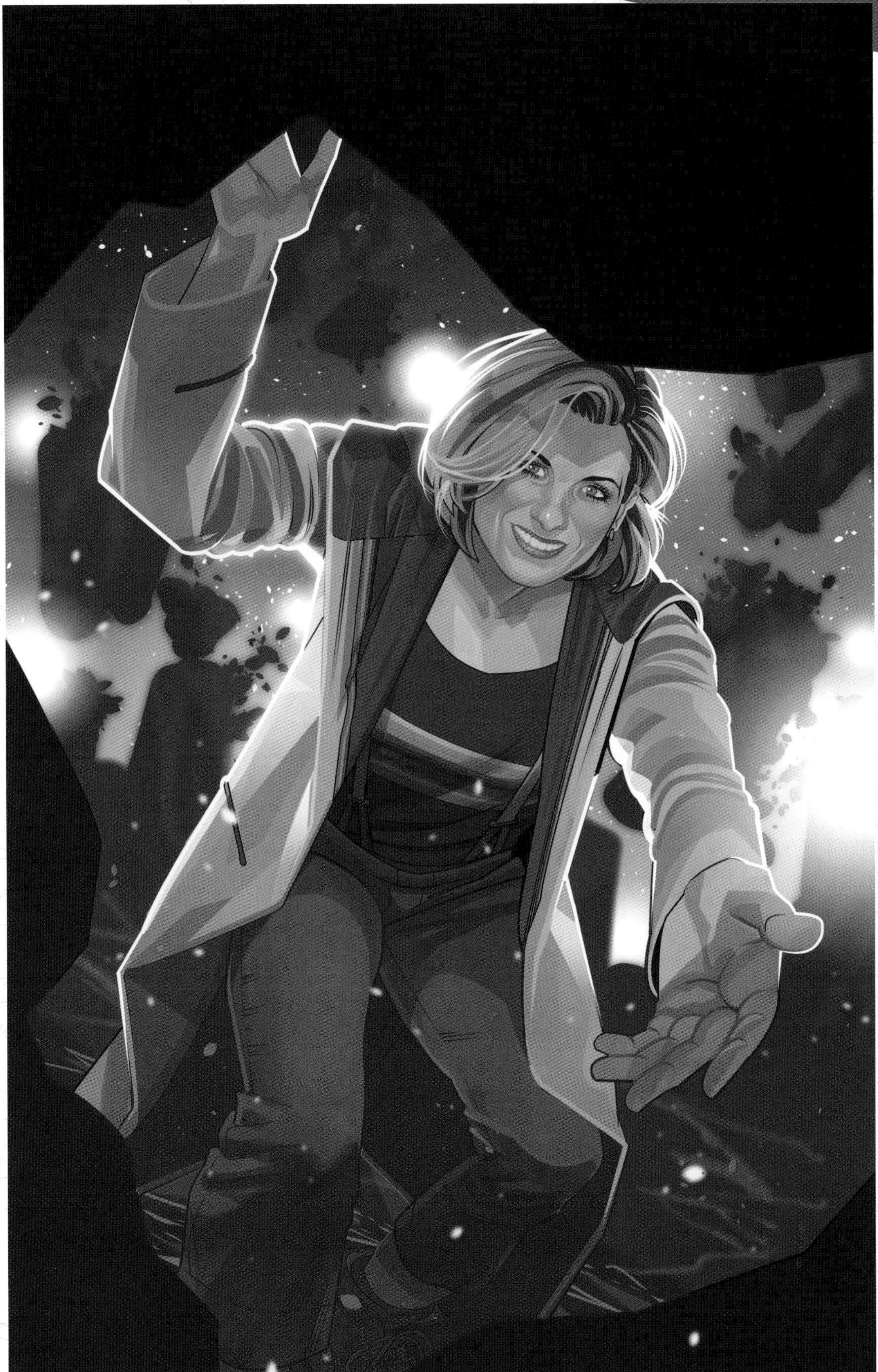

ISSUE #1 COVER D • RACHAEL STOTT

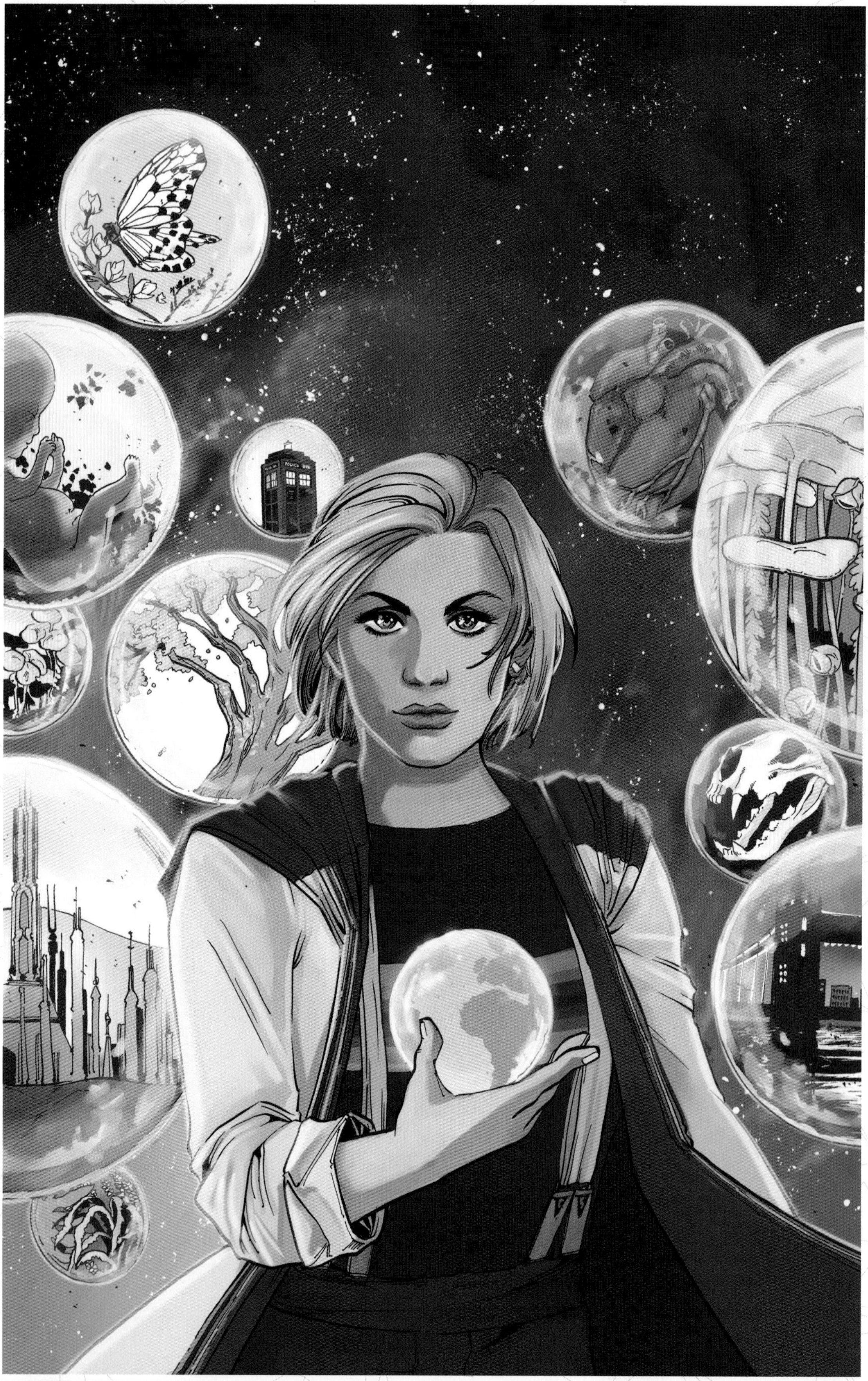
POLICE

ISSUE #1 COVER E • SANYA ANWAR

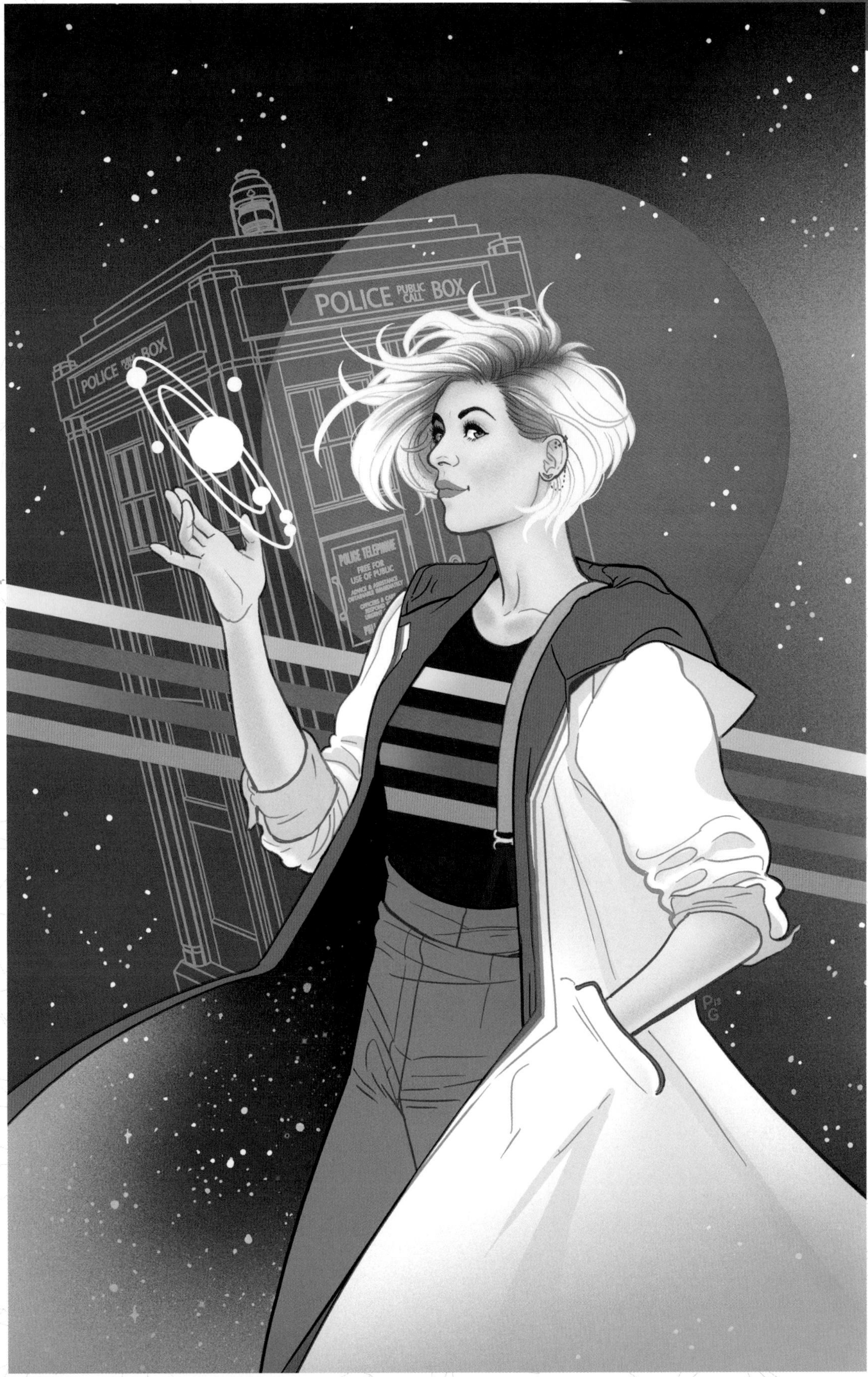
POLICE PUBLIC CALL BOX
FREE FOR USE OF PUBLIC

ISSUE #1 COVER F • PAULINA GANUCHEAU

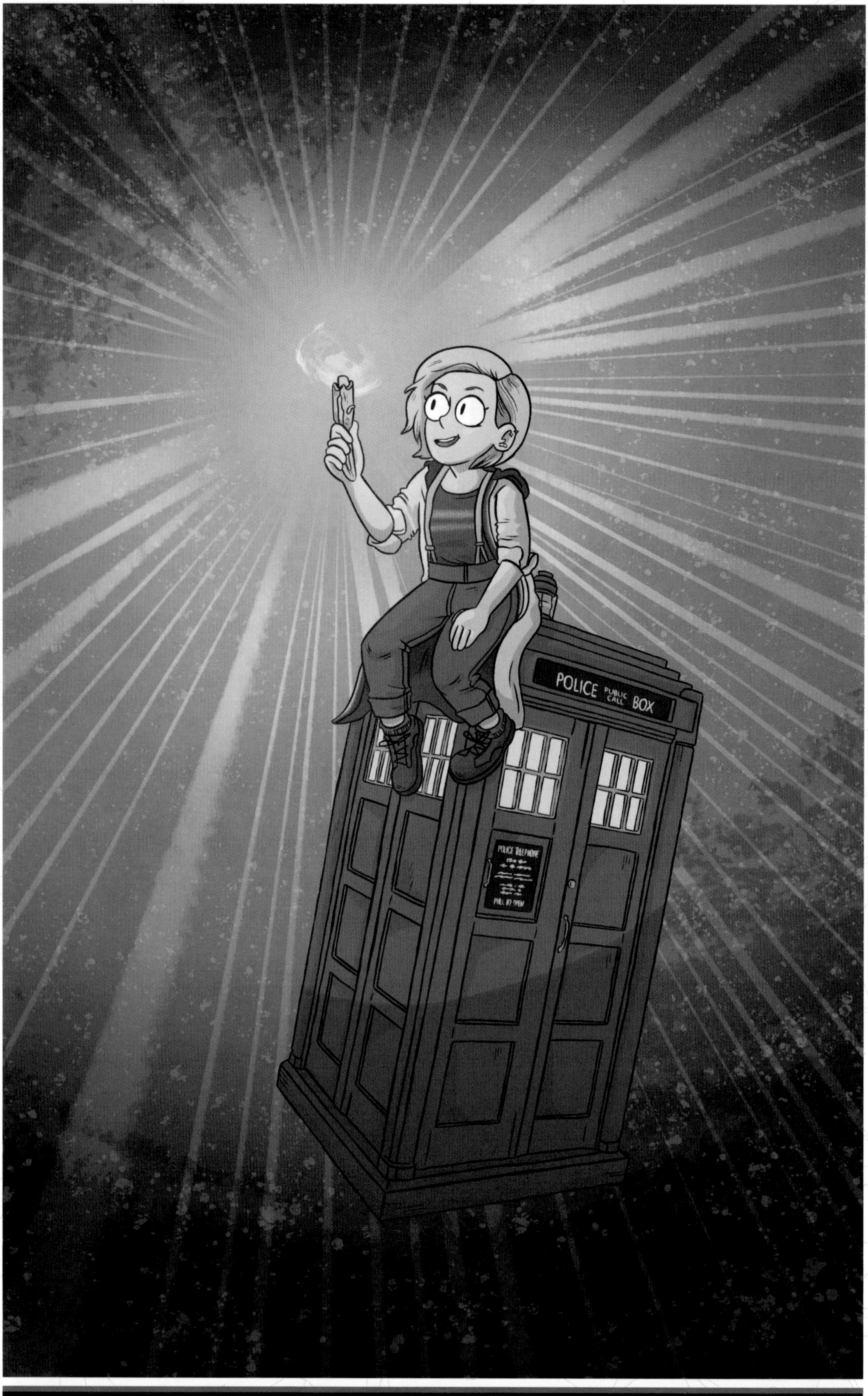
POLICE PUBLIC CALL BOX

ISSUE #1 COVER G • SARAH GRALEY

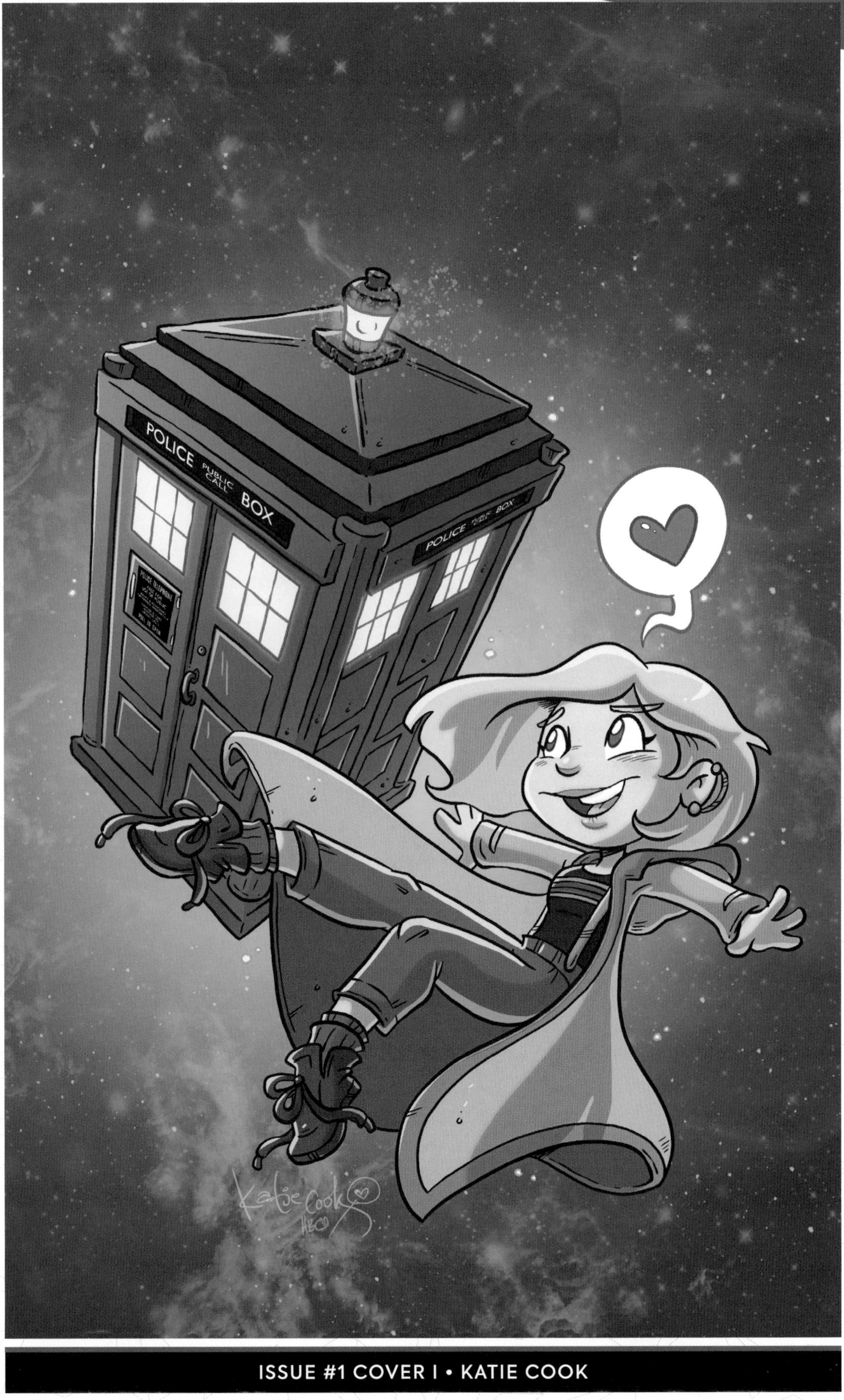
POLICE PUBLIC CALL BOX
POLICE PUBLIC CALL BOX
katie cook

ISSUE #1 COVER I • KATIE COOK

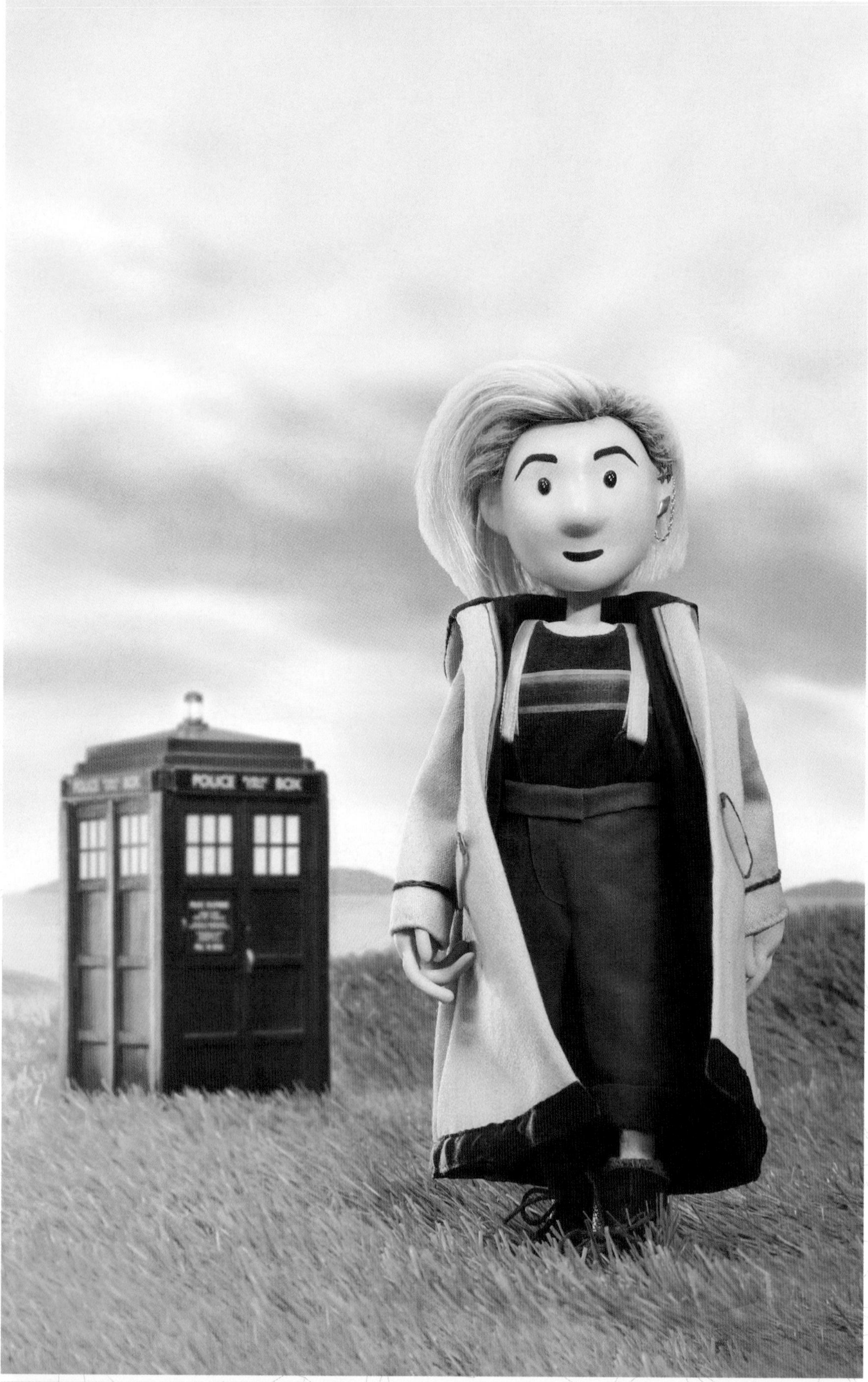
POLICE BOX

ISSUE #1 COVER J • DOCTOR PUPPET (ALISA STERN)

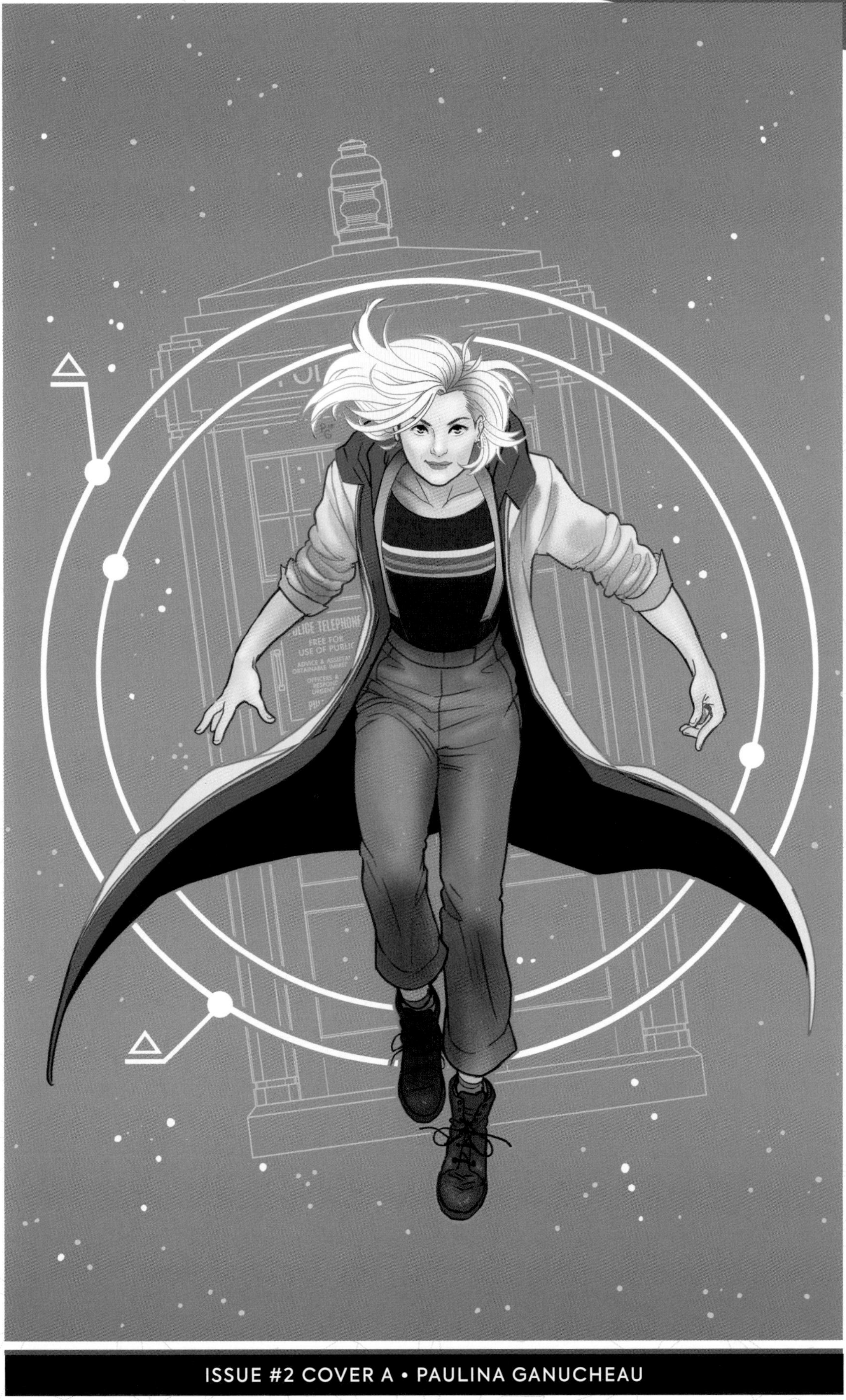
FREE FOR
USE OF PUBLIC

ISSUE #2 COVER A • PAULINA GANUCHEAU

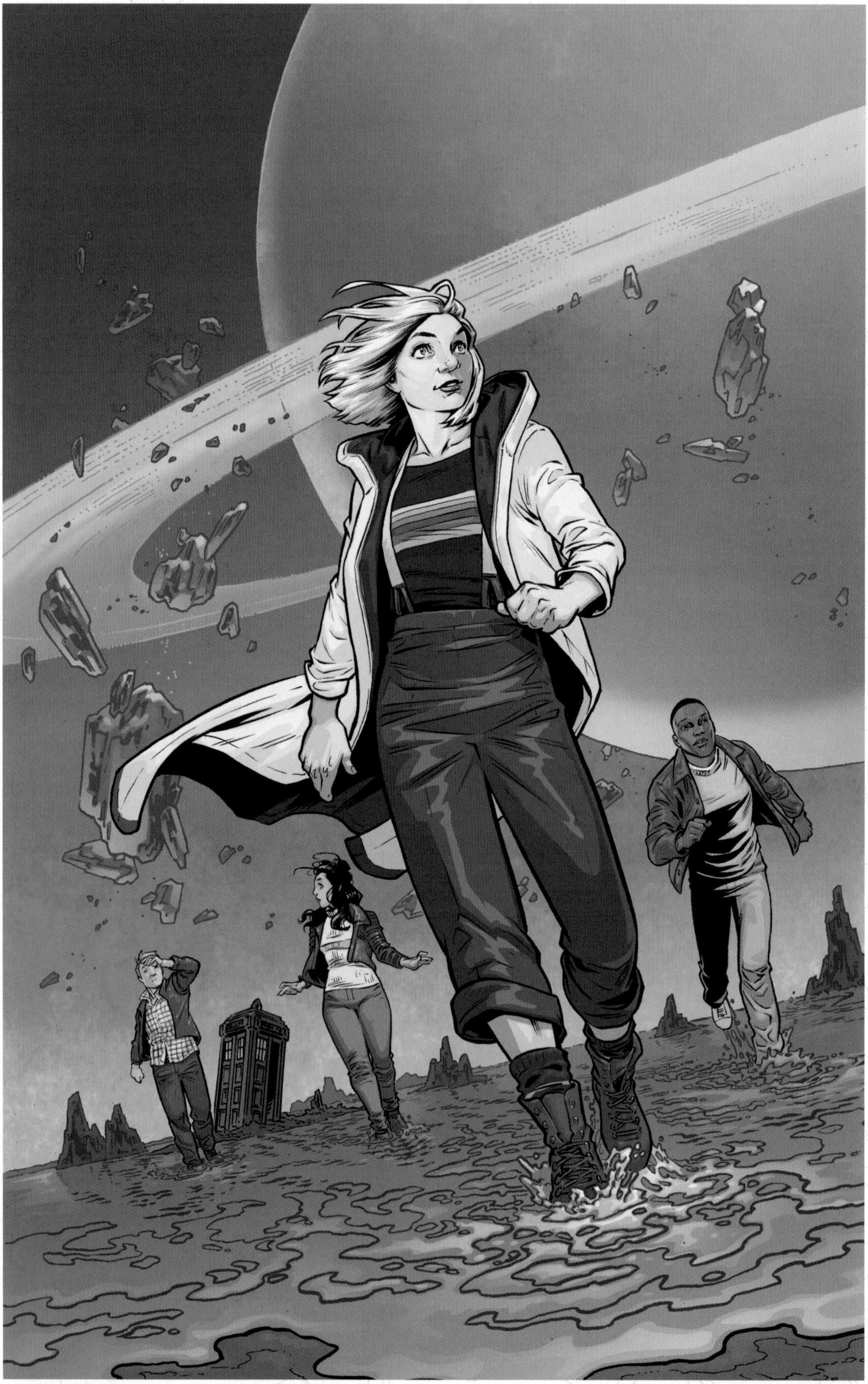

ISSUE #3 COVER A • REBEKAH ISAACS & DAN JACKSON

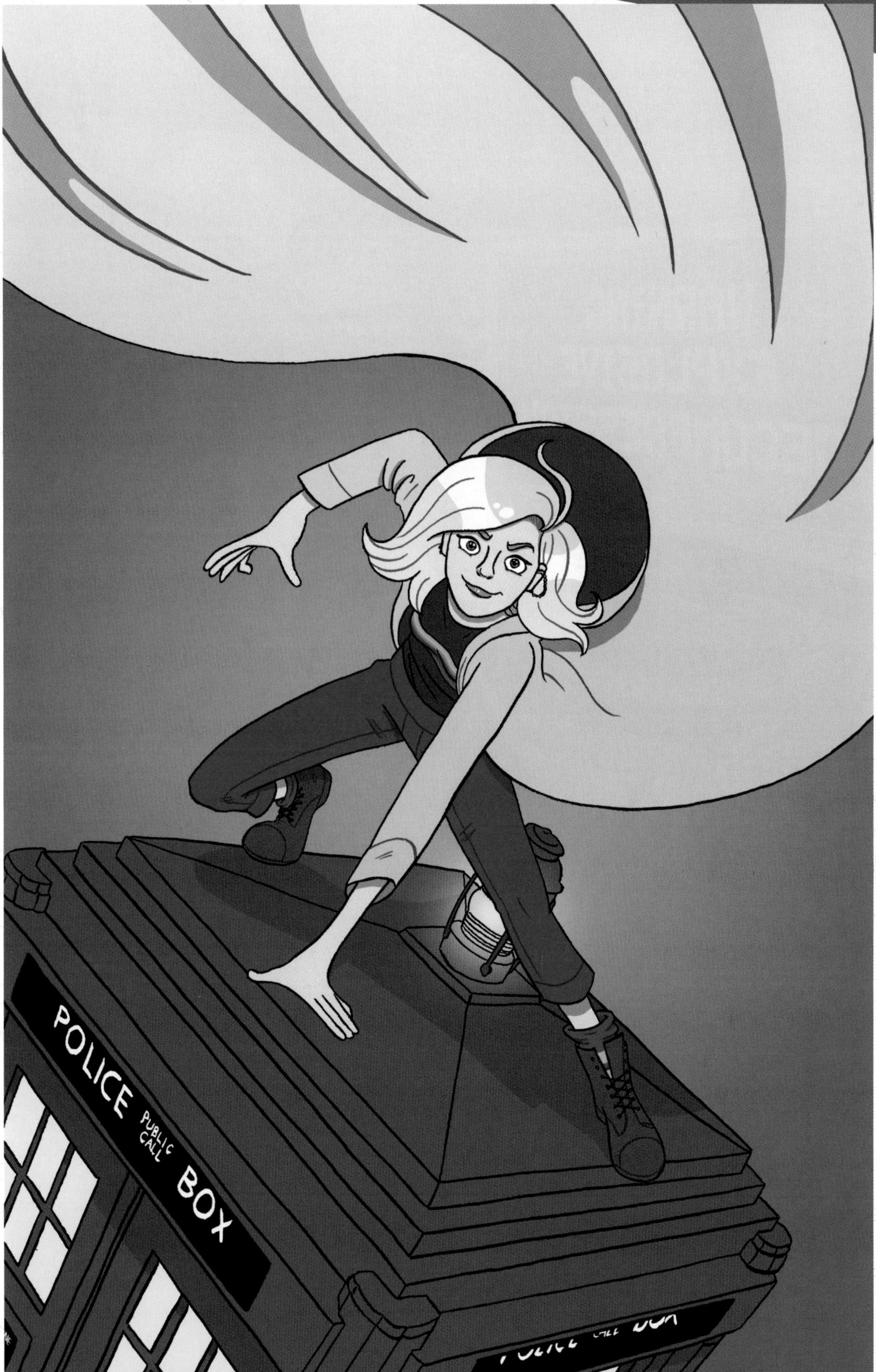
POLICE PUBLIC CALL BOX

ISSUE #3 COVER C • RACHAEL SMITH

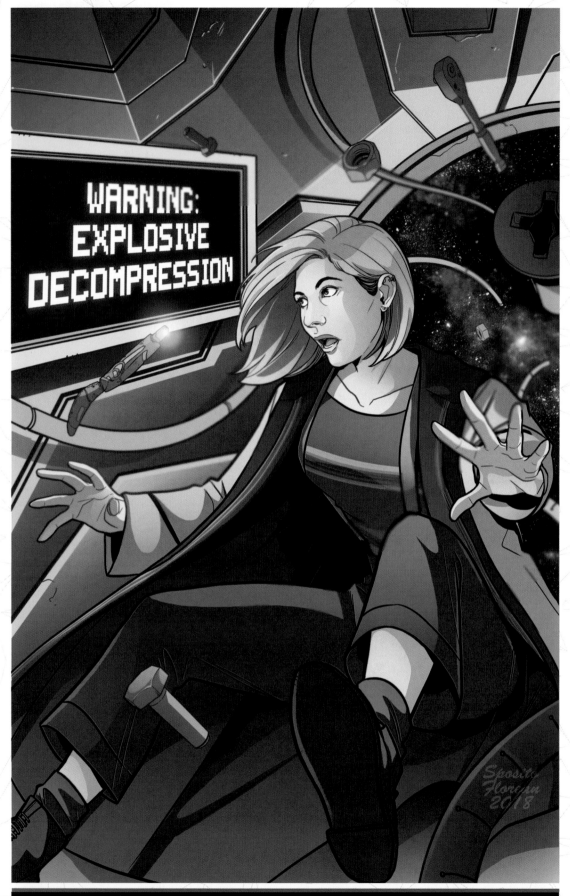

WARNING:
EXPLOSIVE
DECOMPRESSION

ISSUE #4 COVER A • GIORGIA SPOSITO & ARIANNA FLOREAN

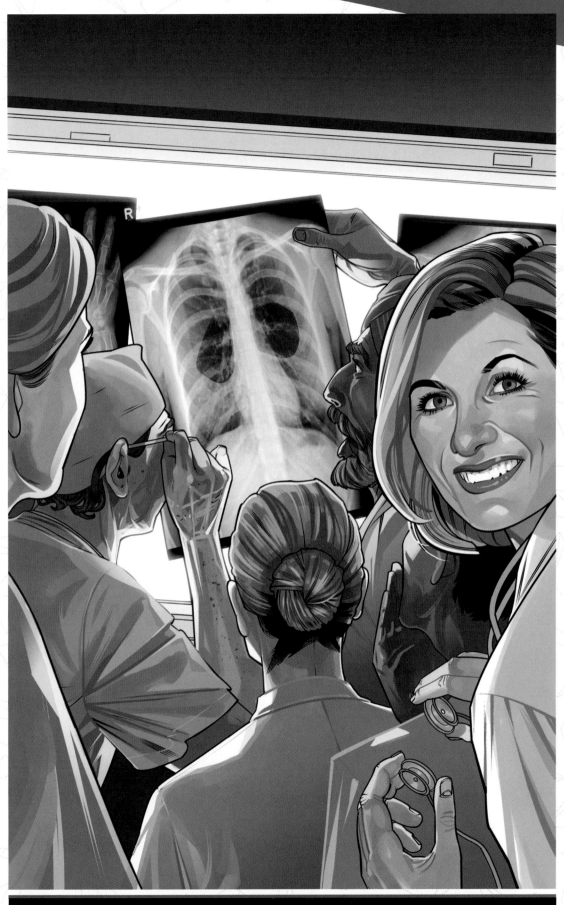

ISSUE #4 COVER C • RACHAEL STOTT

BBC DOCTOR WHO

READER'S GUIDE

With so many amazing *Doctor Who* collections already on the shelves, it can be difficult to know where to start. That's where this handy guide comes in! And don't be overwhelmed — every collection is designed to be welcoming, whatever your knowledge of *Doctor Who*.

THE TWELFTH DOCTOR

| VOL. 1: TERRORFORMER | VOL. 2: FRACTURES | VOL. 3: HYPERION | YEAR TWO BEGINS! VOL. 4: SCHOOL OF DEATH | VOL. 5: THE TWIST |

THE ELEVENTH DOCTOR

| VOL. 1: AFTER LIFE | VOL. 2: SERVE YOU | VOL. 3: CONVERSION | YEAR TWO BEGINS! VOL. 4: THE THEN AND THE NOW | VOL. 5: THE ONE |

THE TENTH DOCTOR

| VOL. 1: REVOLUTIONS OF TERROR | VOL. 2: THE WEEPING ANGELS OF MONS | VOL. 3: THE FOUNTAINS OF FOREVER | YEAR TWO BEGINS! VOL. 4: THE ENDLESS SONG | VOL. 5: ARENA OF FEAR |

THE NINTH DOCTOR

| VOL. 1: WEAPONS OF PAST DESTRUCTION | VOL. 2: DOCTORMANIA | VOL. 3: OFFICIAL SECRETS | VOL. 4: SIN EATERS |

Each comic series is entirely self-contained and focused on one Doctor, so you can follow one, two, or all of your favorite Doctors, as you wish! The series are arranged in TV season-like Years, collected into roughly three collections per Year. Feel free to start at Volume 1 of any series, or jump straight to the volumes labelled in blue! Each book, and every comic, features a catch-up and character guide at the beginning, making it easy to jump on board – and each comic series has a very different flavor, representative of that Doctor's era on screen. If in doubt, set the TARDIS Randomizer and dive in wherever you land!

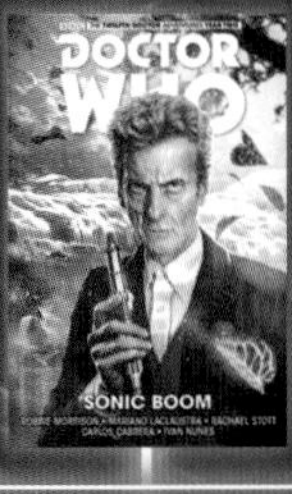
DOCTOR WHO
SONIC BOOM
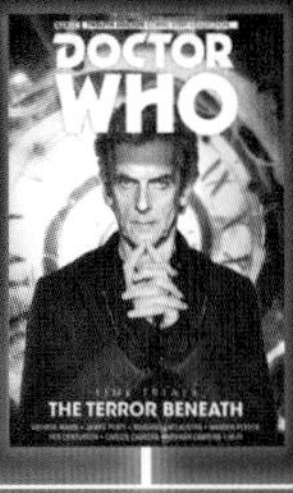
DOCTOR WHO
THE TERROR BENEATH
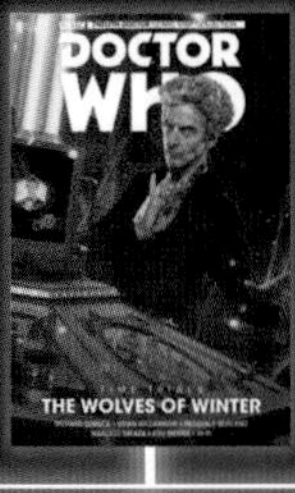
DOCTOR WHO
THE WOLVES OF WINTER
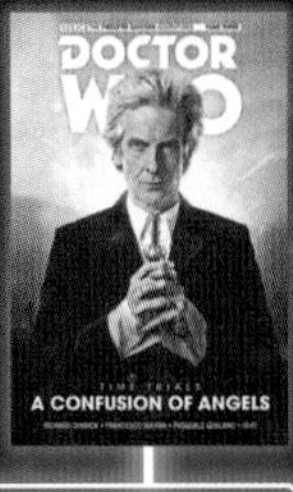
DOCTOR WHO
A CONFUSION OF ANGELS
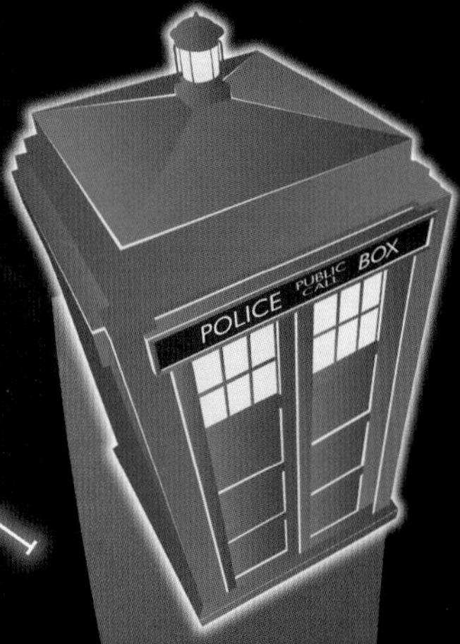
POLICE PUBLIC CALL BOX

VOL. 6:
SONIC BOOM

YEAR THREE BEGINS!
TIME TRIALS VOL. 1:
THE TERROR BENEATH

TIME TRIALS VOL. 2:
THE WOLVES OF WINTER

TIME TRIALS VOL. 3:
A CONFUSION OF ANGELS

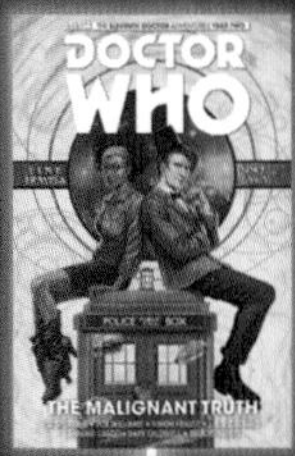
DOCTOR WHO
THE MALIGNANT TRUTH
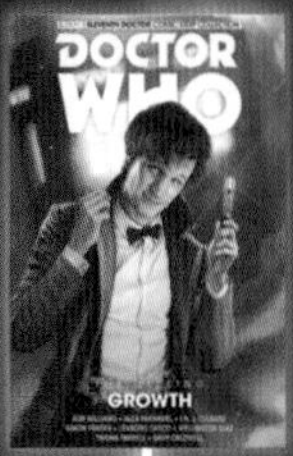
DOCTOR WHO
GROWTH
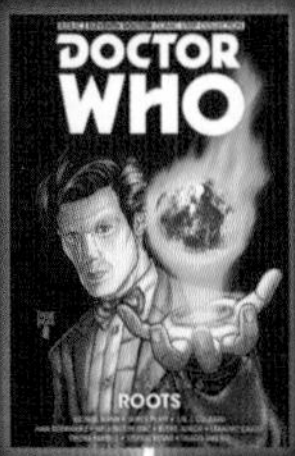
DOCTOR WHO
ROOTS
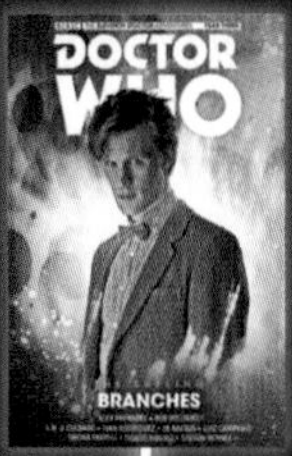
DOCTOR WHO
BRANCHES

VOL. 6:
THE MALIGNANT TRUTH

YEAR THREE BEGINS!
THE SAPLING VOL. 1:
GROWTH

THE SAPLING VOL. 2:
ROOTS

THE SAPLING VOL. 3:
BRANCHES

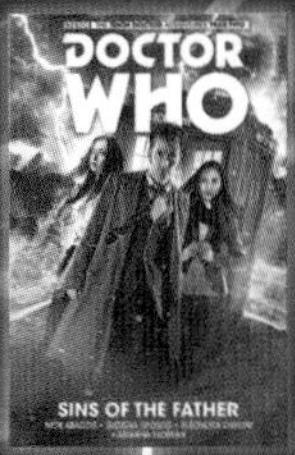
DOCTOR WHO
SINS OF THE FATHER
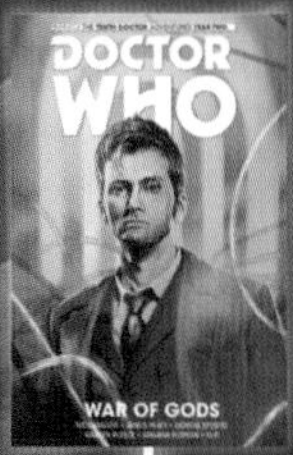
DOCTOR WHO
WAR OF GODS
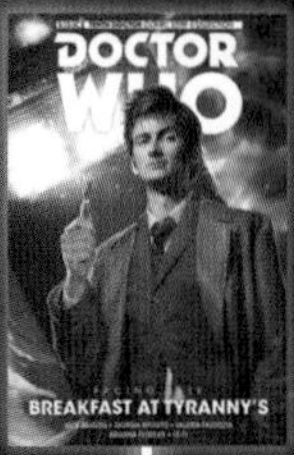
DOCTOR WHO
BREAKFAST AT TYRANNY'S
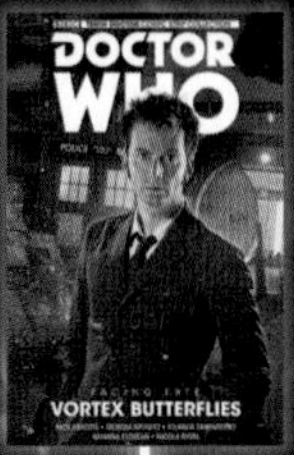
DOCTOR WHO
VORTEX BUTTERFLIES
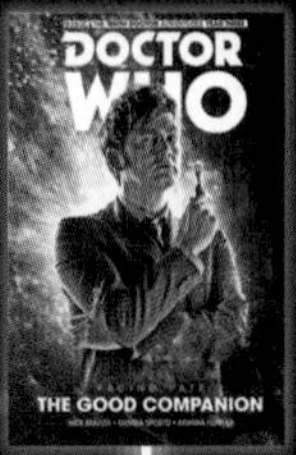
DOCTOR WHO
THE GOOD COMPANION

VOL. 6:
SINS OF THE FATHER

VOL. 7:
WAR OF GODS

YEAR THREE BEGINS!
FACING FATE VOL. 1:
BREAKFAST AT TYRANNY'S

FACING FATE VOL. 2:
VORTEX BUTTERFLIES

FACING FATE VOL. 3:
THE GOOD COMPANION

CLASSIC DOCTORS

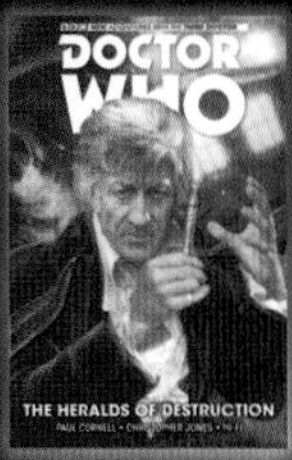
DOCTOR WHO
THE HERALDS OF DESTRUCTION
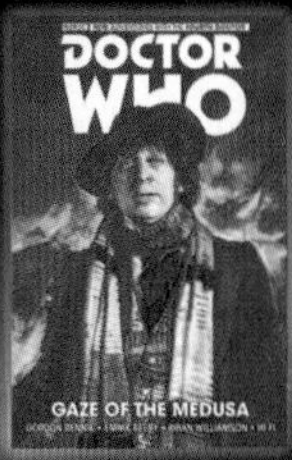
DOCTOR WHO
GAZE OF THE MEDUSA
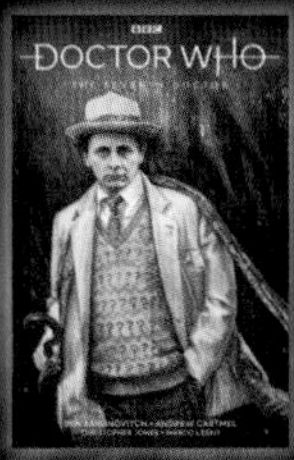
DOCTOR WHO
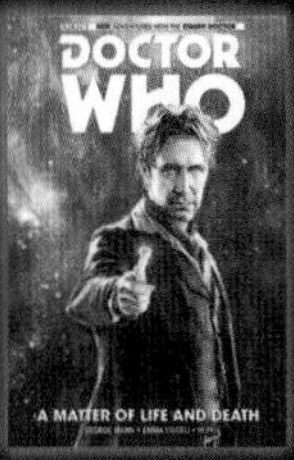
DOCTOR WHO
A MATTER OF LIFE AND DEATH

THIRD DOCTOR:
THE HERALDS OF DESTRUCTION

FOURTH DOCTOR:
GAZE OF THE MEDUSA

SEVENTH DOCTOR:
OPERATION VOLCANO

EIGHTH DOCTOR:
A MATTER OF LIFE AND DEATH

MULTI-DOCTOR EVENTS

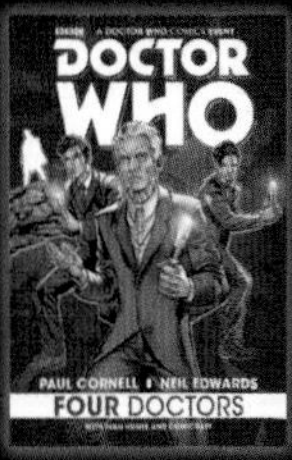
DOCTOR WHO
PAUL CORNELL · NEIL EDWARDS
FOUR DOCTORS
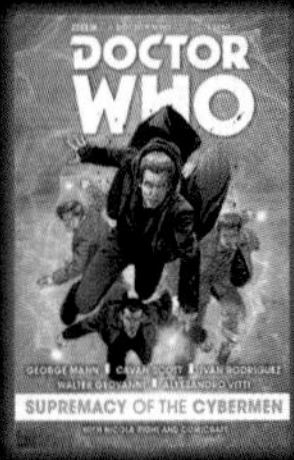
DOCTOR WHO
SUPREMACY OF THE CYBERMEN
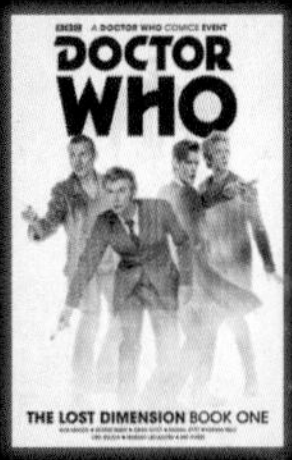
DOCTOR WHO
THE LOST DIMENSION BOOK ONE

FOUR DOCTORS

SUPREMACY OF THE CYBERMEN

THE LOST DIMENSION (BOOKS ONE & TWO)

BBC
DOCTOR WHO
THE THIRTEENTH DOCTOR VOLUME 0

ON SALE NOW

RICHARD DINNICK • MARIANO LACLAUSTRA • GIORGIA SPOSITO • BRIAN WILLIAMSON
ARIANNA FLOREAN • IOLANDA ZANFARDINO • NEIL EDWARDS • PASQUALE QUALANO
CLAUDIA IANNICIELLO • RACHAEL STOTT • CARLOS CABRERA • ADELE MATERA • COMICRAFT

Cover by Claudia Ianniciello

FROM RICHARD DINNICK • MARIANO LACLAUSTRA • GIORGIA SPOSITO
BRIAN WILLIAMSON • ARIANNA FLOREAN • IOLANDA ZANFARDINO

The Many Lives of Doctor Who

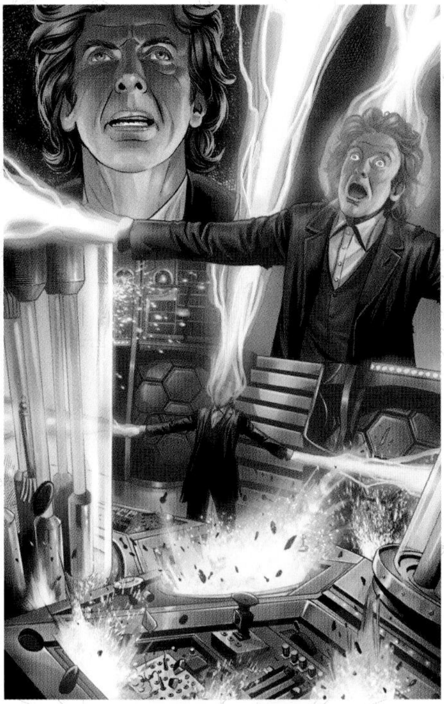

As the Twelfth Doctor regenerates into the Thirteenth, they flash back across their many lives and multiple incarnations – revealing brand-new stories from every era and face of the Doctor to date!

Written by **Richard Dinnick** (*The Twelfth Doctor*) and illustrated by a fantastic selection of mind-blowing artistic talents, this is the perfect introduction to *Doctor Who* for new readers, and the ultimate celebration of the series for long-term fans!

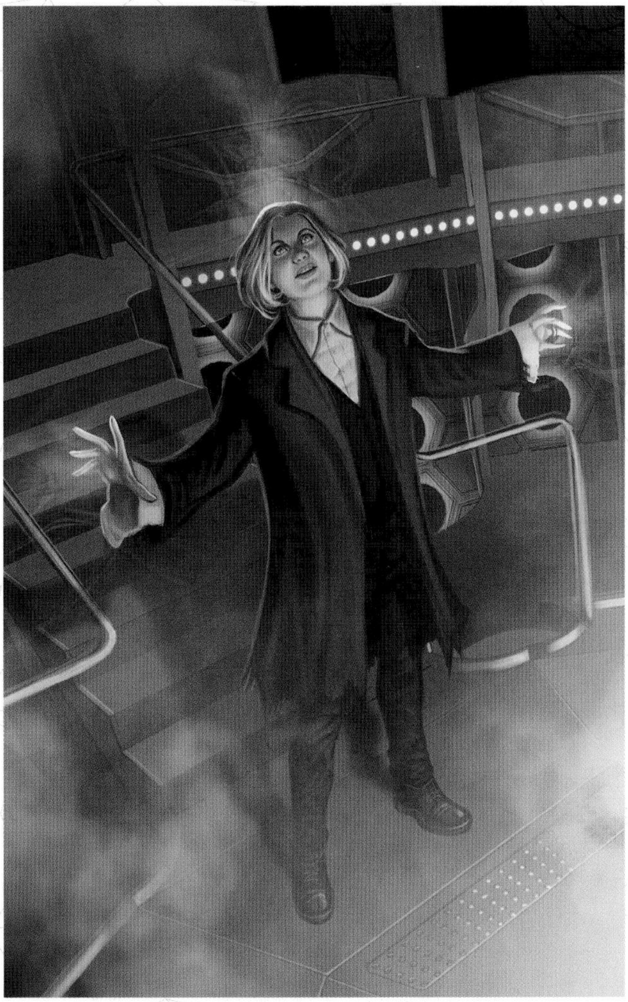

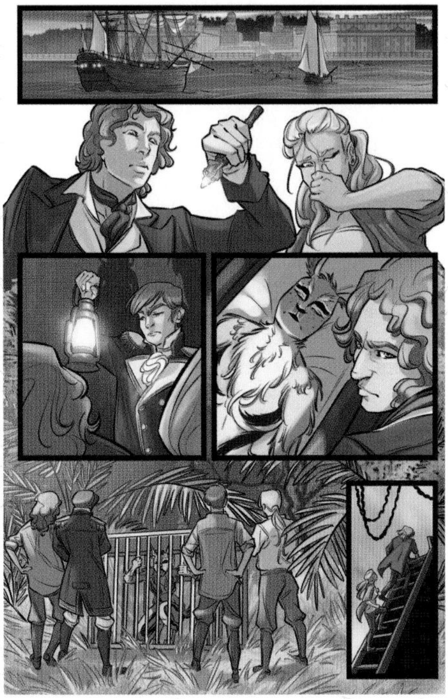

NEIL EDWARDS • PASQUALE QUALANO • CLAUDIA IANNICIELLO
RACHAEL STOTT • CARLOS CABRERA • ADELE MATERA • DIJJO LIMA

Three amazing new adventures with Doctors Ten, Eleven, and Twelve – and the first, mysterious appearances of Perkins!

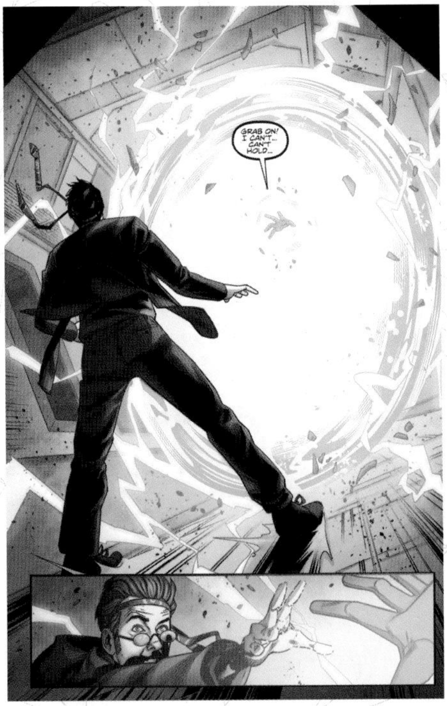
GRAB ON! I CAN'T— CAN'T HOLD...

The **Tenth Doctor** battles a horrific corporate weapon on a spaceship full of ghosts! The **Eleventh Doctor** uncovers a steam-powered robot conspiracy in Victorian-era San Francisco! And the **Twelfth Doctor** and Bill face chaos on the streets of London, as a creative power runs amok!

Writer **James Peaty** and artists **Iolanda Zanfardino, Pasquale Qualano,** and **Brian Williamson** conjure three gripping new tales, all expertly colored by **Dijjo Lima.**

And the road leads directly into this ***Thirteenth Doctor*** series, as writer **Jody Houser,** artist **Rachael Stott,** and colorist **Enrica Eren Angiolini** deliver a series of short stories that feature the first appearances of Perkins!

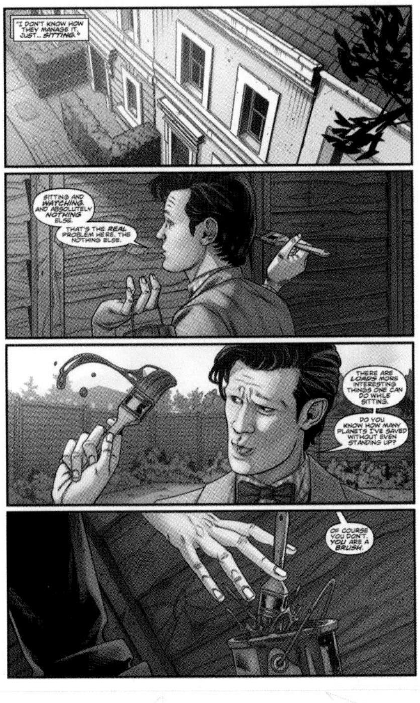
"I DON'T KNOW HOW THEY MANAGE IT. JUST... SITTING."
SITTING AND WATCHING. AND ABSOLUTELY NOTHING ELSE.
THAT'S THE REAL PROBLEM HERE. THE NOTHING ELSE.
THERE ARE LOADS MORE INTERESTING THINGS ONE CAN DO WHILE SITTING.
DO YOU KNOW HOW MANY PLANETS I'VE SAVED WITHOUT EVEN STANDING UP?
OF COURSE YOU DON'T. YOU ARE A BRUSH.

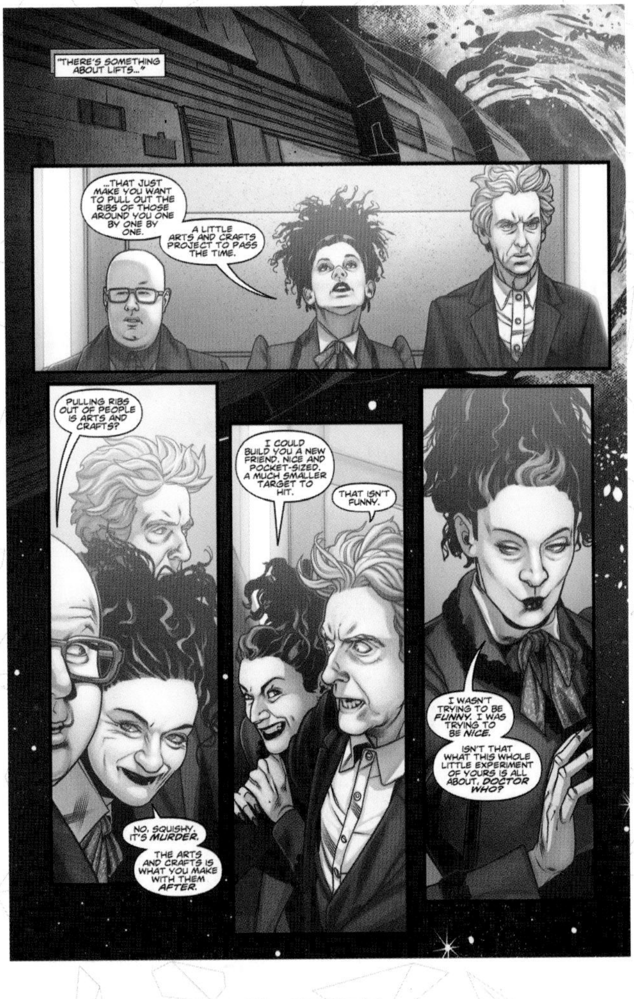
"THERE'S SOMETHING ABOUT LIFTS..."
...THAT JUST MAKE YOU WANT TO PULL OUT THE RIBS OF THOSE AROUND YOU ONE BY ONE BY ONE.
A LITTLE ARTS AND CRAFTS PROJECT TO PASS THE TIME.
PULLING RIBS OUT OF PEOPLE IS ARTS AND CRAFTS?
NO, SQUISHY. IT'S MURDER.
THE ARTS AND CRAFTS IS WHAT YOU MAKE WITH THEM AFTER.
I COULD BUILD YOU A NEW FRIEND. NICE AND POCKET-SIZED. A MUCH SMALLER TARGET TO HIT.
THAT ISN'T FUNNY.
I WASN'T TRYING TO BE FUNNY. I WAS TRYING TO BE NICE.
ISN'T THAT WHAT THIS WHOLE LITTLE EXPERIMENT OF YOURS IS ALL ABOUT, DOCTOR WHO?

WITH JODY HOUSER • RACHAEL STOTT
ENRICA EREN ANGIOLINI • COMICRAFT

BBC

DOCTOR WHO

THE THIRTEENTH DOCTOR

Biographies

Jody Houser

is a prolific writer of comics, perhaps best known for her work on *Faith* for Valiant, and *Mother Panic* for the Young Animal imprint at DC Comics. She has also written *Star Wars: Rogue One, Star Wars: Age of Republic, Amazing Spider-Man: Renew Your Vows,* and *Spider-Girls* for Marvel, *The X-Files: Origins* and *Orphan Black* for IDW, and *Stranger Things, StarCraft,* and *Halo* for Dark Horse.

Rachael Stott

is a British artist who has worked on some of the most high-profile titles in comics, including *Star Trek, Planet of the Apes, Ghostbusters,* and *Doctor Who.* She has also worked on comics covers for titles like *Archie Comics.* A past winner of the Best Newcomer Award at the British Comics Awards, Rachael continues to enjoy critical acclaim for her brilliant work.

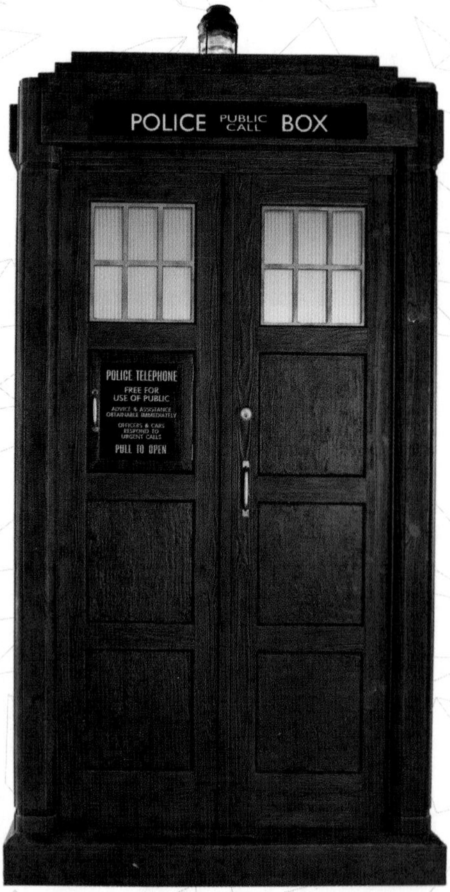
POLICE PUBLIC CALL BOX
POLICE TELEPHONE
FREE FOR USE OF PUBLIC
PULL TO OPEN

Enrica Eren Angiolini

is a colorist and illustrator from Italy. Enrica's rich colors go from strength to strength, as demonstrated by her work on *Warhammer 40,000, Shades of Magic: The Steel Prince,* and her cover work for Titan Comics, Dark Horse, and Aspen Comics.

Giorgia Sposito

is a rising star artist and inker from Italy who, as well as illustrating many adventures of the Tenth Doctor, has worked on titles such as *Independence Day, Charmed,* and *Wonderland.*

Valeria Favoccia

is an upcoming Italian comics artist whose credits include *Doctor Who* and *Assassin's Creed.*